WITCHCRAFT
OUT OF THE SHADOWS

A COMPLETE HISTORY

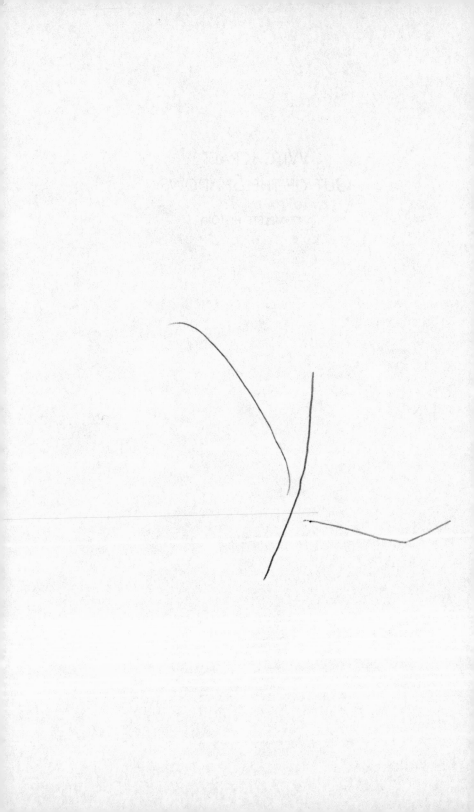

WITCHCRAFT
OUT OF THE SHADOWS

A COMPLETE HISTORY

LEO RUICKBIE

ROBERT HALE · LONDON

© Leo Ruickbie 2004
First published in Great Britain 2004

ISBN 0 7090 7567 7

Robert Hale Limited
Clerkenwell House
Clerkenwell Green
London EC1R 0HT

A catalogue record for this book is available from the British Library

2 4 6 8 10 9 7 5 3 1

Typeset in 9½/12½pt Sabon by
Derek Doyle & Associates, Liverpool.
Printed in Great Britain by
St Edmundsbury Press Limited, Bury St Edmunds, Suffolk.
Bound by Woolnough Bookbinding Limited.

CONTENTS

ILLUSTRATIONS

Between pages 160 and 161

Picture Credits

Leo Ruickbie: 1, 2, 3, 8, 10, 11, 12, 14. Ernst and Johanna Lehner: 4, 5, 6, 7, 13. Ron Cooke: 9

INTRODUCTION

One figure, above all, has haunted the human imagination since humans began to imagine: the witch. Witchcraft[1] has always been with us, but where did it come from and where is it going? And whilst witchcraft may always have been with us, has it always been the same thing to all people? In the following pages we will explore the theme of witchcraft, investigating the fantasies and realities behind its practice and persecution, and charting its emergence as one of the most radical and fastest growing religions of our age.

> Shall we write about the things not to be spoken of?
> Shall we divulge the things not to be divulged?
> Shall we pronounce the things not to be pronounced?
> Julian, *Hymn to the Mother of the Gods*[2]

Forget the modern world, forget electric light, forget central heating, forget penicillin, forget the computer and television, when we enter the 'Age of Shadows' we are in a time when light came from flickering candles, when heat came from smoking wood fires, when good health was a matter of luck not medicine, when information was controlled by priests and kings, when one lived in a world of shadows and whispers. We need to think ourselves into this world as much as we can in order to understand the extraordinary events we are about to encounter. The people we will meet here looked different, thought differently and lived different lives from you and me. It was once said that the past is another country, but it is more than that, it is another planet peopled by aliens.

Most alien of all was witchcraft. We have all suffered misfortune of one kind or another from time to time, but did you blame a witch for the problem? Did you accuse a neighbour of casting evil magic? Did you call for her to be hanged or burnt because of it? We all ponder the question of God from time to time, but have you ever sacrificed a black lamb at a crossroads to the Goddess of Witchcraft? Have you ever signed a pact with the Devil and danced at his Sabbath? All of this and more has happened, or been alleged to have happened, in the name of witchcraft.

As we travel back through time in our investigation of witchcraft we also travel back through language. We have not always had our words 'witch' and 'witchcraft'. They date from the Old English period (roughly from the fifth century CE (Comon Era) to the Norman Conquest in 1066), although their roots lie in the prehistoric Indo-European origins of our language. For hundreds of years 'witch' and 'witchcraft' have denoted maleficent magic and the users of it, and in that definition they can be found in other ages before the words were coined as we understand them now. The general belief that much human misfortune lay in the hands of magic-users and supernaturally endowed persons is thought to date back as far as the Palaeolithic Age (the Old Stone Age, approximately 10,000 BCE to 5,000 BCE), if not farther.[3]

The word 'witch' emerged out of the Indo-European root *weik*, along with 'guile', 'wile' and 'victim'. From this root grew four branches: *wih-l*, *wihl*, *wik* and *wikk*. In Old English *wih-l* developed into *wigle* 'sorcery' and *wiglera* 'sorcerer', which in turn led to our modern 'guile'. In Old Norse *wihl* became our modern 'wile'. In Old High German *wik*, 'holy', became *wihen* and modern *weihen*, 'to consecrate'. Finally, the branch *wikk*, meaning 'magic, sorcery', grew into *wikken*, 'predict', in Middle German and *wicca* (and its feminine form *wicce*), meaning 'witch', and *wiccian*, 'bewitch', in Old English. The word is tentatively connected with the idea of 'priestess' through the connotation of the German *weihen*, 'consecrate', and the distant echo of English 'victim', from the Latin *victima*, originally someone ritually killed. However, it first appears in English in its earliest identifiable form in the *Laws of Aelfred* of 890 CE as *wicca*, meaning specifically a male wizard, and only later, through *wicce*, transferred itself to the female sex.[4]

This Anglo-Saxon heritage is joined by a Classical strain – in particular the word 'magic' itself, which has come to us from the Greek *magoi*, a term used to identify a Persian priestly caste, but also words such as *pharmakon*, which now describes for us the benign practice of pharmacy and pharmacists, yet which could be applied in the ancient world to magic-users and poisoners.

This ambivalence of healer and poisoner implicit in *pharmakon* represents much of the ambivalence intrinsic to their magical figures. As we shall see, the prime exemplars of witchcraft in the ancient world – Hecate, Circe and Medea – were of a social, moral and religious complexity that later interpretations of witchcraft were unable to comprehend, or unwilling to acknowledge.

Whilst many of the origins of our ideas of witchcraft may lie in the god-filled world of ancient Greece, the origins of our outright repression of witchcraft lie in the East, in that fertile crescent that fed the ancient Hebrews and bred the cult of Christ. Whilst magic-users thronged the old world of Europe as both heroes and villains, exemplified best perhaps in the shape of Odin and Loki, it was not until the Christians came that magicians were universally branded 'witches' in the sense of malefactors and, under a simplistic moral dualism, consigned to the ranks of Satanism.

Out of this 'Age of Shadows' a new interpretation of witchcraft was to emerge, but only after the fires of persecution had gone out, only after the Christian Church's vice-like grip on European thought and imagination had eased, could this new interpretation arise. In the second part of this book, 'Born of Shadows', we examine how this revolution in thought came about, how it developed, and how ultimately it led to the creation of the modern religion of Witchcraft.

We look at the gradual development of this reinterpretation of witchcraft from diabolical heresy to Pagan survival, reversing the original Christian perversion of surviving, even thriving, Pagan religious observances as Satanic monstrosities. Yet just as the original Christian perversion of Paganism was predicated on wilful misunderstanding, so this new interpretation of witchcraft was not overly concerned with hard evidence.

However, this new interpretation met with a revival of magic, albeit deeply Hebraic and often Christian tainted magic, which provided a practical basis for these new theories. The two might have developed along their separate paths, a history of witchcraft and a practice of magic, had it not been for the direct intervention of one man, Gerald Gardner. Although he is widely claimed to be 'the Father of Modern Witchcraft', close analysis of his work reveals a tremendous debt to the vision, poetry and magick of an individual dubbed 'the Wickedest Man in the World', Aleister Crowley. We explore the relationship between these two men and the extent to which they created a new religion.

Although the creative vision and compelling voice that Crowley supplied gave the heart and soul to this new Gardnerian Witchcraft, his reputation was still too sulphurous and thus too potentially damaging to its reputation and, more than that, too obvious. Gardner's claims for his new Witchcraft could not stand the discovery of Crowley's hand behind it. It was one of Gardner's most enthusiastic disciples, Doreen Valiente, who covered-up the Crowleyan borrowings and helped launch Wicca as more believably the Old Religion.

Yet we will see that Wicca's own structure and Gardner's own style contributed to what could have been the nascent religion's destruction, but instead led to its greater promulgation and greater strength in action. In this we will have brought the history of Wicca up to date, but whereas most other literature on the subject comes to an end at this point, we go on in the third part, 'Empire of Shadows', to examine and explore the questions which are too often left unasked: who are the modern Witches, what do they do, and how many are there; what is their theology and what is their deeper experience of their religion; and finally, how do they define the magic that they practise, what do they use it for and what effect does it have upon them? Moreover, instead of simply gleaning this information from published sources we delve deeper into the reality of Witchcraft by asking the Witches themselves.

The first three parts of the book thus take us from the earliest beginnings of witchcraft in Western civilization through its darkest hours of witch-hunting – what have come to be known as the Burning Times – during the medieval and early modern period; and from there to what might be called the rebirth of witchcraft as Paganism, as the Old Religion and ultimately as Wicca; and finally to the now worldwide 'Empire of Shadows', an empire of the spirit, of magic, and of the triumph of the freedom of religious choice.

Then, in the Conclusion, 'Old Ways, New Directions', we will investigate the future of Witchcraft, exploring the unfolding social trends of post-Christianization and re-enchantment. Read on and watch witchcraft emerge from the shadows of the past, the shadows of persecution and misunderstanding, into the light of the future.

PART ONE

AGE OF SHADOWS

THE EARLY HISTORY OF WITCHCRAFT IN EUROPE

1. THE BIRTHPLACE OF ALL SORCERIES: WITCHCRAFT, WITCHES AND GODDESSES IN ANCIENT GREECE

Witchcraft has no origin, it has always been with us. Yet like the roots of our very civilization itself we can trace where it has come from and how it has developed over the millennia. And as with our civilization, so too do many of our ideas about witchcraft find their most identifiable beginnings in ancient Greece.

The birthplace of all sorceries and enchantments, that was what the writer Apuleius called the province of Thessaly in Greece.[1] 'Thessaly was a rural district much noted for its peculiarities, including Mount Olympus, the home of the gods, but sorcery and enchantment were not confined there. Everywhere in the ancient Greek world there was magic and everywhere there was magic there were those who worked it. Lying where it does, jutting out into the Mediterranean, Greece was a launch-pad for trading across the known world and an antenna for all its faiths and philosophies. The wandering heroes of Greece came into contact with the Magi (*magoi*) of Persia, the priests of Egypt and stranger peoples at the edges of the world, and learned their forbidden arts and came to worship their strangest gods.

The Goddess of Witchcraft

I call Einodian Hecate, lovely dame,
Of earthly, watery, and celestial frame.[2]

Magic was not the preserve of women in the ancient world, but in the tales of the heroes, warriors who preferred the drawn sword to the wand, the magic-users they encountered were almost always women – an arrangement greatly enjoyed by Odysseus, though the ruin of Jason. Nor was magic the preserve of goddesses: Hermes was the greatest magician amongst the Olympians. Yet it is a goddess who has become most closely associated with witchcraft: Hecate, 'She Who Works Her Will'.

Hecate, Goddess of the Moon and of the Underworld, mistress of magic, represented the dark of the moon in contrast to Diana, who portrayed its fulsome, silver beauty.[3] She was said to walk the earth at night, invisible to all save the watch-dogs that barked their alarm at her approach. Others say she walked abroad with a torch to light the way in the company of the spirits of the departed and a pack of baying hounds of her own. Crossroads and lonely places were sacred to her. Like the moon she was depicted as having three faces, but whereas the moon was seen as waxing, full and waning, Hecate was horse, dog and boar; and, as changeable as the moon, she could also be dog, horned maiden and goat.[4]

The ancient Greeks principally worshipped twelve gods, who were thought to live on Mount Olympus in Thessaly, and were thus known as the Olympians.[5] Hecate was not one of the Olympian gods, although the Greek mythologists later incorporated her into the pantheon. The poet-hero Orpheus brought her worship into Greece some time in the seventh century BCE, but she was an older deity worshipped by the Carians in south-western Asia Minor. This accounts for some of the confusion and overlap with the other lunar goddesses of the Greeks. The record of her worship spans from the eighth century BCE to the fourth century CE, a period of some 1,200 years and it is not surprising that both her representation and characteristics changed over this time.[6]

'Again, Phoebe came to the desired embrace of Coeus,' and the

16

Orpheus

Orpheus, the legendary Thracian poet, was the son of Oeagrus and Calliope, or by some other authorities the son of the god Apollo. It was said that he could cause inanimate objects to dance with the power of his music. However, his many adventures came to a tragic end when he dared venture into Hades (Hell) to rescue his dead wife Eurydice and bring her back to life. As he led her out of the infernal regions he forgot the orders of Pluto (God of the Underworld) and, anxiously turning round to see if Eurydice was still behind him, caused her to vanish for ever. The women of Thrace on hearing the news tore Orpheus to pieces during the Bacchanalia, the rite of the wine god Bacchus much noted for its orgiastic elements.[7] The myth can be read as an initiatory drama: journey to the underworld (the classic 'harrowing of Hell') and orgiastic dissolution of self – archetypal shamanic motifs.

---

result, according to Hesiod, was Hecate.[8] Phoebe and Coeus were Titans, a pre-Olympian race of beings vanquished by Zeus and imprisoned in Tartarus, which was the lowest Hell, as far beneath Hades as Hades was beneath the earth.[9] This parentage put Hecate on a par with Zeus and the other Olympian gods. Hesiod relates that Zeus honoured her above all others and bestowed upon her a share of the earth and the sea, and a glorious reception in the starry heavens.[10] Yet these gifts were not so readily Zeus's to give, for Hecate had prior claim: 'She holds, as the division was at the beginning, privilege both in earth, and in heaven, and in sea.'[11]

The Ancient Titles of Hecate

Propylaia, the One Before the Gate
Einodia, In the Road (i.e. at the crossroads)
Propolos, the Attendant Who Leads
Phosphoros, the Light-Bringer
Kourotrophos, the Child's Nurse
Chthonia, Of the Earth[13]

Hecate is not generally thought of as 'tender-hearted',[12] – the Greeks often addressed a ferocious deity in euphemistic terms – but it

17

was in her power to be beneficent. However, Orpheus's 'lovely dame' was nevertheless 'pleased with dark ghosts' and elsewhere a 'terrible queen' who devoured beasts, roamed mountains, loved desolation and danced with the dead amongst their tombs.[14] As her worship developed in the ancient world her chthonic, underworld, powers came more and more to the fore so that this once beneficent equal of Zeus became the 'Lady of Tartaros', patroness of wickedness and black magic.[15] Her cult grew in ways that to our eyes seem bizarre and monstrous and the young maiden Orpheus found in the East became a three-headed creature, wreathed in serpents, 'Nocturnal and Infernal', who feasted on hearts and flesh, and spread madness, the subduer of mankind 'before whom Daimons quake in Fear'.[16]

Hecate's worship was widespread: 'For to this day, whenever anyone of men on earth offers rich sacrifices and prays for favour according to custom, he calls upon Hecate.'[17] She sat with kings to aid them in their judgement. She gave victory to warriors. She made winners of athletes. She rewarded fishermen with good catches. She blessed the husbandman and goatherd with increased stock. She was indispensable to parents as the nurse of the young. And all these things were in her power to take away. As her ancient titles suggest, Hecate presided over the crossroads of life, the moments of birth and death, guiding the spirit into incarnation and leading it into the grave.

Whilst Thessaly was renowned for its witches it was not noted for its temples to Hecate. The Thessalians venerated a goddess known by the title Einodia, meaning 'in the road', who was only later identified with Hecate.[18] In Caria, whence Orpheus reputedly brought her worship, a sanctuary to Hecate at Lagina drew large crowds,[19] but later Roman popularity for the site and extensive rebuilding in the first century BCE has destroyed most of the early archaeological evidence. At several sites in the northern and central Aegean area Hecate appears in a guardian role to other cultic sanctuaries, as at the Athenian Acropolis, Eleusis, Argos, Selinus, Samothrace and Didyma. The earliest archaeological record of Hecate worship is a tantalizing altar inscription dated to the sixth century BCE in the sanctuary of Apollo Delphinios in Miletos on the coast of modern Turkey, some 50 km from Lagina. The sites are scattered, the evidence scant, little remains to indicate what the true worship of Hecate might have been.

The Sacred Days of Hecate

The Greeks observed two principal days of Hecatean worship: the Celebration of Hecate of the Moon on 13 August, a day on which she was called upon to protect the harvest; and the Day of Hecate at the Crossroads on 30 November. The Romans after them honoured Hecate on the 29th of every month, on what was called the Moon of Hecate.[20] In Roman-occupied Ionia (part of modern Turkey) a religious calendar found at Erythai near Ephesos from the fourth or third century BCE specifies offerings to Hecate to be made on the first, second, and seventh days of every month.[21]

In the second century CE the Greek traveller and geographer Pausanias identified Aegina as the then principal centre of Hecate worship.[22] Aegina was an island lying off the coast of the headland of Attica on the Greek mainland, not an oar's pull from Athens, the heart of Greek civilization. An annual festival founded by Orpheus, involving 'mystic rites' (*Ecatica phasmata*) was held at Aegina and, though details are scarce, it is thought to share features with the orgiastic rites of Dionysus and the Corybantes,[23] and with later depictions of the witches' Sabbat.[24] Here the artist Myron (flourished *c.* 460 BCE) fashioned a single-bodied, single-headed statue of Hecate. Pausanias ascribes the triform Hecate to Alcamenes and tells us that the Athenians called this statue Epipurgidia, 'on the tower'. These images were honoured in the same manner as at Eleusis, that other famous cultic centre: with sacrifices.[25]

Hecate liked the blood of black lambs and black dogs to be shed in her name,[26] and depending on the worshippers' intention would demand different offerings: 'For doing Good, offer Storax, Myrrh, Sage, Frankincense, a Fruit Pit. But for doing Harm, offer Magical Material of a Dog and a Dappled Goat (or in a similar way, of a Virgin Untimely Dead).'[27]

She was also propitiated with 'suppers', small dishes of food left at her favoured spot, the crossroads, by supplicants and worshippers at the dead of night, in the dark of the moon. These dishes would consist of the remains of purificatory sacrifices, sometimes including garlic. Chicken hearts, honey cakes, fish and eggs might also be left as offerings, especially on the last day of the month. Special statues or pillars called *Hecateae* were erected at crossroads in her honour and to invoke her aid as 'the One Before the Gate' to protect travellers from harm.[28]

Night was the proper time for the invocation of Hecate. Night, then as now, was the proper time for all anti-social magic. Under the reign of darkness the Grecian witch could vent her darkest desires. Also called upon by the barbarous names Bombo, Gorgo and Mormo,[29] Hecate was not just a creature of the night, but its queen, as this ancient invocation shows:

> Come infernal, terrestrial, and celestial Bombo, goddess of the crossroads, guiding light, queen of the night, enemy of the sun, and friend and companion of the darkness; you who rejoice to hear the barking of dogs and to see blood flow; you who wander among the tombs in the hours of darkness, thirsty for blood, and the terror of mortal men; Gorgo, Mormo, moon of a thousand forms, look favourably on my sacrifice.[30]

It has been conjectured that the name Bombo is onomatopoeic, representing both the sound of the magical instrument used to invoke her, the rhombus,[31] and the sound she made upon appearance – *Bombo!*, like a sonic boom, a spiritual boom caused by the goddess puncturing ordinary space and time, the sound of the veil between the worlds being torn apart.

Hecate was not only worshipped in the ancient world, but also invoked for her magical powers. Whilst Orpheus intoned, 'Propitious grant our just desire's success', others more directly called upon her powers, and not always for the success of just desires. Fragments of magical papyri from the third or fourth century CE reveal a Hecate who could protect the magician (and also protect him from Hecate), aid him in divination, save him from death, inflict insomnia upon his enemies and cancel the spells of others.[32] Even though of an apparently later period all the familiar elements of Hecatean invocation feature in this spell. As always the proper place for invocation is the crossroads and the proper time is night. However, Hecate is given the additional title of Ereschigal, a Babylonian goddess, and strange words appear, the so-called Ephesian Letters – *askei kataski*, etc. – which have never been deciphered.

The Charm of Hekate Ereschigal[33]

... name ... a favour charm, a charm to dissolve a spell, an amulet, and a victory charm: 'aa emptôkom basum, protect me.'

Charm of Hekate Ereschigal against fear of punishment: if she comes forth, let her say: 'I am Ereschigal,' holding her thumbs, and not even one evil can befall her. But if she comes close to you, hold your right heel and say: 'Ereschigal, virgin, dog, serpent, wreath, key, herald's wand, golden is the sandal of the Lady of Tartaros,' and you will prevail upon her.[34]

'Askei kataski erôn oreôn iôr mega semnuêr bauï', (three times), 'Phobantia, remember, I have been initiated, and I went down into the chamber of the Dactyls,[35] and I saw the other things down below, virgin, dog,' etc. Say it at the crossroads, and turn around and flee, because it is at those places that she appears. Say it late at night, about what you wish, and it will reveal it in your sleep; and if you are led away to death, say these things while scattering seeds of sesame, and it will save you.

'Phorba phorba breimô azziebua'. Take bran of first quality and sandalwood and vinegar of the sharpest sort and mould cakes. And write his name upon them, and so hide them, saying into the light the name of Hekate, and 'Take away his sleep from so-and-so,' and he will be sleepless and worried.

Against fear and to dissolve spells: Say, [text missing]

From being the equal of Zeus, King of the Gods, Hecate has descended in the religious imagination to reside almost entirely in the dark netherworld. Her wide-ranging influence and beneficent powers forgotten, she has become the epitome of evil. This image of Hecate as the Goddess of Witchcraft became so firmly and so widely entrenched that when Shakespeare came to write *Macbeth* more than 2,000 years later he chose her as the goddess his three witches invoked, a choice, what is more, that was immediately recognizable by his audience. Yet for other reasons, as we shall see, the great nocturnal and infernal queen, even in this debased form, was entirely ignored by the inventors of the modern Witchcraft religion of Wicca in the twentieth century.

The most renowned, most feared witches of the ancient Greek world were the daughters of Hecate, Circe and Medea.[36] Although they were traditionally related, the term 'daughters of Hecate' is perhaps more indicative of their religious loyalties than their parentage. For whilst genealogy is difficult to establish in the mythological era, as we saw with Hecate herself, what is clear beyond doubt is that both Circe and Medea were priestesses of Hecate, and that they drew their power from her and invoked her in their rites. Nor were they Hecate's only daughters in this more liberal sense. Greek and Roman legends and history abound with tales of Hecatean women: Ovid's Dipsias, Horace's Sagana, Canidia who drew down the moon, Erichtho who could cause the dead to speak, Cassandra who could see the future,[37] Pamphile who could change herself into a bird and Theoris who was burnt for fear of her dread art. Yet Circe and Medea remain the pre-eminent daughters of Hecate in the ancient world, immortalized in the great myths of Greece, just as seductive and instructive now as they ever were, and just as powerfully definitive of the character of the witch.

The Witch of the Wailing Island

And you, too, daughter of the Sun, Circe the witch,
come and cast cruel spells . . .[38]

Circe, whom Homer called 'Circe of the lovely tresses', 'the beautiful Circe, a formidable goddess' and 'the formidable goddess with a woman's voice', sister of the wizard Aeëtes, daughter of the Sun and Perse, Daughter of the Ocean,[39] – it appears her parentage was contested – dwelt on the island of Aeaea ('wailing'), the 'sepulchral island'.[40] A goddess in her own right, Circe was yet married to a mortal, a king of the Sarmaritans.[41] The union was not a happy one and it was for his murder by poison that she was banished to this island of wailing. Her name means 'she-falcon', a bird of omen in Greece, and is thought to be an onomatopoeic attempt to render its cry, 'circ, circ', into Greek.[42] The wailing she-falcon circling round, the circle (*circos*) casting enchantress, she built a palace for herself on Aeaea, and turned all who set foot there into animals.

She is the archetypal temptress. Noted for her beauty, her lovely hair, her sweet voice, she sits at the centre of her island weaving and waiting for incautious wanderers: '. . . And they heard Circe inside singing in a beautiful voice, as she worked at her great, godly web . . .'[43]

Her spinning shows her to be in control of men's destinies. The web imagery that Homer uses when describing her is suggestive: it symbolizes Circe's waiting trap. Her web is her beauty, her silken hair its entrapping threads, her sweet voice an intoxicating venom. She lures her victims into her palace and throws them off their guard with a fine banquet. As her guests dine on the drugged food and fall under its spell they 'lose all memory of their native land'. She then strikes them with her wand, transforming them into beasts: swine, wolves or mountain lions.

> Who knows not Circe,
> The daughter of the sun, whose charmed cup
> Whoever tasted, lost his upright shape,
> And downward fell into a grovelling swine? [44]

We first encounter Circe in the tale of Odysseus where, as bewitching temptress, she is ultimately both a magical test of heroic ambitions and an initiatrix into dark mysteries. She embodies that Hecatean ambivalence of protectress and destroyer, of helper and fiend. Yet her trap is not an unwelcome one. Her palace is surrounded by shape-changed men who, instead of raging against their plight, act in a most gentle and uncomplaining manner. It is only Odysseus who rejects her animal paradise, her reverse Island of Doctor Moreau. Odysseus exemplifies both the overcoming of temptation and the transcendence of man's animal desires in his confrontation with the bewitching, web-weaving, falcon-feathered goddess of prey:

> Tell me, Muse, of the resourceful man who wandered very far after he had sacked the holy city of Troy.[45]

During his long voyage home after the Trojan War, he came by chance upon Circe's island. Not knowing where he was or who dwelt there he sent a party of his men to investigate the source of the smoke that rose from the dense woods in the island's interior. Only one of them returned. The reconnaissance party had found a palace surrounded by wild, but apparently tame, beasts – wolves and mountain lions – and on hearing a lovely voice from within had entered, never to re-appear. Odysseus set off after them, driven by a hero's courage and a captain's need for a crew. As he made his way through 'the enchanted glades'[46] he fortuitously met Hermes, the Messenger of the Gods.[47] Hermes explained to Odysseus how Circe worked her magic and taught him a counter-spell to use against her. Against the drugged food he provided Odysseus with an antidote, a plant called *moly*: 'It had a black root and a milk-white flower. The gods call it Moly, and it is an awkward plant to dig up.'[48] This herbal counter-attack had the added advantage of disabling Circe's magic wand. Hermes also told Odysseus that when near defeat Circe would invite him to her bed, an offer that he should swiftly accept, but warned him to make her swear an oath by the 'blessed gods' not to try any trickery before releasing her from the power of his counter-magic. So by magic rather than brawn the hero overcame the witch, released his men (who as swine have been kept prisoner in a pen) and learned from her the art of necromancy, vital to his being able to return home again and end his incessant voyaging.

The ritual drama of Odysseus and Circe begins with the sacrifice of a stag, the archetypal embodiment of nature, an event shared with other Greek myths, notably that of Diana (another moon deity, or another name for the same) and Actaeon. However, in the case of Actaeon and Diana, the protagonist hero is torn to pieces, whilst in that of Odysseus and Circe, the hero wins the maiden and saves his people. After killing the stag, which Odysseus's crew marvelled at for its great size, the next stage in the drama is animal transformation. This takes place as part of a feast and may be seen as an orgiastic possession, with Circe's drugged guests taking the part of swine, synonymous with debased animality. In the later trial accounts of witchcraft, the Devil was commonly worshipped by orgiastic feasting marked by animal transformation, and witches themselves were frequently accused of going in the form of animals to work mischief, either as werewolves, or more often as less monstrous creatures. In the case of Odysseus the encounter with Circe is an essential preparatory and initiatory ritual that enables him to acquire the art of necromancy. However, he resists orgiastic transformation through the use of a counter-charm, and having broken Circe's power exacts a promise from her before sexually concluding the ritual. So, whilst this ritual drama may be seen as a rite of Circe, or of Hecate with Circe as her priestess, it cannot be overlooked that Odysseus is favoured by Hermes against the power of

Hecate as represented by Circe, and the rite can therefore also be seen less as a cultic ritual and more as a religious battle between opposing magical deities, or indeed a confusing overlap of the two.

Animal transformation in the rite of Circe is not confined to swine-form; Homer relates that Circe's castle is surrounded by men in the form of mountain lions and wolves that behave like dogs. The dog is the animal sacred to Hecate and one we would have more readily expected than the swine, which seems peculiar to this special rite of Circe. Traditionally, the lion, wolf and swine represent pride, greed and bestiality. Yet for Odysseus's men the process of animal transformation has the effect of making them younger and more handsome when they resume human form. It would seem that orgiastic possession and descent into sin has beneficial results: their freedom to give full vent to a bestial characteristic releases pent up, and hence dangerous, nervous energies. Such catharsis, or purification of the emotions, was a central component of Greek tragic drama and later became the foundation of modern psychoanalysis. More than a myth, this rite of Circe is a complex psycho-drama of magic and religious ritual involving psycho-active substances and sex that positively transforms the participants.

Odysseus's highly symbolic encounter with Circe supplies us with possibly the only insight into what went on during those orgiastic rites of Hecate that Orpheus introduced into Greek culture and are now only dimly remembered as being somewhat akin to the infamous debaucheries of the Dionysiacs and Corybantes. What is more, it embodies all the essential ingredients that would later be identified with the witches' Sabbat: feasting, animal transformation, orgy and sexual initiation.

The High Priestess of Murder

The witch-goddess of the edge of the world, Medea had a fearsome reputation. Yet her tragic plight invites our sympathy. She is a passionate woman driven to extreme actions by love and the betrayal of love. She is a witch capable of defeating dragons and monsters with her sorcery, and of overcoming men by her cunning and ruthlessness. She is a goddess revered by the Aryan tribes of Parthia. She is the child and priestess of Hecate, and Circe's niece.

She is the daughter of the wizard-king Aeëtes and princess of an exotic eastern kingdom.[49] But ultimately she is a fool for love.

Named the 'wise' or 'cunning one,' she was wise in the lore of herbs and cunning in her schemes.[50] She knew which herbs could kill or cure and she knew which words could move heaven and earth at her whim. The Greeks called her *polypharmakos*, an expert enchantress, 'knowledgeable in many evil things'.[51] A chariot drawn by winged serpents conveyed her across the night sky, leaving broomsticks to more humble witches. At midnight, with her hair flying and dancing barefoot under the stars, she howled her threefold incantations. She invoked the forces of darkness – the very night itself and infernal Hecate – and the forces of nature – the gods of the forest, of the earth, wind and water – to pervert the natural order of things, making rivers flow backwards, storms appear in clear skies, trees turn upside down, rocks fall from the mountainside, the solid earth quake, the dead return from their graves, and the moon crash down from the heavens.

Medea's Magic

To protect against fire. Medea makes a paste from the Colchian crocus that protects against fire-breathing bulls.

To turn an army against itself. Medea defeats an army of warriors who sprang from dragon's teeth sown upon the ground because she knows that a stone quoit (a ring used in games and thrown at a peg) thrown amongst them will cause them to turn their swords against each other.

To overcome dragons. Using secret words and the juice of freshly cut juniper, Medea stupefies the dragon guardian of the Golden Fleece.

To level giants. When the giant Talos threatens to sink the Argo Medea tricks him into drinking a sleeping potion, believing it will make him immortal.

To poison enemies. Medea infuses a goblet of wine with the deadly poison aconite in an attempt to murder the hero Theseus.

To restore lost youth. Medea's most powerful magic is the Charm of Rejuvenation, a great spell to reverse the ravages of time and restore the flush of youth.

We first meet Medea in the story of Jason and the Argonauts and their famous quest for the fabulous Golden Fleece. Here she is a princess, the daughter of Aeëtes, King of Colchis, living in the city of Aea on the coast of the Black Sea in that part of the world now known as Georgia, which was for the ancient Greeks the farthest limit of their world, where the sun in his chariot rose to light the world. The Greek mythologists subsume her role beneath the heroic quest of Jason for the Golden Fleece, but it is only by her magic and cunning that Jason succeeds, and not only in acquiring the Fleece.

Medea enables Jason to overcome the impossible tasks set by her father to prevent him from winning the Fleece. She smears his body with a flame-retardant herbal paste to protect him against the fire-breathing bulls he must yoke and use to plough the Field of Ares. She tells him the trick that allows him to defeat the armed warriors who spring up from the dragon's teeth he sows in the freshly ploughed earth. She drugs the monstrous guardian of the Fleece, allowing Jason to steal it. She facilitates their escape by cutting up her own brother and casting him into the sea, forcing the pursuing Aeëtes to abandon the chase to collect his dismembered son's remains.[52] Finally, she wins Jason back his father's usurped kingdom by tricking the impostor's daughters into cutting him to pieces.

The Charm of Rejuvenation

Medea builds two altars of turf, the one on the right to Hecate, the one on the left to Hebe, goddess of youth, and ties them with vervain and other plants. She digs two pits, one to catch the hot gush of blood from the black ram she sacrifices and the other to catch her libation of milk and wine. She sets her cauldron over a fire and throws in the ingredients of her spell as the poet Ovid tells us in his *Metamorphoses*:

'. . . roots cut from Thessalian valleys, seeds, flowers, dark juices . . .; stones from far East, sands washed by Ocean's reflux, hoar-frosts from moon-lit nights; owl flesh and feathers; entrails of werewolf changeable to man; Cynphus River snakes' scaly membranes; liver of long-lived stag; and she adds above all, head and beak of a crow more than nine lifetimes old.'[53]

And she does all this because she loves Jason and has extracted a promise from him before the altar of Hecate to marry her. Yet here Jason has used a little magic of his own and with the aid of Aphrodite, goddess of love, he charms the heart-strings of this foreign princess upon their first encounter. Like Odysseus with Circe, Jason wins through the use of magic and again at the price of a sexual bargain. Yet where Odysseus keeps his, Jason proves faithless. Having won the Fleece and regained his father's kingdom, Jason spurns Medea for the embraces of another woman.

There is no more classic example of Medea's guile, of her cold-blooded temperament, than the vengeance she wreaks upon the faithless Jason. Reminding him of his pledge made before the altar of Hecate, Medea gives him a second chance, but he brushes off his hasty oath, scorning the great infernal goddess as well as her priestess. Medea feigns submission whilst plotting deadly revenge. She has her own children by Jason present his new bride with a gown. The hapless bride dons the garment, which Medea has coated with incendiary spells and before the assembled wedding guests bursts into flames. Only Jason escapes the ensuing conflagration, which wastes the royal palace. Her fury unsated, Medea has further horrors planned. She slaughters their children and leaves the wailing Jason to mourn over their corpses as she flies off in her serpent-drawn chariot.

She goes on to further adventures, but Jason is ruined. His wife and children are dead; therefore his royal heirs and the means to replenish them have been destroyed. After some forlorn wandering, Jason comes across the old *Argo* beached upon the shore and as he sits in its shade pondering his loss he is ignominiously crushed by the boat toppling on top of him (one detects the impish finger of some god in that accident). Medea, by way of several colourful incidents including the attempted murder of her stepson Theseus, curing Heracles (Hercules) of his wife- and child-slaughtering madness, and teaching snake charming to an Italian tribe, eventually returns to Colchis, and in restoring her deposed father to the throne, atones for her original crimes. The hero Jason is ultimately destroyed by his unheroic faithlessness, whilst the anti-hero Medea is redeemed by her own heroic homecoming. So a full reading of the myth beyond the familiar gung-ho Jason and the Argonauts story reveals a complex tale that subverts the usual heroic conventions.

There are other interpretations of Medea's story available to us, ones that see her as the initiatrix into Medean mysteries, the facilitator of kingly ambitions and the foundress of a religious cult, that of Hera Akraia. Medea uses her greatest spell, the Charm of Rejuvenation, to destroy Pelias and return the kingdom of Iolcus to Jason's father Aeson, and again to restore the ageing man's youth. As such it is a test of royal legitimacy: the false king dies horribly, the true king is restored. She again played a similar role in Athens. After leaving Jason she married Aegeus, King of Athens, and conspired to poison her stepson so that her own children by Aegeus might gain precedence. She was discovered in her crime and fled the kingdom, but strangely this attempted murder was commemorated by the erection of an expensive monument. So the deeper significance of Medea's attempt to murder the young heir is her testing of the genuineness of his claim, since it is in the process of lifting Medea's poisoned chalice to his lips that he is recognised as Aegeus's heir. Looking again at the Jason myth in this light we see Medea fulfilling a similar role. She initiates Jason through ritual ordeals (the fire-breathing bulls, dragon's teeth warriors and confrontation with the final guardian) into mysteries represented by his ownership of the Golden Fleece, an act that allows him to return to his homeland and reclaim the kingdom for his father. Indeed, there is also a version of the myth in which she directly uses the Charm of Rejuvenation upon Jason himself.

The cult of Hera Akraia, however, seems to serve a different purpose. Medea's murder of her own children establishes the annual ceremony of 'hiding' fourteen children in the sanctuary of Hera Akraia to propitiate a potentially destructive goddess. Yet here again a change of status is involved. The fourteen children, drawn from noble families, are confined as they reach puberty for a period of a year. Thus they are transformed from children into adults and come into their station in life as members of the aristocracy.

Medea's parentage is uncertain; we are unsure as to who exactly she was. We first hear of her in the mythic quest of Jason and the Argonauts, where she is simply a mortal woman though still of royal blood, but learn from other sources that she was regarded as the daughter of the goddess Hecate and indeed as a goddess in her own right. This variation may represent a theological development. Like

Hecate, she is not Greek, but whilst Hecate retains her divine position as the Greeks grow in power and influence, Medea the goddess
is ousted by the Olympian Hera and demoted to the mortal realm.
This perhaps explains why a ritual she is credited with founding is
devoted not to herself but to Hera Akraia.[54]

Almost every point in one story of Medea can be contradicted by
other sources: Medea endlessly cuts up and rejuvenates herself. Yet
we always see her through Greek eyes: the exotic foreign princess
who comes from where the sun rises out of the earth; the dangerous
witch with unnatural powers; the heartless murderess without
compassion or remorse. We do not see her through her own eyes: a
royal princess of a noble, god-descended house; a passionate lover
driven beyond reason by love; an abandoned wife, humiliated by the
one to whom she had given everything; a priestess whose most sacred
goddess is profaned.

Parricide, infanticide, regicide – Medea's murderous wrath is yet
tempered by the tragedy of her situation. We recoil at her deeds, but
sympathize with her plight. Whilst certain interpretations have tended
to dominate – Euripides's Medea as the wronged woman, for example
– we see in her again the archetypal ambivalence of the witch figure –
hero's helper and hero's enemy – and we see gathered around her the
fear of magic and the suspicion of female power. Medea still has
messages for us today, messages of love and loyalty and the destructive
power of both, but to the student of witchcraft she teaches that the
witch will always work her will in the creative imagination.

'Remember, if ever you make it back home, the name of Medea, and
so I shall remember you when you are far away.'[55]

The witch-goddesses of the ancient world were not entirely bad –
neither pure evil, nor pure good. They were not devils, nor yet angels.
They were morally complex beings capable of a wide range of actions
and feelings. They had to be wooed by magic, but once won over were
generous in their bounty. We have few details of the Hecate cult, but
from the tales of Circe and Medea it appears that their assistance
involved a sexual bargain which if broken or betrayed led to dire retribution. Although not strictly equivalent, this can be seen as something
of a forerunner of the pact with the Devil that featured so strongly in

medieval and early modern accounts of witchcraft. Indeed through Hecate, Circe and Medea we have met many of the elements characteristic of these accounts: night as the proper time of magic; the animal transformation of celebrants; feasting, orgy and sexual initiation; and the power of the witch to pervert the normal course of the universe. What we have yet to add is a male leader of these rites. The accounts of Odysseus with his stag's horns and Jason with the ram's horns of the Golden Fleece paint them as magician-priests of horned gods, but it is with the witch-goddesses that they make their pacts. And we have yet to add a leader of pure evil. Although feared and occasionally reviled, the moral complexity of the witch-goddesses could never allow them to represent just one side of the moral equation.

2. EAST OF MIDGARD: WITCHCRAFT, MAGIC AND RELIGION AMONGST THE PAGAN TRIBES OF NORTHERN EUROPE

In the mythological imagination of the northern Europeans, East of Midgard was their very own 'birthplace of all sorceries', the home of the greatest and most feared witch, Angerbode. Encircled by impassable mountains and trackless forests, the peoples of Northern Europe held witchcraft dear, both as the font of wisdom and as the scapegoat of disaster.

As the Romans marched across Europe they encountered a tribal people inhabiting the dense forests, marshes and plains of Gaul and Germania who practised magic.[1] Witchcraft amongst the Germanic tribes was the province of gods and kings, like Odin (Woden), the Father of the Gods, and Erick of the Windy Hat, King of Sweden, as well as the preserve of wicked old women like Angerbode, who mothered the wolves that would eat the sun and moon (the fearful race of Fenrer). Magic was an ambiguous practice and some elements of it were more acceptable to the community than others. As we saw in ancient Greece, a hero like Jason might with impunity practise magic occasionally, but an exotic foreign woman like Medea, who practised it all the time, was immediately suspect.

The Prophetess of the Forest

The warrior tribes of the northern forests believed their women were endowed with prophetic powers. What was persecuted as witchcraft by Christianity was celebrated as natural by the Pagan peoples of Europe. But even before Christianity's corrupting effect, religious differences between Pagan Rome and the rest of Europe would lead to bloody slaughter.

The earliest extant accounts of these tribes derive from the Roman period, most famously that of Tacitus in his *Germania*, written during the first century CE.[2] The richest source of myth and legend, the *Eddas*, were not discovered until the seventeenth century and do not date from such an early period as Tacitus. The *Elder Edda* is believed to have been written in the ninth century CE, the Younger in the thirteenth century CE, and is unfortunately tainted by Christianity. Thus not only is the geographical area vast, but the sources are disparate and greatly separated by time. It is immensely difficult, therefore, to reconstruct the position of magic and witchcraft in the tribes of northern Europe.

Evidence of their magical practices, however, pre-dates the written sources even of Tacitus. Yet if interpretation is difficult in later times, when such sources are available, it is even more problematic in the earliest times when only mouldering archaeological scraps survive to hint at the rich and complex cultures of prehistory. A funeral site dating from the Bronze Age (2000–500 BCE) revealed a most suggestive scene: a woman's body buried with the claw-joint of a lynx, a weasel's bones, snakes' spinal cords, horses' teeth, a twig from the rowan tree, a knife blade broken in half and two pieces of iron pyrites, all apparently of magical qualities which possibly point to her being a sorceress or shamanic figure.[3]

Let us begin with Tacitus, for we, like him, despite the Anglo-Saxon blood in many of us, are strangers to this land and approach like travellers from some far off place. Tacitus's Germany was encompassed by the Rhine to the west which separated it from Gaul, by the Danube to the east which separated it from Rhoetia and Pannonia, by the sea to the north and by mountains to the south. He found the Germanic peoples living in scattered communities, the bravest men much given to idleness when not warring with one another and letting the old men and women do the domestic work. Theirs was a war economy, founded on tribute and plunder from the vanquished, and hence bravery and skill at arms were their most cherished qualities. In this it was akin to the Romans' own economic system, but the Germans were, like the ancient Greeks, a society of heroic warriors where individual prowess was esteemed above all else. The Romans, on the other hand, were a tightly drilled and highly disciplined fighting force of units, not individuals. This Roman collectivization and standardization of military might allowed them to sweep aside the less efficient armies of heroic individuals.

The Germanic tribes followed a lunar calendar, worshipped a multitude of gods in sacred groves and relied heavily on divination to decide important matters. Their chief gods were Tuisto, who was born of the earth, and Mannus, his son, the forefathers of the German peoples. But they also venerated many others that Tacitus only distinguishes by the classical appellations of Mercury, Hercules, Mars and Isis. Their worship was not uniform: the Aestyan nations honoured the Mother of the Gods and wore the symbol of the wild boar as emblematic of this; the Reudignians, Aviones, Angles, Varinians, Eudoses, Suardones and Nuithones all worshiped Mother Earth; the Naharvalians worshiped Alcis. To Mercury they were wont to offer human sacrifice on certain holy days, whilst Isis was said to be worshipped by the tribe of the Suevians.

Whatever their particular gods, the Germanic peoples generally set aside sacred groves for their worship and as repositories for their images. These representations of their gods were, when dire need arose, carried into battle to ensure victory. They were not cast in any human likeness. The sacred grove itself became the god, as Tacitus explains:

> From the grandeur and majesty of beings celestial, they judge it altogether unsuitable to hold the Gods enclosed within walls, or to represent them under any human likeness. They consecrate whole woods and groves, and by the names of the Gods they call these recesses; divinities these, which only in contemplation and mental reverence they behold.

However, it is the German people's love of divination that Tacitus finds most remarkable. They believed their womenfolk to be endowed with prophetic abilities and would frequently consult them. Indeed, they went as far as to single out two women of exceptional ability, Veleda and Aurinia, and worshipped them as divine. But, it is 'to the use of lots and auguries [that] they are addicted beyond all other nations'. Tacitus describes how a twig is taken from a fruit tree, (he does not specify the variety, which would have been important), cut in two and inscribed with 'so many several marks'. A priest for the people, or a father for his family, then takes these pieces and casts them upon a white cloth. With eyes heavenward the gods are reverentially invoked before the diviner picks up each piece three times and interprets their meaning. They would also see portents of the future in the flight patterns of birds and hear it in their calls. The behaviour of the milk-white horses kept in the sacred groves also told those skilled in such matters of things to come.

To decide other matters the community assembled at either the full or new moon because this time was held to be most propitious for beginning any transaction. This rulership of the moon over their events was mirrored in their custom of marking the passage of time by counting the passing of nights rather than days. Tacitus remarks that 'with them the night seems to lead and govern the day'.[4]

The Place of German Women
Although a fierce warrior race, the Germanic tribes revered their womenfolk. According to Tacitus:

In history we find that some armies already yielding and ready to fly, have been by the women restored, through their inflexible importunity and entreaty, presenting their breasts, and showing their impending captivity; an evil to the Germans then by far most dreadful when it befalls their women. So that the spirit of such cities as amongst their hostages are enjoined to send their damsels of quality, is always engaged more effectually than that of others. They even believe them endowed with something celestial and the spirit of prophecy. Neither do they disdain to consult them, nor neglect the responses which they return. In the reign of the deified Vespasian, we have seen Veleda for a long time, and by many nations, esteemed and adored as a divinity. In times past they likewise worshipped Aurinia and several more, from no complaisance or effort of flattery, nor as Deities of their own creating.

The People of the Oak

At the time of Tacitus's writing the Gauls were a largely vanquished people subdued by German and Roman onslaughts, and considered effeminate and of little account. A hundred years earlier when Julius Caesar encountered them he found them more formidable foes and it took him eight years to subdue them (58–50 BCE). It is from Caesar's campaigning that we learn much about the Gallic druids. They were a priestly class, comparable in esteem to the nobility and organized under the authority of a single individual, and administered justice as well as religion.

Druid means 'knowing the oak', for the priests of the Celtic tribes kept the sacred oak groves and harvested the miraculous mistletoe that twined itself about the trees.[5] Within the grove the druids held court, administering justice, foretelling the future of the tribe and negotiating with the gods on their behalf. Our sources about their practices are few, written by Greeks and Romans and scattered over many centuries, from the earliest accounts of the second century BCE until their virtual extinction in the fourth century CE. We have nothing in writing from the druids themselves because theirs was a secret and orally transmitted culture. But their power must once have been vast. The Celtic tribes stretched from Britain and Ireland across Europe through Gaul, the Balkans and Asia Minor, and the druids stood next to their gods, the equals of the warrior nobility and endowed with great power, both spiritual and temporal.

They were undoubtedly ancient; Diogenes Laertius, writing in the third century CE, reported that they were considered a venerable institution even in the fourth century BCE. They were also undoubtedly important; the Greek philosopher Dio Chrysotomus (*c.* 40–112 CE) compared them to those other great mystical castes of ancient times, the Persian magi, Egyptian priests and Hindu brahmin. However, we have only the sketchiest details of what they did.

Most accounts agree that they were the keepers of the traditional wisdom of their community and versed in theology, moral philosophy and the interpretation of natural phenomena. They read omens and conducted sacrifices in the proper manner; they kept the calendar and knew astronomy; and they were learned in herbal medicine and poetry – doctors, poets, priests and astronomers all in one. Modern writers have speculated that they were a shamanic caste practising ecstatic dancing, drumming, chanting and voluntary possession, which is plausible though not conclusive on the limited evidence we have.[6]

The magic of the druids derived from their knowledge of herbs, particularly mistletoe, and of wonders like the magic egg formed from the spit of enraged snakes (which was guaranteed to procure success in court and the favours of princes). They would foretell the future by observing hares or the flight of crows and eagles, or by watching the death throes of sacrificial victims and examining their entrails. During religious festivals they would interpret dreams. With druids chanting round him the dreamer would drift into sleep (or possibly some sort of hypnotic trance induced by the tone and rhythm of the chanting) and upon waking would describe his dream for the druids to decipher.

The ritual cutting of the mistletoe was perhaps the greatest event in the druids' religious calendar. During the summer and winter solstices, when the moon was six days old, the chosen druid, in a white robe, would climb the oldest, most mistletoe-wreathed oak. With a golden sickle in his left hand, its crescent shape reflecting the thin slice of the moon in the sky, he would cut a sprig of the sacred plant. It would be caught in a white cloth before it fell to the ground. Two white bulls would be sacrificed and a great feast held.[7]

Known as golden bough, Devil's fuge, thunderbesom (*donnerbesen*) and the witch's broom, the mistletoe was popularly used to protect against witchcraft, i.e., maleficent magic, although nowadays it is likely only to be met with at Christmas in the hand of some hopeful looking for a kiss – a pale imitation of the druids' original fertility rite. The plant aroused such awe because of its apparent ability to propagate itself magically and grow without touching the earth, which marked it as a plant apart. It was believed to descend from heaven in a lightning bolt: amongst the Norsemen it was sacred to the God of Thunder, Thor. This association lends it the folkloric quality of being able to protect a house from storms. However, its seeds are propagated by bird droppings and because it feeds parasitically on its host plant it can grow without being rooted in the earth.[8]

Mistletoe Medicine

Mistletoe's Latin name is *viscum album*. Its twigs and leaves contain a viscotoxin that slows the heart rate and dilates the arteries producing a sedative effect and lowering the blood pressure. It also sedates the nervous system and may be beneficial in the treatment of tumours. A toxic effect on the liver has been reported, although the evidence remains contradictory. The white berries are highly poisonous and in general the plant should be used with caution – in the United Kingdom it is a restricted herb and may not be purchased openly. The sedative action of the green and woody parts could have been exploited during druidic ceremonies to induce trance states.[9]

Sacrifices of animals and humans would entail burning them alive in wickerwork cages (sometimes themselves in the form of a man), stabbing them, impaling them, or shooting them with arrows. The three-fold death of hanging, stabbing and drowning that one often meets with in British folklore and legend (especially in the death of Merlin – a contrary tradition to his imprisonment in the glass island) may itself be an echo of Celtic sacrificial practices.

The Romans, repelled by the druids' practice of human sacrifice (though they themselves had only banned it by senatorial decree in 97 BCE) and all too aware of the extent of their influence, outlawed druidry by order of the Emperor Claudius in 43 CE. Julius Caesar had broken their power in Gaul by 58 BCE and in 60 or 61 CE the Roman legions laid waste to their holy sanctuary of Mona (Mon) on the island of what is now called Anglesey. Tacitus describes how black-robed druidesses urged on the Celtic warriors and cursed their Roman attackers with great shouts and screams.[10] The Romans were terrible in victory and having won the field of battle, destroyed the sacred groves and massacred the druids. As a spiritual and political force they were finished and gradually declined into obscurity.

Of these ancient peoples, then, we know little of their religious customs and even less of their magical practices. Their lunar assemblies and sacred groves point to elements that we will meet with again in medieval accounts of Witchcraft: nocturnal meetings governed by the moon and in wild rural locations echo descriptions of the witches' Sabbat; and the ancient druidic fire festivals that would mark the dates for the Sabbats' celebration. However, the echoes are faint, apt to be misinterpreted, and it is only several hundred years later when Christianity has spread itself through the once vigorous sinews of the Roman Empire and the written word become dominant, at least amongst the ecclesiastical and governing classes, that we glean any more information.

There is some evidence from later sources that these Pagan peoples of northern Europe, although thoroughly steeped in magic, did not tolerate what we nowadays call black magic. Amongst some tribes of Pagan England we find such practices outlawed. The Germanic tribes generally slandered their enemies as practitioners of evil magic and an early tradition records that one King Filimer, upon conducting something of a census of his people, was alarmed to discover a large number of sorceresses (*alrunae* or *haliurunae*) amongst them. These he banished to the barren plains of Scythia, where they copulated with the demons inhabiting that wasteland and produced the Huns.

We see, then, that even amongst the Pagan peoples of Europe before their conversion to Christianity, the magic which worked against the health of people in the community or against the good of society was proscribed and punishable, and that accusations of this kind of magic were frequently employed for political reasons (such as against the Huns, or by Fredegond against Clovis). More particularly this black magic, not yet properly 'witchcraft', does not form a religion in itself but takes place within a predefined religious context, although outside the range of what is socially acceptable. It is not until Christianity takes root that we learn of the disciples of Diana riding through the air at night, but it is not necessarily because of Christianity that we do so.

The Wicked Witch of the East

> East of Midgard, in the iron forest,
>   Sat the old witch.
> She fed the fearful race
>   of Fenrer . . .
>
>   Lodfafner's Song[11]

Lodfafner describes a figure familiar to us, like Shakespeare's 'midnight hags' in *Macbeth*, or the Wicked Witch of the West in *The Wizard of Oz*. Angerbode, like Lucan's Erichtho, is the personification of evil, which must, perforce, be ugly and old. She inhabits a place beyond the world of the ordinary (Midgard, the middle garden, is the home of man), a fantastic region where nature is forged from the swordsmith's deadly metal, and consorts with the demonic enemies of the gods and mankind. She stands in direct contrast to an historical figure like Veleda, the revered prophetess of the Germans, and together they give us an example of the seemingly eternal archetypal conflict between good witch and bad.

However, the Nordic material introduces much that is new: the association of cats with witchcraft practices; the riding of broom-sticks (as well as other things including distaffs and wolves); the Wild Hunt, or nocturnal procession of spirits; and the Walpurgisnacht (May Eve) revelry on mountain tops. All of these feature strongly in the medieval construction of diabolical witch-craft.

The importance of the Norse material is often overlooked in pref-erence to Classical sources, but the Classical elements of the construction of diabolical witchcraft are often no more than learned glosses upon indigenous north European practices and beliefs (e.g. the substitution of Diana for Holda). It is in the crucible of Christianizing northern Europe that the construction of the heretical, anti-Christian witch becomes both possible and necessary: possible because of the beliefs of the Pagan peoples of this area and necessary in order to eradicate those beliefs (largely through their inversion as is commonly held – the deity to devil hypothesis – but not entirely by these means).

The ambivalence of magic, especially a certain sort of magic, and its reputation as the province of women is strong in the Nordic material. However, it is Odin, chief of the gods, called All-father, who is renowned for his discovery of the runes (recounted in the *Havamal*) and his skill at rune magic (*runemal*), but also infamous, at least amongst the gods, for his use of a special magical technique called 'seething', *seiðr* (pronounced 'say-ther') in Old Norse. Other practices include *galdr* and *spá*. *Galdr*, literally 'to sing', was the name given to magical chants, which were, like *runemal*, usually performed by men. *Spá*, or *spae*, is the particular art of telling fortunes (*ørlög*) most often through intuition and was usually practised by women who were called *spá-kona* (*spá*-wife) or *völva* ('prophetess', or 'sybil'). Some of these apparently distinct practices converge, such that *seiðr* could be used to tell fortunes, *galdr* could be used in *seiðr*, and *runemal* could be sung or form part of *seiðr*, and a *seið-kona* was often, perhaps euphemistically, called a *spá-kona*.[12]

The runes, used nowadays principally for fortune-telling, were originally symbols of great magical power. T.S. Elliot in *The Music of Poetry* described them as 'very practical formulae designed to produce definite results, such as getting a cow out of a bog', or, we might add, victory in battle. Their origins are ancient, lost in mystery. Prehistoric rock carvings known as *hällristningar*, which date from the second Bronze Age (*c*. 1300 BCE) can be found throughout Germany and Scandinavia, but are especially common in Sweden. These pre-runic symbols depict human beings, parts of the body, animals, weapons, solar motifs and other less identifiable abstractions. These prototypes form the basis of the runic system as we know it today, a system that was still in everyday use until some 300 years ago.

> These runes I know, unknown to king's wives
> Or any earthly man. 'Help' one is called,
> For help is its gift, and helped you will be
> In sickness and care and sorrow.[13]

Three versions of an ancient rune poem exist in Anglo-Saxon, Icelandic and Norwegian that details the qualities of the Futhark runes (known as Futhark after the first six runes - f, u, th, a, r, k - in the series to distinguish it from other systems), but it is through the *Poetic Edda* that Odin speaks to us of rune magic (*runemal*) directly.[14] To foretell the future the runes were inscribed on stones, pieces of metal or wood (reminiscent of the practice recorded by Tacitus of the Germans) and cast upon a cloth. As charms they were carved upon shields, weapons, drinking cups and ships' prows.

Reading the Runes

Arranged in three groups (*aettir*) of eight letters each, the traditional Futhark is the most common arrangement of runes, although in Britain the Anglo-Saxon alphabet expanded to encompass some thirty-three letters, or runic symbols. Modern rune-masters, such as Ralph Blum, often use what is known as the Blank Rune, an uncarved stone representing the Unknown.

Freyr's Eight

wealth	aurochs	thorn	mouth	riding	torch	generosity	bliss

Hagal's Eight

hail	trouble	ice	summer	yew tree	dice-cup	sedge grass	sun

Tyr's Eight

Tyr	birch tree	horse	man	sea	Ing	possessions	day

While deep in Jotunheim, most fell,
Are Fenris, Serpent, and Dread Hel,
Pain, Sin, and Death, her children three . . [15]

Loki (meaning 'fire'), the Norse god Christians identified with Satan, secretly married Angerbode, or Angur-boda (meaning 'anguish boding'), in Jötun-heim, the frozen homeland of the giants, and together they produced three terrible offspring: Fenris the wolf, the serpent Iörmungandr and Hel, the goddess of death - the personifications of pain, sin and death. Loki and Angerbode concealed their brood in a cave, but they grew so monstrously huge that Odin could not help but spy them from his seat in Asgard. Their parentage and their size spelt nothing but trouble and Odin descended upon the cave, throwing Hel into the dismal depths of Nifl-heim where she could reign over the nine dread realms of the dead, and hurling Iörmungandr into the sea where he grew so vast that he encircled Midgard and could bite his own tail.[16] Seeing the results of his hasty actions, Odin took Fenris back to Asgard, where he hoped kindness would tame him – a nice example of an early, enlightened criminal rehabilitation programme – but it failed.[17]

The worst and coldest winters blow from Siberia across northern Europe, that is from the east, where the frost-giants waft cold blasts of wind to blacken tender buds and chill the hearts of men, but it was in the far north, where night reigned longest and the ice never melted that the entrance to Nifl-heim and Angerbode's Ironwood lay. In the psycho-geography of the Other World, Angerbode could be both east of Midgard in Jötun-heim and in Ironwood; such was her reputation that she dwelt simultaneously in the worst of places.

It took nine nights' journey for even the swiftest of the gods (Hermod) on the fleetest of steeds (Sleipnir) over rough roads and frozen wasteland to reach the river Gïoll, the boundary of Nifl-heim. Across the river was a glass or crystal bridge suspended upon a single hair, guarded by the gaunt Mödgud:

A maiden horrible to sight,
Fleshless, with shroud and pall bedight.

Across the bridge was Ironwood 'where stood none but bare and iron-leafed trees' - not to mention the snarling, bloody hound called Garm who lived in a cave nearby. Here amongst the razor-wire foliage Angerbode fed her grandchildren, the sons of Fenris, the wolves Hati, Sköll and Managarm, with the bones of adulterers and murderers' marrow. No more malignant and horrible a being than Angerbode, the mother of death, can be conceived.[18]

In the translation of 'Lodfafner's Song' quoted earlier, Angerbode is called a 'witch,' a word of Anglo-Saxon derivation; in the Norse sagas the term was seið-kona (seið-wife), or seið-man. This word seiðr with its connotations of black magic was derived either from the root that gives us our modern word 'seethe', or from that which gives us 'seat' or 'sitting'.[19] The idea of seething may be derived from the practice of boiling sea water to extract salt and lends itself to the familiar image of brewing potions in the bubbling cauldron, especially in Shakespeare's memorable lines:

> Double, double, toil and trouble;
> Fire burn and cauldron bubble.[20]

The derivation from the root meaning 'sitting', which incidentally also gives us the French séance, is possibly a reference to the seið-hjallr, the high seat or platform that the magical practitioner would sometimes ascend to perform seiðr.[21]

Seiðr was powerful magic. It could foretell the future, curse and empower. Odin was known to practise it, but he had learned it from another of the gods, one of the Vanir, Freyja.

> Óðinn had the skill which gives great power and which he practised himself. It is called seiðr, and by means of it he could know the fate [ørlög] of men and predict events that had not yet come to pass; and by it he could also inflict bane on men, or loss of soul [hamingja] or waning health, or also take wit or power from some men, and give them to others.[22]

Whilst Freyja may have taught it to Odin, other references in the sagas point to a Finnish (Lappish or Saami) origin and the practices themselves resemble what is known of shamanic techniques and elements of Saami religion.[23] Finnish wizards were renowned shape-changers who could journey in the spirit to far-off places, enchant arrows so that they never missed or returned to the bow that loosed them, and who could raise storms. The most famous Finnish wizard was Rossthiof (literally 'the horse thief') who would use his magic to waylay travellers with 'phantom-like monsters' and 'invisible snares' so that he might rob and murder them. He could 'mutter incantations, at the mere sound of which the sun hid behind the clouds, the earth trembled and quivered, and the storm winds howled like a pack of hungry wolves'. He was finally overcome by the god Hermod, but his range of powers reminds us of the attributes of those Hecatean sorceresses met with in the previous chapter. This suggests less a similarity of origin, more a similarity of type.[24]

Although it was practised by the chief of the gods, *seiðr* had a dark reputation, such that Loki could turn to Odin and accuse him thus: 'They say you have practised magic in Samsoe, that you have made spells like any Vala: you have wandered through the country disguised as a witch. What, I say, could be viler in a man than this?'[25] There was something unmanly about it, whether because by its power a Norseman could circumvent the glory of battle to smite his foes (and only those who died in battle went to Valhalla), or because there was an unmasculine sexual element to it. In the *Ynglingsaga* it is said that 'this sorcery is attended by such *ergi* that manly men considered it shameful to practise it'. *Ergi*, the adjectival form of *argr*, meant to be willing or predisposed to take the female role in sexual relations with another man. It may refer directly to a homosexual element in *seiðr*, or it may be a metaphor for spirit possession, which in Voudun is called being 'ridden' by the spirit and hence a passive state in which control is surrendered to another.[26] Thus it was 'taught to priestesses'.[27]

> Heidi men call me when their homes I visit,
> A far seeing Völva, wise in talismans.
> Caster of spells, cunning in magic.
> To wicked women welcome always.
>
> The Song of the Sybil[28]

Heidi, or Heid, was a generic name applied to *seiðr-kona*, thus we read of another Heid who with Ham raised a storm to kill Frithiof.[29]

Heiðr is etymologically of the same root as our words 'heath' and 'heathen'. Other common names for witches were Ljot and Huld or Hulda. Ljot meant 'ugly', whereas Huld(a) meant 'hidden' or 'secret'. In a memorable scene a certain Högni turns to his companion and fearfully asks, 'What fiend is this coming towards us?' His companion answers, 'It's old Ljot on her way.'[30]

The dress of the *völva* was something fantastic. In *Eiriks Saga Rauða*, a woman called Thorbjorg, who also has the title of Little Volva, is described as wearing

> . . . a blue mantle fastened with straps, and stones were set all in the flap above; on her neck she had glass beads, a black lambskin hood on her head with white catskin inside; and she had a staff in her hand with a knob on it; it was made with brass and stones were set above in the knob; she had a belt of touch-wood, and on it was a large skin pouch, and there she kept safe her talismans [*taufr*] which she needed to get knowledge. She had on her feet shaggy calfskin shoes with long thongs and large knobs on the ends of those. She had on her hands catskin gloves, and they were white inside and shaggy.[31]

The blue cloak is an important element. The colour blue was associated with death in the Norseman's mind, hence it marks the *völva* as having an affinity with death, either to communicate with the dead, or to cause the death of the living. The use of catskin is important too because the cat was sacred to Freyja, the patron goddess of *seiðr*. The use of black lambskin cannot help but remind us of Hecate, but the association derives from our historical perspective rather than reality. The hood of whatever material was instrumental in producing trance states and could reputedly make its wearer invisible. Again our unique perspective presents another comparison, amusing but suggestive, between the blue and white colours of the *völva* and the blue and white of the Virgin Mary.

Thorbjorg had nine sisters, all of them *spá-kona*, but she lived alone. During the winter months she would make a round of the feasts, foreseeing the future for the curious. It was at just such a feast that the farmer Thorkell approached her, wishing to know when the bad harvest that blighted his fortunes would come to an end. The reading took place in the man's home and Thorbjorg was received with courtesy and respect, as was the custom. A high seat was prepared for her with a hen's feather cushion. A special meal was prepared for her of porridge made with kid's milk and a dish of the hearts of all living creatures (the text adds 'which were available,' so the symbolism may be more important than the content). She ate with a brass spoon and a knife of walrus ivory capped with two copper rings. However, she had still to sleep in Thorkell's house before she was able to foretell his future. Thus it was on the following evening, when the sun was setting, she called to her those women who knew the wisdom chant employed in *seiðr*, the so-called Varðlokur, or Warlock Song.[32] The women gathered round Thorbjorg's high seat and formed a circle. The chanting appeased the spirits ('many of the powers are now satisfied') and the veil was lifted from Thorbjorg's inner sight: 'And now many of those things are shown to me which I was denied before, and many others.'[33]

Another description of a *seiðr* practitioner, in the *Grettis Saga Ásmundarsonar*, recounts the casting of a curse against a certain Grettir using incantations and rune magic. The *seiðr-kona* selected a large tree stump 'as large as a man could bear on his shoulder' from the flotsam on the shoreline. The men rolled the trunk over to reveal a smooth, burnt-looking surface and carved out a flat surface for her. Taking out her knife she cut runes into the wood, then cut herself and reddened the runes with her blood. She quietly spoke incantations over them and then, rising, walked anticlockwise, 'backwards against the sun' round the tree, and 'spoke many potent words'. Under her direction the men then pushed the tree trunk into the sea to complete the spell such that 'Grettir should suffer hurt from it'.[34]

Heidi 'with *seiðr* played with minds'.[35] *Seiðr* could cause forgetfulness, create illusions, instil fear and dull wits. Deceiving the sight, the technique known as *sjonhverfing*, was a frequent ploy. The Finnish wizard Rossthiof was adept in creating phantoms to frighten travellers, but it could also be used to hide something, especially an individual fleeing pursuers. Just such an instance occurs in the *Eyrbyggja Saga*, where Katla uses *seiðr* to hide her son, Odd, from a gang of men determined to kill him. The magical ruse is daring and shows Katla to be confident in her skill at *seiðr*. As Odd's would-be murderers (led by a certain Arnkell) approach the house, she has Odd sit by her, under strict instructions not to move, whilst she continues her spinning. Arnkell and his men burst into the house and search it thoroughly, but find nothing except Katla sitting spinning, a distaff beside her. The men depart, but not satisfied return a second time. Katla is in her porch combing Odd's hair, but they see her grooming a goat. Again they leave and again not quite satisfied return. This time Odd was lying in a pile of ashes, but all they see is Katla's pig sleeping there. Arnkell suspects something is amiss: Katla, he thinks, has waved a goatskin round their heads, as he puts it. Arnkell enlists the help of Geirriðr, another *seiðr-kona* and Katla's bitter enemy. Katla catches sight of her blue *seið-kona*'s cloak through the window and realizing that her deceptions will no longer be effective, hides Odd in the dais.

However, Geirriðr has a trick of her own, and putting a sealskin bag over Katla's head negates all her power and Odd is at last discovered. The tale ends badly for Katla and Odd who are then slain by Arnkell. Yet the tale is instructive, for we learn that Katla's magical ability to deceive the sight of others is connected to her own ability to see and that when this is removed her magic fails.[36]

One of the special methods of *seiðr* was to cover oneself with a cloak or similar garment like a blanket, or an animal skin, or even just a hood. Communication with the *seiðr*-worker 'under the cloak' was strictly prohibited, especially speaking the name of the practitioner, as any interruption to the procedure could have dangerous consequences (one thinks of modern-day trance mediums who similarly should not be interrupted). Both entrance to and return from the trance state was often signalled by an unusually large yawn, which has been suggested as indicative of the soul (*hamingja*) leaving the practitioner's physical body through the mouth.[37] This technique was practised more by men than women, and especially by the male *skald* to foretell the future, discover hidden truths, attack others, or cast spells. The greatest power could be raised by going 'under the cloak' on top of a barrow or grave site, when it was known as *utiseta*, 'sitting out', or *sitja a haugi*, 'to sit on a barrow'. However, where there was greatest power, there was also greatest danger. Sitting out on a barrow could expose the magicians to attack by the ghost (*haugbui*) of the deceased buried in the barrow and they were often found gibbering lunatics in the morning.[38]

The Nordic witch left her body in the form of an animal or as pure spirit to attack her enemies, protect the home, or learn new information. The *seiðr* expert could either take the form of an animal, or project her spirit into one, favouring the walrus, seal or whale at sea, and upon land, one of Freyja's associated animals, such as the cat, wild boar, or falcon. The practice was called *gand-reið*, meaning 'riding the *gand*', a *gand* being a 'chant incantation' or 'enchantment'.[39] It could involve riding broomsticks, distaffs, or even wolves, although this must have proved somewhat hazardous. This chant-riding was also known as 'faring forth', i.e. travelling in the spirit either into an animal, or to initiate an attack like hag-riding, causing nightmares.

Two stories from the Sagas exemplify this particular power and its inherent dangers. The first is from *Kormaks Saga* and involves the witch Thórvaig:

> The two brothers had but left the roadstead, when close beside their ship, up rose a walrus. Kormak hurled at it a pole-staff, which struck the beast, so that it sank again: but the men aboard thought that they knew its eyes for the eyes of Thórvaig the witch. That walrus came up no more, but of Thórvaig it was heard that she lay sick to death; and indeed folk say that this was the end of her.[40]

The second story follows a similar pattern, but reveals more about the actual practice of *seiðr*. It concerns the hero Frithiof, noted for his blue cloak, who fell foul of a certain King Helge for wooing his sister. Helge was apparently something of a sorcerer himself:

> *His wizard-spell,*
> *Potent to command*
> *Fiends of earth or hell.*[41]

Even so be recruited the witches Heid and Ham to summon such a storm as the world had never seen before or since to sink Frithiof as he sailed aboard his magic dragon ship *Ellida*.

The witches retired to the *seiðhjallr* with 'charms and sorcery'. The wind rose and the storm came on. *Ellida* ran before the winds at great speed, engulfed in a darkness so deep that the bow could not be seen from the stern or vice versa, and wracked with driving spray, biting frost and drifting snow. Panic gripped the crew as they lost all bearings. Frithiof climbed the mast to try and find out where they were. Wiping the spray from his eyes he called down to his fellows, 'I see a marvellous sight. A great whale circles the ship, and I suspect that we must be near some land, and he would not let us near the land. Methinks that King Helge does not deal with us in friendly wise: it is no loving message that he sends us. I see two women on the whale's back, and they must wield this hostile storm with their worst spells and magic.'

Frithiof spoke to his magic ship and understanding too well his command *Ellida* bore down on the whale and its witch riders, setting a ramming course. The whale was unable to avoid the fast-approaching ship and *Ellida* smashed into him, reddening the sea with his blood and that of the witches. The wind dropped away in an instant, the waves lost their froth and grew gentle, but back on shore 'while the two sisters were at their incantations they tumbled down from the *seiðhjallr* and both their backs were broken'.[42]

In the first instance the witch takes the form of a walrus, in the second the witches project their spirits to ride a whale, but in each there is a direct physical consequence of their spirit form being attacked. Faring forth was a powerful technique, but it was no less risky than physical confrontation. However, for the witch, transformation into, or the harnessing of, an animal confers a greater strength and available muscle power than she would otherwise have.

Whilst spirit attacks against men as alert and valiant as Kormak and Frithiof were bound to be a difficult contest, the witch could also choose to fare forth at night and assault much more vulnerable sleeping victims. Such was the *mara*, a witch, or a thing sent by a witch, to do violence to a man as he slept - for men were most often the victims, although tales tell of animals and even trees being ridden by the *mara*. *Mara*, in Old English *mare*, is the nightmare, called the 'night-hag', the 'riding of the witch', or in French *cauchemar*, 'the fiend that tramples'. This *mare* is not a female horse, but an evil spirit, and the nightmare was held in dread. Only in the sixteenth century did it become merely a bad dream. It could take any form or no form at all, but preferred the shape of a hag, a cat, a horse or a darker shadow in the night. It would gain access to the victim's bedchamber through the keyhole, through a chink in the window or down the chimney, but apparently only through round holes; it disdained anything rectangular or irregular. If one listened carefully it could be heard coming: a click in the lock, a patter across the floor, or a sinister 'sshh, sshh'. Then it pounced, always too quickly to be avoided. The victim would feel a great weight upon him, often as if rolling over from the feet. Sometimes it felt as if his mouth and nose were being stopped up; sometimes as if he were being squeezed so tightly as to make movement impossible.[43]

In contrast to the unsuccessful magical attacks made by Thórvaig and the duo Heid and Ham the Sagas also record the more effective use of the nightmare as a spiritual weapon. The witch Huld kills Vanlandi most horribly with a *mara* in the *Ynglingasaga* (ch. 13) after he refuses to return to Finland. Drifa summons Huld to make Vanlandi return to Finland and instructs her to kill him if he refuses. As Huld works her spell Vanlandi feels a strong urge to return to Finland, but his friends prevent him and persuade him that this urge has been forced upon him by witchcraft. Vanlandi is then taken by an overwhelming sleepiness and lies down to rest. No sooner has he drifted off to sleep than he calls out saying a *mara* is riding him. His men try to help and take hold of his head, but the *mara* tramples on his legs so that they nearly break; so his men seize his feet, but the *mara* presses so forcefully upon his head that it extinguishes his life.

As well as faring forth at night to hag-ride their victims the Nordic practitioner of *seiðr* was also thought to take part in a singular and most suggestive nocturnal event, the idea of which has persisted down all the long centuries. A central aspect in the later formulation of diabolical witchcraft in the Middle Ages was the nocturnal flight or procession of witches. The idea was an ancient Nordic one, but of course where the Pagan saw deity, the Christian saw diabolism. The Wild Hunt, as it was known, was led by Odin. It was thus no mean sideshow, no devilish antithesis to the divine order, but an integral part of the religion of the North.

Odin means 'wind', or, metaphorically, 'spirit', and he was imagined to rush across the world like the wind on his eight-legged steed Sleipnir. In the night when the wind howled and blew with gale force the Norseman heard the cry of the Wild Huntsman and his followers riding through the land, and the baying of their hounds. His followers were spirits like Odin, the spirits of the dead or the projected spirits of witches. Those wise in *seiðr* would ride out at night upon a boar, a wolf or a fence-rail to join the *trolla-thing*, the spiritual convocation of their fellows.[44] A passage from the *Eddas* gives an account of such an event:

> Ketill was roused at night by a great uproar in the wood; he ran out and saw a sorceress with streaming hair; being questioned, she begged him not to balk her, [for] she was bound for a magic [meeting], to which were coming Skelking king of spirits from Dumbshaf [and other spirits].[45]

The leaders of the Wild Hunt change from place to place and time to time. In Mecklenburg it was led by Frau Gode, or Wode, a female form of Odin/Woden, the White Lady who rode a white horse and whose appearance portended great good. In Holland it was Vrau-elde. In northern Germany it was the goddess Nerthus of whom Tacitus wrote. In southern Germany it was the 'bright one', Perchta, Berhta or Berta (or in masculine form as Berthold, Herlechin or Herne). In some parts of Scandinavia it was Huldra who led her train of wood nymphs. Uller, the God of Winter, Hunting and Archery, and, as befits the ruler of such a season and such sports, the God of Death, led the Wild Hunt in Odin's absence, when the snow lay thick on the ground. The Anglo-Saxons called him Vulder. In some parts of Germany they knew him as Holler, the husband of Holda.[46]

Hölle is German for Hell, which in turn comes from the Indo-European root *kel* meaning to cover or hide, and gives us the names Holler, Holla, Holda, Huld, Hulda, Herla and Hel. The Norse recount how Hel would travel across the land at night press-ganging souls for her pale army. She would ride out on her white, three-legged horse to round up the dead, or in times of pestilence and famine would use a rake to gather them in. In times of still greater distress, like plague, it was said that she rode a broom.[47]

The Wild Hunt could presage both good fortune and disaster, most often disaster - the gods of death seldom gave anything to mortals. It was regarded with great dread; the brave joker who scoffed when the Hunt was afoot soon found himself swept up and away for ever, but if a living (non-witch) entered into the spirit of it in good faith, with a shout of his own added to the tumult, he received an unusual reward for his effort. An old German folktale about a miller tells how when once he was working alone and late into the night he heard a great commotion outside and, stepping out above the slow-turning waterwheel, he saw nothing but the dark and the wind bending the tree-tops. He yelled wildly back and heard a voice on the shrieking wind cry, 'If you want to hunt, you can join the ride!' From out of the night someone, or something, threw what looked like a long stick at him. He caught it and saw that it was a woman's leg, a bright-red shoe on the dainty foot.[48]

The Wild Hunt

Still, still shall last the dreadful chase,
 Till time itself shall have an end;
By day, they scour earth's cavern'd space,
 At midnight's witching hour, ascend.

This is the horn, and hound, and horse
 That oft the late peasant hears;
Appall'd, he signs the frequent cross,
 When the wild din invades his ears.

The wakeful priest oft drops a tear
 For human pride, for human woe,
When, at his midnight mass, he hears
 The infernal cry of 'Holla, ho!'

        Sir Walter Scott

Catskin clad, singing the Warlock Song, seething her enchantments in a cauldron and working magic against the sun, under the cloak and riding the chant, faring forth as a trampling fiend, flying on fence-rail and broomstick in the Wild Hunt with Holler, such was the 'witch' from East of Midgard. A marginal figure wont to live alone, regarded with fear and loathing (remember the *ergi*), even within her own community, the Pagan *seið-kona* was the blueprint for the Christian witch; and the fear of the witches' Wild Hunt would become the basis for the unstinting witch hunt that would ravage Europe. Yet more tears would be dropped for the deeds of that wakeful priest than ever washed the ground at the cry of 'Holla, ho!'

3. SOUTH OF HEAVEN: WITCHCRAFT IN MEDIEVAL AND EARLY MODERN EUROPE

The Witches of the European Dark Ages come flying towards us out of the past's Stygian mire in a wild cavalcade, riding devils and broomsticks, followed by black cats and poisonous toads to be consumed in the fires, not of Hell, but of fear and hatred, greed and lust. For all they lived and for all they died, too often too soon and too horribly, they were only part real. Worshippers of strange gods, healers with strange powers, they come from stranger times when rumour and suspicion were judge and executioner, when fear and loathing were law and order.

We have already seen how what was later called the witch was regarded in earlier times, from ancient Greek goddesses and priestesses to Roman hags, and from revered *völvas* to despised fomenters of ruin. These complex, diverse, ambiguous and at times confused images from myth and folklore and everyday life formed the blueprint for the construction of the diabolical witch who, in league with the arch-fiend, was bent on the destruction of Christendom. At first these figures, both the people themselves – the Hecatean priestesses and far-seeing *völvas* – and the beliefs connected to them formed the front line in the battle against Christian missionaries and

Christianizing conquerors. Their practices were outlawed and the beliefs connected to them declared false. Their persistence could, under Christian interpretation, mean only one thing: Satanic rebellion. As the Bible has it: 'Rebellion is as the sin of witchcraft.' (1 Sam. 15:23)

The process did not happen overnight and did not take the same form in every corner of Europe. However, a curve can be drawn from initial Pagan persecution to a high point of Christian heresy from about the eighth to the sixteenth century CE, when it diminishes but does not disappear, even today, as a glance at the news will testify.[1]

Christianization did not just reinterpret the witch. We have seen how the witch was already someone in close association with the gods of death and the Underworld. The gods of death and the realm of the dead in Pagan theology were not necessarily evil – death was an accepted and inevitable part of life. However, when the Christians turned the Underworld into the place of eternal damnation ruled over by the fallen angel Lucifer, the witch found herself associating with demons and the souls of the damned. The realm of the ancestors, the home of the dear departed, the place where knowledge could be found and power gained became the dungeon of God and the encampment of evil. Christianization reinterpreted the entire cosmos. The 'birthplace of all sorceries' became the 'root of all evil' and East of Midgard became South of Heaven.

The Yoke of the Gospel

In Rome, in 381 CE, the Senate proscribed the 'worship of idols' and in Gibbon's memorable phrase Rome submitted to the 'yoke of the Gospel'. The real turning point occurred in 313, however.[2] It was in that year that the then emperor of Rome, Constantine the Great (274–337), decriminalized Christianity. After a series of battles he seized complete control of the Roman Empire in 324. Constantine was followed by Theodosius in Christian piety, who zealously undertook to stamp out Paganism: he banned sacrifices, divination from the examination of entrails and the immolation of corpses. The temples were closed and their property seized.

The contagion spread throughout the empire. In Gaul, Martin, Bishop of Tours, led an army of monks to destroy the temples, the statues of the gods and the sacred groves of the Pagans. In Syria the infamous Marcellus levelled any temple within his reach, although one particular one, the Temple of Jupiter by its size and excellence of construction caused him no end of difficulties in destroying it – difficulties which the superstitious rabble ascribed to the defence of a black demon guarding the place. Marcellus then gathered his army and, bolstered by gladiators, set about the countryside, slaughtering every Pagan they could find. At Carthage the Temple of the Celestial Venus was invaded and converted into a Christian church.

In Alexandria the Christians feared to take the Temple of Serapis, a formidable fortress that also housed the famed Alexandrian library. Here the Pagans, roused by the philosopher Olympius, mounted a spirited defence of their faith, but it too was eventually broken and the victorious Christians raided the great repository of ancient learning and burned every book. The temple was likewise destroyed. Religious artefacts cast in gold or silver were melted down and the huge statue of Serapis was thrown to the ground and burnt.

It is said that the fact that there was no apparent retribution from the divinities for this public destruction of Pagan sites contributed to the populace's acceptance of Christianity. However, faced with such violent displays of the Christian faith most had little choice and it cannot be overlooked that the Romans had for several centuries been vigorous in their subjugation of local centres of spiritual power, as evidenced by the destruction of the druids.

In 387 a dissolute 33-year-old whose only accomplishments had hitherto been vice and profligacy sought escape in Christian baptism and went on to become one of the most famous and vehement prose-lytizers of the early Church. His name was Augustine of the North African city of Hippo, and is now honoured for his Christian piety as St Augustine. The period in which he lived (354–430) was the high point of the destruction of Paganism and through his prolific writings he was to become one of its major instruments.

The early Church was presented with a problem, which had only been partly solved by the supposed defeat of Simon Magus by St Peter, that is, the existence and persistence of magic and, most significantly,

57

its apparent use by Jesus and the Apostles. Simon was a contemporary of Jesus of Nazareth and the foremost magico-mystic of his day. Whereas Jesus had been executed as a criminal and his claim to be the Son of God dismissed, Simon enjoyed a popular following and wider recognition of his identical claim to be the Son of God. He was, therefore, a deadly rival to early Christianity. It was only the single-minded effects of Peter, who seemed to dog his every step, that led to his undoing. Called before the Emperor Nero (sometime before 64 CE) to prove their competing claims, Simon and Peter engaged in what can only be described as a magical duel. Simon sought to demonstrate his divinity with an ascent into heaven and apparently succeeded in rising into the air from a specially constructed platform. Nero was impressed, but Peter used his own art to bring Simon crashing down to his death. He was given the title 'Magus' in the New Testament (Acts, 8: 9–13): it was not intended to be complimentary, but rather tarred him as a fraudster. Butler (1948:76) thinks Simon to be fictitious, but there is no compelling reason to suppose this, despite the evident propagandistic uses he is put to in the Acts. What the story of St Peter demonstrated was that his God-given power was superior to the alleged infernal provenance of Simon Magus' magic, but it still left the problem of magic *per se*. Augustine was able to provide a solution.[3] He argued that the apparent similarity between the miracles of the saints and the operations of magicians was simply that – appearance only. Whilst the magician performed amazing feats for his own aggrandizement, the saint does so for the greater glory of God; and whereas the magician's power derives from pacts made with his controlling entity, or from crimes committed in its name (he specifically mentions poisoning), the saint acts in accordance with the will of God. It is a weak argument, but it was the best the Church had. It also introduced the idea of the pact, which was to become central to the later concept of the Satanic witch.

Although the most famous clerical injunction against witchcraft of the first millennium, the Canon Episcopi was supposedly drawn up in the fourth century CE, it has been shown to date in fact from the early tenth century. Our earliest legal proscriptions of witchcraft in non-Roman Europe date from the eighth century. Although zealous monks had ravaged the Gaulish temples and groves in the fourth century CE, the Christianization of the northern fringes of the Roman

Empire took considerably longer. Although St Columba arrived in Iona in the Western Isles of Scotland in 563 and St Augustine (of Canterbury) visited Britain in 597, England did not accept the yoke of the Gospel until the seventh century CE. Germany resisted until the ninth century and Scandinavia was not fully subjugated to the cross until the twelfth. Estonia was not Christianized until as late as the fifteenth century. Even in cases of apparently early Christianization the picture was far from uniform; for example, the general ignorance of the English peasant on Christian matters was reported as a cause for concern up until the seventeenth century.[4] Throughout Europe Christianity's hold was anything but absolute. Whilst monarchs and chieftains bent their knee to Rome and passed laws to demonstrate their faith, the 'common' people, the 'pagans' and 'heathens', the people literally of the countryside and heaths, retained their own beliefs and paid little heed to the showcase statutes, difficult as they were to enforce.

One of the earliest documents from this period of the Christianization of Europe which demonstrated the Church's growing hostility to the practices of the Pagan populace was the penitential of St Theodore, c. 600 CE.[5] He went further than the existing laws of the Holy Roman Empire, which already proscribed harmful magic, to extend punishment to the practice of beneficial magic. He specifically codified the punishment for a particular magical cure: 'If any woman puts her daughter upon a roof or into an oven for the cure of fever, she shall do penance for seven years.'[6] He was also rather concerned by the number of people cavorting about at New Year dressed up as stags and bulls, and added some extra penance for anyone caught being so 'devilish'.

New Year Idolatries

If anyone at the kalends of January goes about as a stag or a bull; that is making himself into a wild animal and dressing in the skin of a herd animal, and putting on the head of beasts; those who in such wise transform themselves into the appearance of a wild animal, penance for three years because this is devilish.[7]

From his newly built cathedral in Canterbury St Theodore was evidently addressing some very real and prevalent practices. He is both particular in their detail and concerned enough to establish especial punishments for them. It is notable that his reasoning against the practice of dressing as an animal at New Year is because it is 'devilish'. At a stroke the Pagan practice is identified with Satanism and judged accordingly. Such was the sophistication of the theological reasoning demonstrated by the Church for more than a thousand years.

In Spain, the Council of Toledo, which met in 633, was less concerned about cavorting parishioners being devilish, than about its own priests overstepping the mark:

> If a bishop or priest or deacon or anyone belonging to holy orders is discovered consulting magicians, diviners who interpret thunder and lightning, people who divine by inspiration (and especially those who interpret the flight of birds), those who cast lots, those who profess any such skill, or anyone practising any similar act: let his punishment be loss of rank and confinement in a monastery where he may expiate by perpetual penitence the crime of sacrilege he has incurred.[8]

Even the threat of life imprisonment failed to eradicate the problem. The Council meeting again in 683 found it necessary to forbid priests from stripping altars and closing churches to punish God (Pagan priests had done exactly the same in their temples). When it sat down again in 694 a new outrage was brought to its attention and immediately outlawed: certain priests were saying the Requiem Mass for living persons in order to bring about their untimely end. (The involvement of the priestly class is a recurrent theme and it affected all ranks: even a pope could be tried for necromancy, as Gregory VII was in 1080.)

In France Childeric III's edict of 743 eroded some of the distinction between magic and Paganism by treating them as much the same. The Pagan practices proscribed included sacrifices to the dead, but also sacrifices to the holy martyrs and confessors which were taking place in close proximity to the churches themselves. So part of the problem for Christian rulers seemed to be that the people were approaching Christianity in a Pagan manner, and some of these measures rather than being directly intended to eradicate Paganism, were more concerned to try and save Christianity.

Childeric III was not the only one who found it necessary to defend Christianity with the weight of the law. In that same year, 743, from the heart of the Empire, the Synod of Rome outlawed the Pagan practice of leaving small offerings of food out for minor spirits because, in a display of logic akin to St Theodore's, these spirits must be devilish. Rome was feeling particularly threatened that year. In a letter to St Boniface dated 1 April 743, what we now call April Fool's Day, Pope Zacharias lamented that 'New Year celebrations, divinations, amulets, incantations, and other practices . . . observed in accordance with non-Christian practice' were being performed in the Church of St Peter the Apostle and throughout the city of Rome.[9]

Childeric III's problem with Pagans treating Christian saints like Pagan deities was not his alone. The Council of Leptinnes, convened in 744, issued its List of Superstitions, forbidding the making of sacrifices to saints. The Council also thought it necessary to introduce a new clause into the baptismal recitation for the catechumen to 'renounce all the works of the demon, and all his words, and Thor, and Odin, and Saxnot, and all evil beings that like them'.[10] Almost a hundred years after St Theodore, the argument had not changed a jot, but it had become most specific. The highest gods of the northern peoples, Odin, Thor and the Anglo-Saxon Saxnot were singled out for theological abuse and redefined as pernicious.

The Confessional of Egbert, c. 750, gives another example of the struggle against popular belief: 'If a woman works *drycraeft* [sorcery] and *galdor* [enchantment] and [uses] magical philters, she shall fast for twelve months.' The penalty for successful magic was even more severe: 'If she kills anyone by her philters, she shall fast for seven years.'[11] Unless they fasted in the Muslim manner, from dawn to dusk only, these protracted fastings could only be euphemisms for execution by starving to death. It is notable that, like St Theodore a hundred years before him, Egbert singles out women as the practitioners of magic. We cannot just dismiss this as misogyny as some writers have done; that is too easy a judgement, too fitting for certain political agendas, and too limited as an explanation. For two individuals as influential as an Archbishop of Canterbury (and later a saint to boot) and a king, so separated in time and office, to associate a particular sex with magic suggests something more tangible than emotion, more enduring than dislike. The simplest explanation is that magic at this period was the particular province of women. We have already seen that amongst the Germanic tribes women were accorded respect born of their presumed prophetic power, and that amongst the Scandinavians women were, for tortuous mythological reasons, the chosen practitioners of certain magic arts (*seiðr*).

Pagan practices were persistent, and the measures introduced were insufficient to eradicate them completely. With the populace flouting the religion of their supposed betters, with the Church itself being undermined by a preference for Paganism even in its own rituals and observances, the measures against Paganism increased in severity.

The chivalric avatar Charlemagne, King of the Franks, and Holy Roman Emperor from 800, responded to the continued threat of Pagan magic to Christianity with draconian measures. Like Childeric III before him he was specific in his prohibitions, but he went further in the degree of punishment to be meted out. In a series of edicts (the Capitularia) dating from about 789, Charlemagne singled out for reprobation the modelling of images in wax, summoning 'devils', raising storms, cursing and blighting crops, causing milking cows to dry up, reading the stars, and making talismans and love philtres. He expressly stipulated that those so practising these devilish arts should be stripped of all honour and judged like murderers, poisoners and thieves. Furthermore, their clients should suffer the same penalty. It hardly needs mentioning, but these new laws frequently meant the death sentence for the accused.[12]

In a drastic attempt to destroy the last vestiges of Paganism another act of the Frankish kings, dated 789 CE, referring to Saxony, condemned both the practice of and the belief in witchcraft as a capital offence (*Capitulatio de partibus Saxioniae*). The act specifically detailed the unwholesome habits of the man-eating *strigae* (usually translated as 'witches'), demanding that such creatures be burnt to death for their crimes, but also that those who believed in the *strigae* should be executed as well.

Unless our interpretation of these ancient legal documents is flawed, this is a most bizarre position since the upholders of this law must perforce not believe in the *strigae*, which raises the question, why then execute those accused of it? In addition it should again be noted that these witches are identified as women, *feminam strigam*.[13] In the *Leges Langobardicae*, dating from the reign of King Rotharius, it was categorically stated that witches (*strigae* or *mascae*, 'masked women') could not be capable of the acts of which they were accused.[14] Here we can see the position developing in which both the practice of witchcraft and the belief in it are equally problematic for the Christian authorities. It later became a matter of faith to believe in witches because they are described in the Bible.

The Council of Tours in 813 still found it necessary to condemn the use of magic, in this case to heal the sick and cure animals, but it also expressed the view that such magic could not be efficacious because any good results were simply illusions created by the Devil.[15] The Archbishop of Lyons at this time, Agobard, underlined the point by remonstrating against those who believed that certain individuals could control the weather with their magic. However, a particular crisis at the time, an epidemic amongst livestock, had led the stricken peasantry to accuse Duke Grimald of having sent sorcerers against them. Agobard also took issue with such claims, and his stance against magic takes on a possible political colouring.[16]

In spite of all the laws and penitentials, and, one must assume, the trials and punishments, which unfortunately have not been recorded, the situation did not improve. The Synod of Rome, meeting in 826, complained that people came to church not to attend the Mass but to dance and sing in a Pagan manner.[17] Not only were they treating the saints like Pagan deities, but they were also treating the churches like Pagan temples.

Following Charlemagne's intolerant lead, the Council of Paris in 829 decided to take sterner measures against the recalcitrant people and, citing Exodus 22:18 and Leviticus 20:6 as their authority, granted the courts the power to pronounce sentence of death upon those found guilty of witchcraft. Thus the churchmen enforced what they believed were the laws of God against the legacies of Paganism: all manner of magic, fortune-telling and poisoning. Childeric III's conflation of magic and Paganism was carried a step further by the Council. Magic was specifically the legacy of Paganism, but like

Agobard and the Council of Tours, the Council of Paris also denied that magic was real. However, the references to the use of philtres, drugged food and phylacteries, suggest that something worked, even if it was merely to produce illusions.

Biblical Authority for the Witch Hunt

'Thou shall not suffer a witch to live.' (Exodus 22:18)

'And the soul that turneth after such as have familiar spirits, and after wizards, to go a whoring after them, I will even set my face against that soul, and will cut him off from among his people.' (Leviticus 20:6)

In England at this time, Alfred the Great, King of Wessex, pronounced the death penalty for *wiccan* (witches), and Ethelstan likewise decreed that murder by *wiccecræft* was to be punished with death. In Italy St Barbato warred against the persistent Paganism of the Lombards (a Germanic people from the river Elbe who invaded Italy in 568 CE and founded a kingdom in the Po valley, subsequently overthrown by Charlemagne in 774), and Charles the Bald (Charles II), Holy Roman Emperor, decreed in 873 that all witches, sorcerers and the godless be purged from his realm.[18]

Very Dangerous Evils

There are other very dangerous evils which are certainly legacies of paganism, such as magic, astrology, incantations and spells, poisoning, divination, enchantment, and the interpretation of dreams. These evils ought to be severely punished, as the laws of God ordain. But there is no doubt, as many learned men have witnessed, that there are some people capable of so perverting the minds of others with the Devil's illusions (by giving them philtres, drugged food and phylacteries), that they become confused and insensible to the ills they are made to suffer. It is also said that these people can disturb the air with their spells, send hail-storms, predict the future, take produce and milk from one person to give to another, and do a thousand similar things. If any such be found, be they men or women, they should be severely punished, particularly since, in their malice and temerity, they fear not the Devil nor do they renounce him publicly.[19]

As the final century of the first millennium opened, a most revealing document appeared. It was said to date from the fourth century, although modern scholarship has dated it more accurately to 906.[20] It is widely considered to be one of the most important texts, if not the most important, on witchcraft of the Middle Ages.[21] It first appeared when Regino of Prüm, an abbot in Trier, included in his collection of instructions for bishops, *De synodalibus causis et disciplinis ecclesiasticis libri duo*, a section entitled 'So that the bishops shall expel witches and enchanters from their parishes' (*Ut episcopi de parochiis suis sorteligos et maleficus expellent*), which came to be known as the Canon Episcopi. Whether by genuine error or intentional counterfeit, Burchard, Bishop of Worms, attributed the text to the Council of Ancyra (314) in his *Decretum* (*c.* 1000). In 1140 it was incorporated into the standard text of canonical law, Gratian's *Concordance of Discordant Canons*.

The Canon Episcopi describes how 'some wicked women' are 'perverted by the Devil' and, seduced by his illusions, believe themselves to fly through the night with the Pagan goddess Diana – Burchard later added the name Herodias to the list. A great horde of these women rode beasts across huge distances on certain, unspecified, nights. The Canon exhorts 'bishops and their officials' to do their utmost to drive sorcerers, whether 'man or woman', from their parishes, to 'eject them foully disgraced'.

Cannonade Against Paganism

Bishops and their officials must labour with all their strength to uproot thoroughly from their parishes the pernicious art of sorcery and malifice invented by the Devil, and if they find a man or woman follower of this wickedness to eject them foully disgraced from their parishes. For the Apostle says, 'A man that is a heretic after the first and second admonition avoid.' Those are held captive by the Devil who, leaving their creator, seek the aid of the Devil. And so Holy Church must be cleansed of this pest. Canon Episcopi[22]

We can see that over the years of what were called the Dark Ages, from the earliest ecclesiastical laws in England to the later pontifical councils and kingly decrees, the position on witchcraft, magic and Paganism was hardening. Indeed several popes became so alarmed by this development that they sought to dampen the ardour of their subjects in prosecuting these offences (Leo VII and Gregory VII). We can also see that what was being conducted was not just the persecution of Paganism, but the defence of the Church. The common people were subverting Christian iconography and even places of worship to their own, still Pagan, ends; even Christian priests were consulting magicians and practising magic. This eventually necessitated something of a compromise, or perhaps a clerical gloss on real events, when the festive calendar was standardized to encompass all the major Pagan celebrations and define them as Christian events, even going so far as to shift the birthday of Jesus to comply with Pagan solstitial observances.

As we enter the Middle Ages the Church was still facing widespread residual Paganism and fighting a war on all fronts against it. It certainly helped their cause that they could consolidate these myriad gods and magicians under the banner of a single enemy, Satan. Paganism was ineluctably recast as Satanism and Witchcraft became a heresy. The demonography of the time pictured the arch-fiend in an especially Romish manner (because it was so Classical, so first century CE) as the goat-footed Pan, the popular Dionysus/Bacchus, who so easily fitted in with folk beliefs across Europe of Green Men and Robin Goodfellows.

The Witchcraft Heresy

> Those who try to induce others to perform such evil wonders are called witches. And because infidelity in a person who has been baptised is technically called heresy, therefore such persons are plainly heretics.
>
> *Malleus Maleficarum*, part I, question I.[23]

Whilst it was being forcibly expressed that Pagan magic was illusory, in an attempt to undermine its power and the perception of its power, such an approach left the Church with a problem; why then was it necessary to extinguish it so thoroughly? The causal association with Satan, the claim that these phantasmagoria were the delusions of the Devil, justified the rooting out of Pagan magic. Odin, Thor, Saxnot and Diana whom the Christian writers had explicitly named, were now either demoted to demons in Satan's retinue, or recast as the fiend himself in disguise. Now because the formerly Pagan magicians were really Satanists, and Satan (as the arch-fiend) was a Christian concept, they could be tried and prosecuted as heretics.

It is unlikely that anyone ever sat down and worked this out; the position developed over centuries. But it demonstrates how the Pagan threat was isolated and drawn into the frame of Christian understanding. To an extent Paganism was neutralized by this process; although it was now perhaps more dangerous than ever, at least to the Christian mind, it was no longer in competition with Christianity as an alternative world-view, but became the path of falsity and only amenable to Christian intervention.

This development was also to mark a divide between English and European interpretations. In England the offence of witchcraft continued to be tried in the criminal courts as *maleficia* and, although judgement was occasionally given over to a religious authority to deliver, it did not become a matter for ecclesiastical courts. In continental Europe, however, the idea that witchcraft was heresy gained greater sway and the prosecution of those accused of it was largely the province of ecclesiastical authorities. One visible consequence of this was that whilst witches in England were hanged, on the Continent they were burnt.

It was in the early part of the eleventh century, in 1022 to be exact, in the French town of Orleans, that witchcraft and heresy became irrefutably linked. On trial was a religious group accused of worshipping the Devil, who appeared to them as a beast, as a black man or, in a form reminiscent of the Canon Episcopi, as an angel of light. They worshipped with sex orgies held underground or in abandoned buildings. In the flickering light of their torches they began by chanting a litany of demonic names until the Evil One appeared. They renounced Christ and desecrated the cross. The torches were extinguished and the congregation indiscriminately copulated. Children were inevitably conceived at such meetings and in a parody of the Christian baptismal rite, eight days after they were born they were burnt and their ashes mixed with other ingredients to form wafers that were eaten in a blasphemous, unholy communion.

What the Orleans heretics actually believed appears to have been a dualist doctrine, something akin to Gnosticism, in which the Devil though elevated to a position rivalling the power of God, was not worshipped. However, in reinterpreting Satan's role and influence they did appear to be according him greater power and prominence than was the Christian orthodoxy, and this left them open to the allegations brought against them.

The image was a compelling and enduring one. Almost a hundred years later, in about 1115, Guibert of Nogents in his *Monodiae* described the heretics of Soissons, a French town just a few miles north of Paris, in terms almost amounting to a plagiarism of the Orleans charges. Walter Mapp gave his own variation on the theme and in the process introduced the word 'synagogue' for their assemblies. Writing in 1182 he described, with what appeared to be alarmingly like first-hand knowledge, how the heretics sat in silence, after the watchman had made his first rounds and good people had closed their doors and windows, waiting for their master. They sat round a rope hanging down from the ceiling and after some time a huge black cat would climb down amongst them. As usual, the lights went out and the congregation welcomed the cat with a kiss, 'some [kissing] the feet, more under the tail, most the private parts'.[24]

Towards the end of the century Alan of Lille provided some explanation for these obscene rites. The heretic, he argued, indulged in the orgy to free himself from worldly, which meant Satanic, attachments. It was a purification through perversity. The Gnostics had faced accusations of obscenity in the early centuries of the Common Era, particularly the Barbelognostics. The latter did indeed seem guilty of the charges, and it was clear that their ascetic, world-rejecting faith had a propensity to lead in such generally abhorrent directions. Gnostic doctrines taught that 'flesh must do service to flesh before it can be overcome', that because the body is evil it should be debased through obscenities, that becoming filled with the Holy Spirit one is no longer bound by worldly laws, that those who are not filled with the Holy Spirit are free to sin because they cannot be saved. Medieval heretics like the Cathars amplified this inherent dualism to an extreme degree.[25]

The essentials of witchcraft had at last been established: the pact, night-riding, the obscene kiss, orgies, human sacrifice, and cannibalism. However, the zeal to prosecute wholesale was slower in developing. There were crusades and plenty of heretics – Albigenses, Cathars and Waldenses – to occupy the lords temporal and spiritual;

and there was still the authority of the Canon Episcopi, maintaining the works of the Devil to be illusory, to hold the zealot in check.

The writings of St Thomas Aquinas in the thirteenth century, notably his monumental *Summa Contra Gentiles* and *Summa Theologica*, were to prove instrumental in changing the attitudes of the ecclesiastical authorities to sorcery. His greatest impact was in his refutation of the Canon Episcopi. Speaking perhaps with unbecoming experience in such matters – he had after all studied with the alchemist Albertus Magnus and numerous magical legends have accrued to him – St Thomas asserted that sorcery was real and tangible in its effect. Any work of sorcery implied a pact with the Devil, thus all sorcerers were diabolists and the Satanic witch was born. Contrary to the Canon Episcopi, St Thomas Aquinas believed that witches flew through the air, changed shape, copulated with evil spirits, raised storms and used magic to produce all kinds of wickedness. His views were supported by evidence from the heretics, especially those of Orleans and Soissons, and thus became doubly compelling.

These new and persuasive arguments met with new organizations and imperatives within the Church to form a powerful combination. The Papal Inquisition had been formally established over the years 1227–33, culminating in Gregory IX's appointment of the black-cowled Dominicans as inquisitors, answerable only to the Vicar of Rome. The Dominicans were noted for their intellectual vigour and because of their thoroughness became known as *Domini canes*, the Hounds of the Lord, which is both a Latin play upon the name of the members of the Order, the Dominicani, and an allusion to the peculiar motif of St Dominic, a black and white dog with a torch in its mouth. St Thomas Aquinas was a Dominican.[26]

In 1233 Gregory IX had also accused the Waldensian heretics of meeting with the Devil and engaging in sexual orgies. In 1252 Innocent IV issued the *Ad Extirpanda*, authorizing the imprisonment, torture and execution of heretics, and the seizure of their property, on minimal evidence. However, the escalation into a full-blown witch hunt was temporarily stalled in 1258 by Alexander IV, who refused to grant the Inquisition authority over all cases of sorcery. In what was the first papal bull dealing with sorcery, he gave it authority over all cases of sorcery involving heresy, but refused to grant it power to try other cases. However, witchcraft had already been associated with heresy and the inquisitors simply played upon this connection to extend their judicial authority.[27]

It was not until the beginning of the fourteenth century, after the high-profile posthumous trial of Pope Boniface VIII on charges that included making a pact with the Devil, that the Inquisition was formally empowered to prosecute all acts of sorcery. When Pope John XXII issued the bull *Super illius specula*, he simply made concrete that implicit connection between witchcraft and heresy that the inquisitors had earlier exploited by stating that sorcerers worshipped the Devil and had entered a 'pact with Hell'. His motivation appears to have been his own fear of witchcraft; from 1317 to 1319 John XXII accused a doctor, a barber and a bishop of conspiring to kill him by magic.[28]

In the British Isles during the early fourteenth century there was a series of prominent trials involving the aristocracy and upper classes: 1314–15 saw the trial and execution of John Tannere (also known as John Canne), who claimed to be the rightful heir to the throne; in 1324 Dame Alice Kyteler and ten accomplices were tried for witchcraft; in 1325 Robert le Mareschal and twenty-seven others were tried on charges of using sorcery to try and kill the king; and in 1330, Edmund, Earl of Kent and the brother of Edward II, was tried and condemned for consulting a demon. The trial records of lesser mortals from this period demonstrate that all levels of society were affected. We read, for example, of a goldsmith brought before the King's Bench in 1331 charged with using wax figures to try and kill two people and in 1385 of a clergyman and a tailor accused of dabbling in prohibited magic.[29]

In Italy, in 1387–8, a group of heretics was rounded up in the Lombardy region. Under torture they implicated most of the town in their abominable ceremonies which included the renunciation of Christianity, the worship of the Devil, feasting and orgy. In France, in 1398, the University of Paris showed its endorsement of the papal position by declaring maleficent sorcery to be punishable as heresy if it was accomplished by a pact with the Devil and, of course, they also maintained that pacts were implicit in acts of sorcery and required no formal agreement, whether written or verbal.[30]

The Hammer of the Witches

'It has indeed lately come to Our ears... [that] many persons of both sexes, unmindful of their own salvation and straying from the Catholic Faith, have abandoned themselves to devils...' In 1484, Pope Innocent VIII issued the papal bull *Summis desiderantes affectibus* as a confirmation of papal support for the Inquisition against witches. Although its effect was restricted to Germany, it set a dangerous precedent. In fact, though it was seemingly confined to northern Germany, Innocent VIII was extending the power of the Inquisition over districts formerly outside its jurisdiction and thereby laying the foundation for the extensive Europe-wide persecution of those accused of witchcraft. Furthermore, he appointed two men to defend the faith in these dangerous parts, thereby cementing their reputation and authority, and greatly contributing to the success of their book, a work that was to become the handbook of the persecution of the witches.[31]

In 1485, or 1486 (authorities quibble over the exact date), two doctors of theology, two Hounds of the Lord, Heinrich Kramer and James Sprenger, whom Innocent VIII called 'our dear sons', published the *Malleus Maleficarum*, the 'Hammer of the Witches'.[32] They also reproduced Innocent VIII's bull, attesting to the high origin of the authority invested in them and therefore in their treatise on witchcraft. It was a brilliant example of marketing.

The *Malleus Maleficarum* is a thorough work, dealing with every possible type of witchcraft, the forms taken by witches, the methods of detecting them, how to judge the accused and the punishments suitable for their crimes. In other words, it supplies every sort of detail that the inquisitor investigating witchcraft would need to know. Its popularity is greatly attested by the number of editions printed. Around fourteen editions appeared from 1487 to 1520 and between 1574 and 1669 there were a further sixteen editions, all from the leading presses of the day in Germany, France and Italy. It was the international number two bestseller, second only to the Bible until the success of John Bunyan's *Pilgrim's Progress* in 1678.[33]

The 'Hammer' delivers its resounding impact in three blows. The first strikes out the theological argument concerning witchcraft, principally the source and reality of the power of the witches. The second sounds out the practices of witchcraft, how witches cast spells, how they enter pacts with the Devil and so on. The third hammers out the judicial procedure for prosecuting witchcraft, from selecting judges to the number of witnesses required and the use of torture. Each blow successively drives home the message that witches are to be rooted out, first by presenting the argument for their existence, secondly by demonstrating the wickedness they inflict upon the world, and thirdly by showing the means of dealing with them. The book opens by arguing for the existence of witchcraft. It is not an argument that can be disagreed with; it is not simply a position, because the authors assert that opinions contrary to it are heretical. There is no real discussion, only the refutation and condemnation (if not damnation) of other arguments. Kramer and Sprenger are forging an unbreakable hammer.

At one point the reality of the witches' power is attested to by the severity of its punishment as laid down in the Bible (citing Deuteronomy and Leviticus). The authors argue that such severe penalties would not be necessary if witchcraft were not indeed capable of real effects. There is frequent reference to the Canon Episcopi, but canonical law is not refuted, its interpretation is just challenged – although the result amounts to the same thing. The authority of the Episcopi, almost six hundred years after its composition, is palpable.

The two inquisitors also seek to discover why it is that women are more frequently given over to witchcraft than men, or in their words, 'why a greater number of witches is found in the fragile feminine sex than among men'.[34] They have it on the authority of the Bible that women are the greatest in wickedness: 'All wickedness is but little to the wickedness of a woman': and on the authority of the saints: 'What else is woman but . . . a necessary evil . . . an evil of nature, painted with fair colours'.[35] The two monks consider the argument that women are more credulous than men and that in consequence are a softer target for the Devil, whose chief purpose is to 'corrupt faith'. They also draw upon the Classical authority of Terence to propose that women are intellectually like children (this was probably the case with most of them, but through the lack of education, not want of mental ability), that they have weak memories and are undisciplined. However, they conclude that the 'natural reason' is that women are more 'carnal' than men: 'for though the devil tempted Eve to sin, yet Eve seduced Adam'; and 'all witchcraft comes from carnal lust, which is in women insatiable', a position which they support with more quotations from the Bible.[36] Whilst their arguments may appear ridiculous to us now, Kramer and Sprenger were drawing upon their common experience as inquisitors, in which they found that most of the cases brought before them involved women, hence their somewhat tortuous attempts to try and explain the fact.

Kramer and Sprenger take the established picture of witchcraft and amplify it. Witchcraft is clearly and undeniably equated with heresy, 'which is Apostasy of the Faith', but it is not, if one can put it in such terms, just another heresy; indeed they themselves put it, that witches 'are not simple Heretics, but Apostates'. It is the highest evil: 'The evils which are perpetrated by modern witches exceed all other sin which God has ever permitted to be done.' And again, 'The works of witches exceed all other sins, in hideousness since they deny Him crucified, in inclination since they commit nastiness of the flesh with devils, in blindness of mind since in a pure spirit of malignity they rage and bring every injury upon the souls and bodies of men and beasts.' Because their sins are greater than all others it follows, at least to the inquisitorial mind, that their punishments must be greater than all others here on earth and, of course, in the hereafter.[37]

The Hounds sniff out some extraordinary stories of sorcery and enchantment to demonstrate their arguments, but they characterize witchcraft less as a magic art and more as a power channelled through the witch, ultimately coming from Satan. It cannot be taught, it cannot be learned from books, including, they are at pains to point out, their own.[38] By these means they diminish the power of the witch herself and her magic arts. Woman is weak and wicked and could not, perforce, be capable of such things by herself.

The Mouse Magician
We hear of a certain leader or heresiarch of witches named Staufer, who lived in Berne and the adjacent country, and used to publicly boast that, whenever he liked, he could change himself into a mouse in the sight of his rivals and slip through the hands of his deadly enemies . . . *Malleus Maleficarum*, part II, question I, chapter 15.[39]

In the final part of the book Kramer and Sprenger set out the formalities for beginning a witchcraft trial, give the guidelines for its conduct and the means of passing judgement. They are very particular and correct in their approach, and it is clear that they do not wish the trial of witches to be conducted by kangaroo courts, places of summary judgement, but in a manner lawful and conducive to justice. For instance: a person's sworn enemies are not permitted to stand as witnesses and give evidence against him; as many witnesses as possible should be produced; and the accused should be appointed an advocate, 'for the proof of an accusation ought to be clearer than daylight, and especially ought this to be so in the case of the grave charge of heresy'.[40]

They are very detailed in describing how to interrogate both witnesses and suspect. They give sample cases with the sort of questions to be asked closely described, and alert the questioner to possible grounds for suspicion in the accused's answers. It is this step-by-step process, this level of detail, that makes the *Malleus Maleficarum* such an important work in the development of the witch hunts.

Only with the accused's own confession of heretical witchcraft could the court send her to the stake, but the Inquisitors would not allow her to remain silent. With the acceptance of torture as part of the process, any semblance of justice breaks down. Even silence under torture was considered a further indication of guilt, since the Inquisitors held that witches attempted to preserve their silence with charms.

Kramer and Sprenger had written the textbook for the witch hunts, and the sparks from their 'Hammer' started a thousand fires across the length and breadth of Europe for the next 200 years. The craze reached its height from 1560 to 1660.[41] Estimates vary as to how many died in the ensuing slaughter. In 1598, adding up the figures for the past 150 years, Ludovicus à Paramo estimated that 30,000 had perished. Modern estimates put the total figure somewhere between 40,000 to 200,000, although some rather partisan accounts, relying more on feeling than fact, have stated that as many as 9 million died.[42] The number of trials that took place must have been considerably greater, since not all trials resulted in execution. Indeed, not all executions were judicial, so we must allow for the inevitable lynchings and other summary acts of mob justice. Inevitably, too, given the ravages of time, not all trial records have survived. So we will never know exactly how many died, but when looking at such estimates as we have it is important to consider their relative magnitude: taking into account population increase, 200,000 in the sixteenth and seventeenth centuries, might equate to 9 million today.

Although Kramer and Sprenger approve the use of torture and suggest that it be introduced to the case gradually, proceeding from lighter to heavier tortures as and when the accused proved resistant, they do not detail what those tortures should be. It is almost as if they assume that judicial and ecclesiastical authorities would already have at their disposal a more or less standard set of equipment for torture. Certainly the use of torture was not peculiar to the witch trials, although some practices emerged that were, such as swimming, which in themselves were less tortures and more trials of the crime itself in the same way that the earlier ordeals of the age of chivalry had been. The torturers' art was at its height in the Middle Ages, progressing from bloody outrages to more subtle methods of sleep deprivation in the early modern period. As Leonardo was painting masterpieces and imagining machines for flying in the air, and Shakespeare was writing the crowning glories of English literature, nameless torturers sat sharpening their instruments and heating their irons till they glowed red hot.

The 'swimming' of witches was a typically bizarre example of medieval logic. Like the ancient ordeal by water, the 'swimming' process was thought to demonstrate the guilt or innocence of the accused. The victim was bound and tossed into deep water. If she sank she was innocent (and probably drowned); if she floated (and lived), she was guilty. Perhaps a more agreeable test was that of weighing. The suspected witch was set upon a large pair of scales with a Bible on the other side. If the Bible rose, she was innocent; if the Bible fell, she was guilty.

The examination of witches could prove a torture in itself, although that was not the direct intention. Whilst the examination for the 'witch's teat', the extra nipple she used to feed her familiar, could prove embarrassing, it was not as painful as the practice of 'pricking' for the Devil's mark. This mark was most often invisible, although blemishes were particularly suspect, and was likely to appear on any part of the body. It was supposed to be the place where the Devil had touched the witch in confirmation of her acceptance into the legions of evil. It was commonly thought to be insensible to pain. Accordingly the suspect was pierced and prodded with sharp instruments in search of this spot. In due course it was most often found, but whilst the Chinese had developed this knowledge into the beneficial technique of acupuncture, the superstitious, God-fearing Christians, used it as evidence of diabolical influence.

The direct methods of torture were various, ranging from thumb-screws and racking to the practices of 'waking' and 'walking' whereby the accused was deprived of sleep or exhausted by continual move-ment until a confession was forthcoming. The so-called Witch-house of Bamberg was furnished with the most extreme instruments of torture imaginable: iron-spiked whipping stocks; the strappado, a method of hoisting the victim so that his arms would be agonizingly pulled from their sockets; the rack that stretched the victim, pulling apart leg as well as arm joints; and lime baths that dissolved the flesh. The rack was a Continental, and especially French, favourite. The curious name seems to come from the German *recken*, 'to strain'. In England it was, with gallows humour, known as the Duke of Exeter's daughter, after the device was brought over to England in 1447 and installed in the Tower where the Duke of Exeter was serving as its Constable. Its use in England was abolished in 1640.[43]

Then there was the *turcas*, a device for tearing out fingernails; the spider, a sharp iron fork for prodding and mangling; boots (*bootikens*, and in Scotland, *cashielaws*) for crushing the legs; 'thraw-ing' with ropes bound around the head; the scold's bridle (sometimes also called the witches' bridle) that held the mouth open with a spike depressing the tongue; and water tortures involving pumping the victim full of water, or feeding him salty food and brine. Sometimes it was enough for the accused to be shown the instruments of torture, in other cases, such as that of Alison Balfour in Orkney in 1594, they were forced to watch the torture of loved ones. The torturers' inven-tiveness is remarkable and most depressing.

The first of the English witchcraft acts was passed in 1542, in the reign of Henry VIII. The conjuration of spirits or the practice of witchcraft, enchantment or sorcery was made a felony and hence a capital offence. Edward VI repealed this act in 1547, but Elizabeth I introduced another in 1563 (repealed 1603) after an earlier bill of 1559 failed. Like its predecessor, it emphasized the harmful effect of witchcraft, without any mention of heretical beliefs. However, unlike its predecessor, it deemed only those witchcrafts that resulted in the death of the victim to be capital crimes. A year's imprisonment and four visits to the pillory was the punishment for unsuccessful witches. James I of England (VI of Scotland), himself an authority on witch-craft, introduced another act in 1604, which proved particularly enduring, not being repealed until 1736.

Elements which were familiar, if not essential, to witchcraft on the Continent were rare in England. Only three charges of worshipping the Devil were brought and all of them in the early fourteenth century. Walter Langton, Bishop of Coventry was charged in 1301, but the charges were not sustained by the Papal Commission. The prosecution of the Knights Templar was similarly unsuccessful. Only the case against Dame Alice Kyteler in 1324 was successful and that was tried in Ireland by a French-educated Franciscan monk. The first reference to a pact with the Devil was not made until 1612. The witches' Sabbat, the flying of witches and the use of broomsticks were all rarities in England. The orgy that seemed to so delight Continental persecutors was entirely lacking until Matthew Hopkins unearthed a few cases involving carnal relations with demons in the 1640s. In contrast, the witches' familiar spirit, usually in some physical form like a toad or cat, or even an insect, was characteristic, although not universal, among English witch trials and wholly lacking in Continental ones.

When Shall We Three Meet Again?

FIRST WITCH
> When shall we three meet again?
> In thunder, lightning or in rain?

SECOND WITCH
> When the hurly-burly's done,
> When the battle's lost and won.

THIRD WITCH
> That will be ere the set of sun.

Shakespeare, Macbeth

The battle that Christianity had been fighting against the armies of witchery ended, not with the thunder of the Inquisitors' 'Hammer', but with the judges' gavel. And as the witches appeared, at last, to be vanquished, in the already dying light of Christianity's setting sun, it was not they who stood in the dock. Two spectacular events stand as prime examples of the way in which witch-hunting reached its apogee and in the process burnt itself out in the seventeenth century.

These are the brief career of Matthew Hopkins, Witch-Finder General, and the Salem witch trials in Massachusetts.

Whilst in continental Europe the opponents of witchcraft had their Hounds of the Lord to sniff out the practice, in England, because of the different status of witchcraft, a different figure arose: the professional witch-finder. The most famous, indeed the most infamous, as well as the most successful of these was Matthew Hopkins. The son of a minister, he was born in Wenham, Suffolk, and scraped a living as a lawyer in Ipswich and Manningtree. Until 1645 he appears to have been an unremarkable man. Indeed so little was remarked about him that we do not even know the precise year of his birth. However, from 1645 he enters the scene as a witch-finder by accusing several people of Manningtree of using black magic against him. This seems to have been something like a conversion experience for him. From that day he quit his law practice and set up in the profession of witch-finder with his associate John Stearne.

With a knowledge of James I's *Daemonologie* under their belts and precious little else, Hopkins and Stearne advertised that for a fee they would root out witches wherever they might be. The English Civil War had been raging since 1642 and would not end until 1648, but despite the upheaval that that caused – perhaps because of it – Hopkins and Stearne were not short of work.[44] Hopkins styled himself the Witch-Finder General and claimed to have been appointed to this office by Parliament. He further boasted that he had in his possession the Devil's List of all the witches in England. His claims went unchallenged and his success mounted so that he was soon employing four assistant witch-finders. Together they marauded through the counties of Essex, Suffolk, Huntingdonshire, Norfolk, and Cambridgeshire, torturing suspects and charging outrageous fees.

No doubt inspired by James I's Continent-influenced *Daemonologie*, Hopkins produced the first confessions from witches of having signed a pact with the Devil. His investigations always produced a plethora of witches – thirty-eight in Chelmsford and 124 in Suffolk. He seemed to be constantly searching for a great society of witches. However, his meteoric rise to fame ended in an equally rapid, but catastrophic fall from favour. His excessive ambition and enthusiasm in prosecuting witches, although undoubtedly successful, brought criticism of overuse of torture and overcharging of fees. Where before he had been welcomed he found resistance and by 1646 judges and local authorities were beginning to turn against him. In particular Hopkins's use of 'swimming' met with increasing disapproval.

After 1647 nothing more of any certainty is heard about him except the record of his burial in the graveyard of Mistley church. He had separated from Stearne and returned to Manningtree, and popular tradition has it that he was himself accused of witchcraft, of being in league with the Devil. It was said that his 'Devil's List' had been procured by sorcery. He was 'swum' in Mistley pond and, according to one version, drowned an innocent man, or in another floated as a guilty one, was fished out and hanged. For the record, Stearne recorded in 1648 that his former business associate passed away peacefully in Manningtree after a long illness from tuberculosis.[45]

Although the witch hunts did not end with the disappearance of Hopkins, his brief career brings out those elements that were to turn the tide: growing doubt over the judgements reached and growing distaste over the methods used.

The Salem witch trials present a complex case, about which much has been written and, one suspects, remains to be written. However, it neatly demonstrates the way in which witch hysteria arose and spread, and eventually became exposed as fallacious. Whilst Salem was not the first case of witchcraft in the British colonies, nor the worst, nor the last, it did come to be regarded as essentially the test case for the existence of witchcraft in America. From the initial outbreak in Salem Village in 1692, the accusations of witchcraft spread like wildfire to encompass hundreds of people and even animals across Massachusetts.

The hysterical paralysis and convulsions that struck first two young girls and then others following a failed attempt at fortune-telling was so extreme, so strange and so far beyond the medical knowledge of the time that it was diagnosed as witchcraft-induced. The thought of this unknown enemy amongst them so terrified the people of Salem that when the girls accused several members of the community of bewitching them they were readily believed. However, the excesses of their accusations grew so monstrous that their outrageous claims became unbelievable, despite the willingness to believe them in the first place. As first marginal figures in the community – black slaves and wise women – then pillars of the community fell victim to the accusations, they became increasingly hard to sustain. It was, after all, the pillars of the community who were prosecuting the suspected cases of witchcraft. The final tragic irony was that the eighteen people who were hanged on Gallows' Hill died not because they were witches, but because they refused to confess that they were witches.

The changing climate of both learned and ecclesiastical opinion across Europe and the American colonies spelt the end of the witch craze. Horror at the abuses of the system and growing disbelief in the possibility of the crimes alleged combined in varying degrees and in various places to smother the flames of persecution. However, where many of the witch trials had been brought by pressure from the bottom up, reaction against them came from the top down. Towards the end of the seventeenth century Roger North, brother of the then Lord Chief Justice, remarked on the great fervour for witch-hunting amongst the people, referring to the 'popular rage' for the execution of witches.[46] It was the learned men of the Enlightenment (c. 1690–1790), like Roger North, who viewed the belief in witches as superstition and their persecution as barbarous.

The change in the law brought by the new act of 1736 followed rather than led these changed attitudes. Roger North expressed his indignation at the situation: the judge who dared to question the case against an accused witch was deemed an irreligious man and acting improperly. As early as 1682 his brother, the Lord Chief Justice, complained to the Secretary of State that 'we cannot reprieve them [those accused of witchcraft] without appearing to deny the very being of witches, which . . . is contrary to law.'[47]

Despite problems with the law and the superstitious mob, the last judicial execution for witchcraft in England took place in 1682 and in Scotland in 1727. The last assize court conviction took place in Hertfordshire in 1712 and the woman convicted, Jane Wenham, was later pardoned. The last indictment for witchcraft was brought in 1717, but despite the willingness of twenty-five people to give evidence against the accused, the case against Jane Clarke, her son and daughter, was thrown out of court. Although the courts had turned their back on the witch hunts, the 'popular rage' still continued. The case of the mob lynching of the elderly Osbournes in 1751 in Tring, Hertfordshire, demonstrates the point; significantly, it was the mob's ringleader, Thomas Colley, who was brought to trial, found guilty and hanged.[48]

Elsewhere in Europe the trend was similar, although slower. From the last judicial execution in England it was a hundred years until the last execution in Europe as a whole. Portugal was an odd case, executing its last witch as early as 1626, but not seeing its last trial for witchcraft until 1802. France was closest behind England, executing its last condemned witch in 1683 in Alsace and holding its last trial under the Parlement of Paris in 1693. Estonia's last trial and execution for witchcraft was in 1699. Sweden's last execution was in 1710, although its last trial for witchcraft was as late as 1779. Ireland held its last trial and executed its last witch in 1711, although the persistence of witch beliefs resurfaced in 1895 with the tragic case of Bridget Cleary, the so-called Fairy Witch of Clonmel. Denmark was next, executing its last witch in 1722, but holding its last trial in 1762. Austria and Hungary condemned to death their last witches in 1756, although trials continued to be held until 1775 in Austria and 1777 in Hungary. Poland executed its last witch in 1775 and the following year held what was to be the final trial for witchcraft in that country. Germany as a whole (although it was not yet unified) saw its last judicial execution in 1775 in Kempten and held its last trial in 1792 in Bavaria. Spain burnt her last witch in 1781, but was the last country in Europe to hold a trial for witchcraft, in 1820. Switzerland held its last trial and execution in 1782, the last time a witch was convicted and executed by a European court.[49]

Just as the reasons for the persecution of witches were various, so too were the reasons for its decline. For as many who came forward to denounce the superstitious barbarity of witch beliefs there were as many who still defended the view. We cannot overlook changes within the very fabric of society itself, agricultural and industrial revolutions, and advances in science and medicine. Indeed the success of the medical re-interpretation of former signs of malevolent magic as cases of mental instability or physical ailment was a powerful antidote to the fear of the unknown. These developments in turn contributed to the lessening of local power and the destruction of traditional communities, the decline of religion and the over-all secularization of society. Yet for all that, it was as much a growing repugnance with the old methods of extracting confession as a decrease in the old beliefs that fanned the witch hunts that led to their demise – it goes without saying that without torture confessions were less forthcoming. It was not, then, simply a war of words, for and against the persecution of witches, it was the entire transformation of the civilized world as it was then conceived. Magic did not die out, the world around it changed. But the witches were destined to meet again.

PART TWO

BORN OF SHADOWS

THE ORIGINS OF MODERN WITCHCRAFT

4. CELTIC TWILIGHT AND GOLDEN DAWN: THE REVIVAL OF WITCHCRAFT AND MAGIC

The European witch hunts were over, but witchcraft and the idea of witchcraft would never die out. In the nineteenth and twentieth centuries witchcraft was reexamined, reinterpreted and, ultimately, reinvented.

The fear of magic that resulted in the witch hunts had always been accompanied by an interest in, if not a fascination with, the subject. Even whilst witches were rounded up in their hundreds for trial and execution, people practised the forbidden art: cunningmen and wise women in the lower strata of society, astrologers and alchemists in the upper levels. Even as Elizabeth I passed her own Witchcraft Act she consulted with her court astrologer and magical adept John Dee. As the inquisitors' fires guttered and went out, as the judges turned sceptic and the torturers found themselves unemployed, there arose a great fascination and intrigue with the secret mystical society. Rosicrucians, Illuminati and Freemasons congregated to work their secret rites, drawing royal, noble and common alike into their ranks. The danger of such associations diminished rapidly as the judge's gavel came down on the last witch trials, but the thrill was undeniably attractive, the promise just as compelling.

The Old Religion

As new groups such as the Illuminati arose to proclaim ancient wisdom, old groups became reinterpreted, even revived. The druids, so thoroughly eradicated, were after more than a millennium resurrected.

Witches, so thoroughly persecuted if not quite eradicated, were seen in a new light. As early as 1828 the German Karl Ernst Jarke proposed that witchcraft really had been a Pagan survival. Jarke was Professor of Criminal Law at Berlin University and in 1828 he edited the trial records of a seventeenth-century witchcraft case for publication in a legal journal, adding a brief commentary. It was here that he made the startling, otherwise unheard of and indeed wholly original claim that the witchcraft persecuted in the early modern period had been the tattered remnant of a Pagan religion. It had been the ancient faith of the German peoples, vilified as Satanism by Christianity and reduced to a thing of shreds and patches by the Inquisition. Under these pressures it had, during the Middle Ages, begun to conform to the Christian stereotype and had resorted to Devil worship in earnest. Disgusted by this degeneration of their faith the common people began to denounce it to the authorities.[1]

Jarke's idea was readily taken up. By 1832 a variation of it even found its way into the popular music of the time. In his orchestral piece 'The First *Walpurgisnacht*' (*Die Erste Walpurgisnacht*) Felix Mendelssohn told the story of how Pagan villagers attacked by Christians on May Eve pretended to be witches to scare them away. In 1839 another German advanced a new theory of witchcraft. Franz Josef Mone, Director of the Archives in Baden, argued with Jarke that witchcraft was indeed a Pagan religion, but he diverged from the earlier thesis to advance the theory that it was a foreign religion introduced into Germany by Greek slaves. Based upon the mysteries of Hecate and Dionysus this degenerate cult was loathed by both the Pagans and the Christians who came after them. This explanation preserved the purity of the original Germanic Paganism whilst also accounting for the source and persecution of witchcraft. Unfortunately, neither Jarke nor Mone produced much in the way of evidence to substantiate their claims.[2]

Meanwhile, in Great Britain interest in the subject was revived with the publication of Sir Walter Scott's *Letters on Demonology and Witchcraft* in 1830. Unlike Jarke or Mone, Scott was sceptical, even sensibly dismissive as was the rationalist style, of witchcraft. In his earlier novels (*Ivanhoe*, 1817, and *The Pirate*, 1821) he treated the subject unevenly: Rebecca in *Ivanhoe* is executed as a sorceress because of her knowledge of herbal medicine; whilst in *The Pirate* a traditional wise woman is revealed to be a manipulative conjuror whose powers are a sham and who in the end is led to Christianity. Whilst Scott may have piqued the interest of his readers there was no new interpretation of witchcraft forthcoming, either from himself or his contemporaries. It was the work of a Frenchman that had the greatest impact.

In 1862 the historian Jules Michelet published his *La Sorcière*.[3] This work incorporated his themes of anti-Catholicism, matriarchy and radicalism, and was delivered in an inimitable, almost poetical style.[4] Although it was produced in only two months and was largely lacking in evidence, Michelet saw the book as seminal, noting in his journal: 'I have assumed a new position . . . that of proclaiming the provisional death of Christianity.'[5] The use of the word 'provisional' is interesting; did Michelet fear that, though he had killed it, it would rise again on the third day?

Michelet's witch is a revolutionary heroine, a force for spiritual freedom, women's rights and the liberation of the working classes. He attributes great things to the witch: her store of wisdom gave rise to the Renaissance, and her healing powers founded modern medicine. The witch is his perfect idealization of womankind because every woman is 'a creature of Enchantment . . . a Sibyl; in virtue of love, a Magician'. She enjoys a special relationship with the natural world. At the Witches' Sabbat she 'fulfils every office'. However, the witches worship the very masculine god Pan or Priapus and that this figure was appropriated as the Christian Devil causes Michelet no concern. Indeed, he goes so far as to ask, 'Is not Satan the outlaw of outlaws?' and describes his religion in eulogistic terms: 'He gives his followers the joy and wild liberty of all free things of Nature, the rude delight of being a world apart, all sufficient unto itself.' Witchcraft's degeneration into orgy and child-sacrifice he blames on the influence of nobles gaining admittance to the religion.[6]

La Sorcière has never gone out of print. Although ignored by his contemporary academics, Michelet's heady mix of Paganism and radical feminism made a broad and wide-ranging impact. In America the women's rights campaigner Matilda Joslyn Gage drew upon the book for her own polemical work, *Woman, Church, and State*, published in Chicago in 1893. Gage's witches were Pagan priestesses of the original matriarchal religion that had dominated mankind and their persecution was a war of misogyny in which 9 million women were slaughtered. Like Michelet, Gage abandoned thorough research for polemical passion and political effect.

Another American who was influenced by Michelet was the journalist, literateur and adventurer Charles G. Leland. Born in Philadelphia in 1824, he was a restless spirit, living with the Native Americans and travelling widely across Europe, even taking part in the French Revolution in 1848, before settling in the Italian town of Florence, where he died in 1903. He was a prolific author, best known in his day for a collection of comic verses, *Hans Breitman's Ballads* (1872), but he was the master of a hundred subjects as evidenced by his *Gypsey Sorcery and Fortune-Telling* (1891) and *Etruscan Roman Remains* (1892). However, it was his *Aradia, or the Gospel of the Witches*, a slight book of a little over a hundred pages published late in his career in 1899, that was to be his most enduring legacy.

Leland tells us that in 1886 he had learned of the existence of a document relating the principles of Italian witchcraft and, of course, was eager to get hold of it. He had made the acquaintance of a woman he called 'Maddalena', who he said led a 'wandering life in Tuscany', collecting and passing on scraps of folklore for him, and he now urged her to seek out this rare manuscript.[7] He waited for eleven years before a package arrived bearing the postmark Colle, Val d'Elsa, near Siena in Tuscany, and containing *Aradia, or the Gospel of the Witches*.

It is a remarkable book, filled with mythology, spells, invocations and even directions for holding a Sabbat. In fragmentary form it purports to detail the theology and magic of *La Vecchia Religione*, the Old Religion. It opens with a theogony, the story of how Aradia came into being, and it begins with incest. Diana, 'Queen of Witches' and Lucifer, 'the God of the Sun and of the Moon, the God of Light,' are brother and sister, and the sister loves the brother more than she should. From this love and through the machinations of Diana comes Aradia, and in female counterpoint to the Christians' Jesus, she is sent to earth as a mortal to teach mankind. Aradia is reborn on earth as 'the first of witches known' with the divinely ordained mission to teach the arts of poisoning, crop-blasting and cursing to the oppressed so that they can overthrow the aristocracy, the wealthy and the Christian priests. When she dies she leaves instructions among her followers on how, at the full moon, to summon and worship her mother, Diana.[8]

The Worship of Diana
Whenever ye have need of anything,
Once in the month, and when the moon is full,
Ye shall assemble in some desert place,
Or in a forest all together join
To adore the potent spirit of your queen,
My mother, great Diana.
And ye shall be free from slavery;
And so ye shall be free in everything;
And as the sign that ye are truly free,
Ye shall be naked in your rites,
And ye shall make the game of Benevento,
Extinguishing the lights . . .'

The elements of that worship are familiar – nudity, orgy – but they are portrayed in the text, not as signs of devil-induced debauchery but as symbolic demonstrations of liberty. The rest of the book consists of a confused cosmology, a series of spells and charms of no great account except in their occasional oddities (like a spell to find 'some fine and ancient books, and at a moderate price'),[10] and some final, seemingly random, mythological tales and legends.

Leland took *Aradia* at face value and enthusiastically championed it in a manner reminiscent of Michelet. Its authenticity, however, is naturally disputed. Not only did Leland have a reputation as a dissembler, but his sources could not be checked. He tells us that 'Maddalena' disappeared shortly after he received the manuscript from her in 1897. Eye-witness testimony from Leland's niece confirms that she had seen correspondence from her, lending at least some weight to her existence, albeit biased in origin.[11] However, there has been no independent corroborative evidence, either of her existence, or of the genuineness of her manuscript. Nor has there been any information forthcoming that could support the existence of a widespread society of witches of the sort described in *Aradia* operating in Italy, despite Leland's reference to 'several papers published in divers magazines' as testifying to the fact.[12] None of that really mattered, however, for the story was stronger than the facts, although it would take another fifty years for its impact to be felt.

Aradian Witchcraft

The *Treguenda*. Aradia's followers meet every month at the full moon, calling their Sabbat the *Treguenda*.

Nudity. Aradians eschew clothes to demonstrate their freedom.

The Supper. The Aradians feast on meal, salt, honey, water and wine baked into crescent-shaped cakes.

Conjuration of the Meal. The meal is honoured as the source of life.

Conjuration of the Salt. The salt is conjured as symbolic of truth.

Conjuration of Cain. Cain is conjured as a lunar spirit and asked to foretell the future and change unwelcome destinies.

Conjuration of Diana. Diana is both implored and constrained to deliver the witches' wishes. The Conjuration takes the form of both an address and a dance.

Benevento. Aradia's followers play this 'game', which involves 'extinguishing the lights'.

Invocation of Aradia. At midnight her followers invoke the spirit of Aradia.[13]

In the Vault of the Adepts

Whilst Michelet and Leland shaped the theory of what would later become modern Witchcraft, another group of men were busy forming what would become its key practices. Significantly none of them was a witch, or claimed to have anything to do with witchcraft. They were Freemasons and amateur occultists.

These four men, the Revd A.F.A. Woodford, Dr Wynn Westcott, S.L. MacGregor Mathers and Dr W.R. Woodman, founded the Hermetic Order of the Golden Dawn and set in motion a force that would change the world of the spirit for ever. They were inspired to take this step by the discovery of a cipher manuscript. Accounts vary as to how exactly this discovery was made; some say the manuscript was found amongst the papers of a deceased clairvoyant, others maintain that it was found folded in a second-hand book picked at random from the crowded shelves of a bookshop. Whatever its exact origin the manuscript appeared to contain five skeleton rituals and contact details for a certain Fräulein Sprengel of Nuremberg.

Woodford discovered the manuscript in 1886; he passed it on to Westcott in 1887 to decipher it; Westcott called in Mathers to help him flesh out the skeleton rituals; and Mathers brought in Woodman to assist. By 1888 they had founded the Isis-Urania Temple in London with a charter granted by the mysterious Anna Sprengel. For three years they operated with the assistance of Sprengel, developing the Order and opening temples in Weston-super-Mare, Bradford, Edinburgh and Paris, until a letter arrived breaking the connection forever. It purported to be from Sprengel's colleagues and informed the British occultists that she had died. Her fellow members of the German branch had disapproved of her communication with them and they would now have to continue on their own.

Although they had achieved much, all they had was an outer order, essentially a teaching order; to progress they would have to make their own link with the Secret Chiefs of the Order, super-occultists who could only be contacted through the astral plane and held their exalted office in the Third Order. The next year Mathers announced that he had made such a connection and established a Second Order, the Red Rose and the Cross of Gold. He supplied the rituals of this new order, which had been gained 'by clairvoyance – by astral projection . . . by the table, by the ring and disc – at times by Direct Voice . . . at times copied from books brought before me, I knew not how'.[14] The experience was a dramatic one. Mathers talks of extreme exhaustion, and of blood pouring out of his nose, mouth and even ears.

Mathers was an extraordinary character, larger than life, both in the depth of his knowledge and the height of his ambition. Born in 1854 to a London clerk, he had shown an early interest in the occult. He was an extremely able scholar, producing translations of three key texts from Knorr von Rosenroth's *Kabbalah Denudata* (published as *The Kabbalah Unveiled* in 1887), compiled from many manuscript versions a definitive English edition of *The Key of Solomon the King*, produced a translation of *The Book of the Sacred Magic of Abramelin the Mage*, and published *The Lesser Key of Solomon the King*. His diligent labouring in the great libraries of the British Museum in London and the Bibliothèque de l'Arsenal in Paris gave the world easily accessible versions of the greatest and most renowned of magical texts.

If his learning was remarkable so was his dress. He was a flamboyant figure, frequently to be seen around Paris dressed in full Highland regalia. Enthused by the cultural fashion of the 'Celtic Twilight' then in vogue, he claimed that 'Mathers' was actually derived from the Gaelic *Mo Athair*, meaning 'posthumous one', a euphemism for the banned name of MacGregor, hence his assumption of that name.[15] As well as the name he also assumed the title of Count of Glenstrae, a title he said had been conferred upon his great-grandfather by the French.[16]

The Golden Dawn system was a masterpiece of occult syncretism, drawing together the practices of East and West, the Jewish cabbala, Christian mysticism, Western Hermeticism, Eastern philosophy and Yogic practices, to form what was in effect, with its complex system of examinations, initiations and degrees, a university of magic. The student progressed through the system by demonstrating his understanding of the knowledge required by the Order and by his mastery of the techniques taught. The aim of the Order was to bring the student to a state of spiritual union with his 'Higher and Divine Genius' through High, or Ceremonial Magic.[17]

The Neophyte Ritual

Inheritor of a Dying World, we call thee to the Living Beauty. Wanderer in the Wild Darkness, we call thee to the Gentle Light. Long hast thou dwelt in Darkness – Quit the Night and seek the Day.[18]

This magic was a set of psycho-spiritual exercises designed to transform the consciousness and elevate the soul of the practitioner. It was a thousand times removed from the Goetic or Low Magic, of cursing and destruction, the *maleficia* of the traditional witch. Whilst the great witches of antiquity, Medea and Circe, were downcast goddesses, degenerated into common sorceresses, these new magicians sought to raise themselves up from their soiled mortality and court once more the company of the divine. That they occasionally fell from this ideal is less remarkable than the fact that they mostly stuck to it.

Woodford died before the Isis-Urania Temple had been founded and Woodman before the establishment of the Second Order. When Westcott resigned in 1897 Mathers was left in sole, but not unchallenged, command of the Order. A rebellion by members of the First Order ousted him in 1900, but not before hundreds of initiations had taken place, including such luminaries as the poet W.B. Yeats, the author Algernon Blackwood, the actress Florence Farr, and, of course, Aleister Crowley, who was initiated 1898.

The wickedest man in the world – that was what the magazine *John Bull* called Crowley, and it was certainly an image Aleister Crowley occasionally cultivated and frequently revelled in. A poet, a mountaineer, a chess master, an explorer, a drug-fiend, a pervert, a mystic and a magician, the myriad facets of Crowley's personality cannot quite be captured in the dull lustre of the printed word. Born in 1875 to devout members of the Plymouth Brethren, his life and character for ever bore the mark of religious fanaticism: at times he too waxed fanatical, at others this early exposure drove him to acts of rebellion, relishing every sin in direct defiance of the moralistic monsters of his childhood. He was not, however, the wickedest man in the world. Whilst his experiments with drugs and sex horrified Victorian and later Edwardian society, they would have found a natural home in the cultural climate of the 1960s, and would scarcely cause an eyelid to bat nowadays. He was a man before his time.

His introduction to the Hermetic Order of the Golden Dawn was quite fortuitous. He was holding forth on the subject of alchemy to a group in an alpine tavern when a certain initiate of the Order heard him and challenged his position. Crowley was intrigued, excited even – here was someone who actually knew something about the subject, someone, what is more, who hinted at more. He sought out his company and the two talked more deeply on the subject, but in the morning the alchemist was gone and it was several years before Crowley renewed his acquaintance. It all so nearly did not happen, but it did and the history of Witchcraft has the Fates to thank for it.

Crowley quickly ascended through the ranks of the Golden Dawn, showing a real flair for the complex business of ceremonial magic. Yet his reputation, still in its infancy though suitably wicked, and perhaps also his success in the Order, provoked the enmity of higher-grade magicians like Yeats, and when a schism erupted, Crowley's position as

Mathers' protégé turned the London Temple against him.

This crisis came at a crucial point in Crowley's magical career; he was on the brink of initiation into the highest grade the Golden Dawn could confer in the Outer Order. His exclusion from the Isis-Urania Temple in London prevented him obtaining the Order papers of this grade. He eventually received the initiation from Mathers in Paris, but the affair seems to have propelled him to found his own magical order and now, with a solid training in ceremonial, the spiritual ambition and the ritual flair, he was eminently suitable.

It was whilst he was honeymooning in Egypt in 1904 with his young wife, Rose, that Crowley turned the page of a startling new chapter in his life. In a typically flamboyant attempt to impress, he took Rose to the Great Pyramid and, journeying to its heart, proposed that they spend the night in the King's Chamber. He also could not resist the temptation to invoke the gods before they settled down to enjoy the evening. He wanted, he said, to prove what a great magician he was. He began with the Preliminary Invocation from *The Goetia*:

> *Thee I invoke, the Bornless one.*
> *Thee, that didst create the Earth and the Heavens.*
> *Thee, that didst create the Night and the day.*
> *Thee, that didst create the darkness and the Light.*[19]

With his voice he made a golden glory in the east, red rays in the south, blue radiance in the west and in the north a flame of green, as the barbarous names of power died echoing in the stone tomb.

The invocation proved particularly successful: Crowley recorded that the room became lit with a soft astral light, pale lilac in colour and bright enough for them to extinguish their own torches. In the morning it had gone and they awoke to the sound of bats flitting to and fro.[20] This ritual, slightly frivolous and perhaps somewhat fool-hardy given the location, sparked off a series of events that would change the course of Crowley's life, turning him from minor magician to major prophet.

The Crowleys had just returned from Ceylon (then a British colony, now Sri Lanka), after Rose's pregnancy had diverted them from a proposed expedition into China. Crowley claims to have largely given up magic at this point in his life, though he was apparently still keeping his hand in with stunts like that in the Pyramid.

We left Colombo for Aden, Suez and Port Said on January 28th, intending to see a little of the season in Cairo, of which we had the most delightful memories, and then to sail for England, home and beauty. I had not the slightest idea that I was on the brink of the only event of my life which has made it worth living.[21]

A Paraphrase of the Inscription upon the Obverse of the Stele
Above, the gemméd azure is
  The naked splendour of Nuit;
She bends in ecstasy to kiss
  The secret ardours of Hadit.
The wingéd globe, the starry blue
  Are mine, o Ankh-f-n-Khonsu.[22]

'They are waiting for you.' Rose repeated over and over again in a dreamy fashion. At first Crowley was a little annoyed. He had performed the Preliminary Invocation in their Cairo apartment, with the intention of showing the sylphs (elemental spirits of air). Rose did not see them, instead she just repeated the mysterious message. The next day, not to be put off, he repeated the Invocation, again with the intention of showing the sylphs to his wife. Again Rose repeated the strange phrase, adding, 'It's all about the child . . . All Osiris.' Still annoyed, but more than a little curious, Crowley invoked again the next day and this time discovered who it was who was waiting for him: it was Horus, the hawk-headed, avenging son of Osiris, but as Rose was later to inform him, it was not the usual form of Horus.

They were visiting the Boulak Museum in Cairo for the first time when Rose, again possessed by strange forces, led Crowley past several representations of Horus to exhibit 666, the Stele of Revealing, 'a quite obscure and undistinguished stele', Crowley later observed in his *Confessions*.[23] This tablet, painted with a central frieze surmounting rows of hieroglyphs, revealed to the Crowleys the true identity of Horus as Ra-Hoor-Khuit.[24]

Back in their apartment Crowley performed a ritual dictated to him by Rose, even though it went against all his magical training: Rose was not an accomplished magician nor even an initiate, and Crowley thought the ritual sheer rubbish. The pattern of recent events, however, convinced him to trust in her. After two false starts he was overwhelmed by the power of this new ritual. As he completed it on the third occasion a voice out of nowhere announced, 'The Equinox of the Gods has come.'

Still following Rose's now unquestioned instructions, on 8 April Crowley sat down alone in the apartment and, as their chosen scribe, awaited the message of the gods. From over his left shoulder, coming from the most distant corner of the room a voice loud and strong proclaimed, 'Had! The manifestation of Nuit. The unveiling of the company of heaven.'[25] For three days Crowley sat in the room and wrote down all that he heard. The result was *The Book of the Law*. It announced the passing away of the Aeon of the Dying God – Osiris, or Jesus Christ – and the inauguration of the triumphant age of the Crowned and Conquering Child, Horus as Ra-Hoor-Khuit. This book would also become the foundation stone of modern Witchcraft.

Crowley, however, was not interested in Witchcraft. If anything he had an aversion to it. Some have claimed that he was involved in a coven early in his magical career, but had either been thrown out or left owing to internal conflicts. However, many of the attempts to prove that he was directly involved in Witchcraft are concerned to justify the later use of his writings by Gerald Gardner (whom we shall consider presently), the widely acknowledged 'Father of Modern Witchcraft'. If Crowley was involved he did not mention it, which is unusual for such a prolific autobiographer, and no one has advanced anything more than hearsay as proof of his involvement.

Witchcraft, for Crowley, was a barren, infertile, life-negating practice, illusory in operation. 'It is only the romantic medieval perversion of science,' he wrote, 'that represents young women as partaking in witchcraft.' It was instead the refuge of non-sexual hags. The moon, the patroness of witchcraft (as Diana in its fullness and Hecate in its dark), sums up all he has to say on the subject: it is 'not . . . the feminine correlative of the sun, but . . . the burnt-out, dead, airless satellite of earth'.[26]

He seems overly harsh and dismissive, for the essence of his magical system is the working partnership of male and female. His general respect for the Goddess of Witchcraft, Hecate, is demonstrated by the naming of his first child after her (as well as several other female deities). Crowley dreamt of witchcraft and painted it, he was even engaged by an English aristocrat to cure him of it, but it did not form any part of his master plan. In his 'autohagiography' he stated it simply: 'My own task was to bring oriental wisdom to Europe and to restore paganism in a purer form.'[27]

It was Wednesday, 21 January, 1914, and the two magicians were in their temple: Crowley and his close associate Victor Neuburg, a Zelator of the Order and fellow poet.[28] They were engaged in a series of twenty-four magical experiments over six weeks that Crowley called the Paris Workings. At the stroke of eleven o'clock they began their Eleventh Working, the invocation of Jupiter. A white light swirled about the altar and the old gods spoke: they wished to regain their dominion on earth and the two magicians were to be their instruments, shot like 'fiery arrows' at the 'slave gods' of Christ, Buddha and Allah.[29]

Some months later, with Europe in the opening stages of what was to become known as the Great War, Crowley, now sojourning in the USA, wrote to a brother of the Ordo Templi Orientis (OTO), Frater Achad, in the mundane world an accountant in Vancouver by the name of Charles Stansfield Jones, and suggested to him that he found a Paganism for the masses. He sketched out a rough guide to this Paganism: regular full- or new-moon rituals balanced by solar ceremonies observed at the solstices and equinoxes. 'In this way,' he said, 'you can establish a regular cult.' Crowley believed that 'the time is just right for a natural religion'.[30]

People like rites and ceremonies, and they are tired of hypothetical gods. Insist on the real benefits of the Sun, the Mother-Force, the Father-Force and so on; and show that by celebrating these benefits worthily the worshippers unite themselves more fully with the current of life. Let the religion be Joy, with but a worthy and dignified sorrow in death itself; and treat death as an ordeal, an initiation . . . In short be the founder of a new and greater Pagan cult in the beautiful land which you have made your home.[31]

This was no idle commission. Although not yet thirty, great things were expected of Achad. Through a series of magical operations he had become Crowley's mystical son; and through extensive and intense magical rituals and initiations he rose rapidly up the ranks of Crowley's Order. Unfortunately, he went quite mad and passed beyond the help of his friends. Another man, however, unsought, would arise to accept this challenge. Meanwhile, the ground was still fallow, another writer was required to seed the field of Witchcraft that Crowley had ploughed before its crop could grow to ripeness.

A Sunday School Teacher and the Witch Cult

A formidable spinster, devoted to her work and her mentor, Sir Flinders Petrie, Margaret Murray (1863-1963) made the single greatest impact on the idea of Witchcraft in the twentieth century. The idea was that witchcraft as it was persecuted during the medieval and early modern period was the survival of the pre-Christian Pagan religion of Europe. Whilst Jarke, Mone and Leland had introduced this idea in the nineteenth century, Murray popularized it more effectively in the English-speaking world and, in contrast to Leland, employed the structure of academic argument to demonstrate her thesis; and in contrast to Jarke, Mone and Michelet, she supplied convincing evidence to support it. Her portrayal of the 'witch cult' as she called it, differs in no great respect from Michelet's: it is centred on the worship of a male god, but is the scene of female power.

Having abandoned her former career as a Sunday School teacher, and with the war in Europe preventing her from going out to her archaeological dig in Egypt, Murray was in London and at a loose end. Someone, and in her autobiography *My First Hundred Years* she claimed to have forgotten who, suggested to her that she should look into witchcraft. The result was a series of articles published in the journals of the Folk-Lore Society, the Royal Anthropological Society and the Scottish Historical Review, which culminated in the publication of *The Witch Cult in Western Europe* in 1921 and a more populist restatement of the thesis in *The God of the Witches* in 1933. Yet it was not until the 1950s that her ideas found the audience she sought. *The Witch Cult* sold just over 2,000 copies in the thirty years after its publication.

Dancing Round the Goat

Someone, I forget who, had once told me that the witches obviously had a special form of religion, 'for they danced round a black goat'. As ancient religion is my pet subject this seemed to be in my line, and during all the rest of the war I worked on witches . . . I worked only from contemporary records, and when I suddenly realized that the so-called Devil was simply a disguised man I was startled, almost alarmed by the way the recorded facts fell into place, and showed that the witches were members of an old and primitive form of religion, and the records had been made by members of a new and persecuting form.[32]

The essence of Murray's argument was that because there was a real and genuine fear of witchcraft, and free confession (i.e. without torture) of its practice, it must really have existed. To an extent it did: cunning men and wise women, condemned as witches by the Church, survived up until the early years of the twentieth century. However, she took the Christian description of witchcraft – that it was organized Devil worship – and argued that it was an organized, Europe-wide Pagan religion, demonized and persecuted.

With this idea she brought together trial records from England, Scotland and continental Europe to support her case. She divided Witchcraft into operative and ritual. The first was all spells and charms such as 'are common to every nation . . . and people of every religion', what she called 'part of the common heritage of the human race'. It was the ritual Witchcraft, or 'Dianic cult', defined as 'the religious beliefs and rituals of the people known in late mediaeval times as "Witches" ' that was the subject of her investigation. She concluded that 'the evidence proves that underlying the Christian religion was a cult practised by many classes of the community, chiefly, however, by the more ignorant or those in the less thickly inhabited parts of the country.'[33]

Drawing on ancient sources she concreted this connection between medieval witchcraft and pre-Christian Paganism. So the laws of eighth-century Northumbria, the tenth-century ecclesiastical canons of King Edgar and the eleventh-century laws of King Cnut were trotted out in proof of the continuity of the tradition. Undoubtedly these sources did link what the translators of these texts have called 'witchcraft' and 'paganism', but as we have seen, these terms had very different meanings in the periods mentioned.

The cult, although 'Dianic' after the famous description of night-riding with Diana in the Canon Episcopi (see Chapter 3), worshipped 'the Devil', the male horned god. The prospective witch joined the religion through several marked ceremonies of admission. First the recruit was sponsored by an existing member, or, as was more often the case with men, approached by 'the Devil' in person. Having been approved they would renounce all previous religious vows and take new ones to 'the Devil', to obey him and make over to him both body and soul without reservation. This verbal contract would then be reinforced with a written pact or covenant, signed by the new recruit. Membership would be conferred by baptism or renaming and the taking of the Witches' or Devil's Mark, a tattoo sometimes like that of a hare's footprint and at others just a simple spot. The wearing of a garter was also associated with membership.[34]

Organized in covens of thirteen, the followers of this cult would meet at Sabbats, 'the General Meeting of all the members of the religion' for 'purely religious' celebrations on May Eve (30 April), All Hallows Eve (31 October), Candlemas (2 February), Gule of August (Lammas Day, or 1 August), and also, but not apparently in Britain, at the midwinter and midsummer solstices, 'the festivals of the solstitial invaders', i.e., not of the original cult, and at Easter.[35] A select group would convene more regularly to conduct 'business . . . usually the practice of magic for the benefit of a client or for the harming of an enemy', but again these meetings could be for the 'rites and practices of the cult', or 'for sheer enjoyment'.[36]

The rites themselves comprised acts of homage to the god, such as prostration, curtsies and kissing; and dances, either a jumping dance for the fertility of crops, or an obscene dance for the fertility of animals and women, which would have a musical and sometimes sung accompaniment. These would be followed by feasting, a sacrament of bread and wine, known through the perverted Christian conception of it as the Black Mass, and generally concluded with a sacrifice of the witch's own blood, an animal, a human (usually a child), or the god himself in the form of an animal substitute.[37]

Murray's academic tenure and success as an Egyptologist, and indeed her forceful defence of the witch cult thesis, ensured both its respectability and its longevity. The ideas sketched out as early as 1917 were still holding sway up until the 1960s. She supported her allies and denounced her critics, writing the introduction to Gardner's *Witchcraft Today* which ignored their differences and championed Gardner as one of her followers.

However, her position was fatally flawed. By selective use of the evidence, both of the sources themselves and quotations from them, Murray railroaded history into conforming to her idea of what the witch cult of Western Europe should have been. The breadth of her sources, from England, Scotland, France, Sweden – indeed from across Europe – appear to confer a uniformity upon her description of this cult, but closer investigation reveals that her amalgamated picture distorts geographical peculiarities into universal attributes. For example, she based her structure of the Sabbats on a single case, that of Forfar, Scotland, in 1661, which was entirely unsupported by evidence from other countries or periods. Her argument, challenged from the first by more serious scholars, has now been thoroughly refuted, but not before it left its mark.[38]

Seven Steps to Becoming A Witch

1. Be sponsored by a member or approached by the Devil.
2. Renounce all previous religious vows.
3. Swear to obey the Devil.
4. Sign a pact to this effect.
5. Be rebaptised and take a new Witch name.
6. Be branded with the Devil's Mark.
7. Wear a garter on the left leg (optional).

As the Celtic Twilight dimmed into night and the Golden Dawn brightened into day, all the right elements were in place: a working system of modern magic and a theory of Witchcraft as the ancient Pagan religion of Europe. What they lacked was a unifying force. Jarke, Mone and Leland were long dead, Murray had gone on to write other books, her heart always in archaeology, not religion,

Crowley was past his best and in retirement. Then a series of completely unconnected events beginning in the Far East, like the butterfly's wing beats causing hurricanes on the other side of the world, changed the course of the history of religion.

As they met upon the level and parted upon the square to work three degrees of initiation, concluding their rites with 'So mote it be', little did the Freemasons of Singapore's Sphinx Lodge realize that the colonial adventurer in their midst was to become the 'Father of Modern Witchcraft'. The modern practice and theology of Witchcraft (Wicca) can be directly attributed to the thoughts and actions of this one man, Gerald Brouseau Gardner. A Freemason, novelist, amateur archaeologist and student of religion, he began his career inspecting rubber plantations and regulating the opium trade for the British government in their Far Eastern possessions, spending his formative free time investigating local tribal customs and beliefs. When he retired in 1936, at the relatively young age of fifty-two, he concentrated upon his other interests, but so far there was little to suggest that he would go on to invent the modern Pagan religion of Witchcraft. The riddle of the Sphinx Lodge is the story of Gardner's craft of invention.

5. The Craft of Invention: The Founding of the Modern Religion of Wicca

The founding of Wicca begins with the invention of a tradition, leads to the invention of a founder, undergoes the discovery of both inventions and reinvents itself to survive. Currently Witchcraft is portrayed by its practitioners as a religion of invention, with individual creativity at its core. Understanding the convolutions and convulsions of the birth of modern Witchcraft is central to understanding its character and structure today.

' "Magic! Witchcraft! Stuff and nonsense. No one believes in such things nowadays. It was all burning evil-smelling powders, muttering words. The Devil jumped up, and you sold him your soul. That was all there was to it." But was that really all?' So begins Gerald Gardner's *High Magic's Aid*,[1] and, perhaps, a new chapter in the sociology of religion, if not in history. It certainly did not mark any moment in literature. Yet despite the dreariness of the prose and inadequacy of characterization and plot, this novel achieves its aim: it answers its own question. Gardner portrays witchcraft as something more than devilish pacts and powders. He shows it to have been a pre-Christian fertility cult. His ruse is the use of the past tense. Witchcraft, whatever it was, is not what Gardner intends it to be. In retrospect we see a man in the process of building a new faith.

Witchcraft is no longer what we thought it was. But is it now what Gardner meant it to be?

Five years after *High Magic's Aid* Gardner publicly claimed to be a member of 'one of the ancient covens of the Witch Cult which still survive in England'. Moreover, he claimed to be writing on their behalf: 'Write and tell people we are not perverts. We are decent people, we only want to be left alone . . .'[2]

These decent people, as Gardner explained, 'were the Wica [sic] or wise people, with herbal knowledge and a working occult teaching usually for good'. Furthermore, they were the remnants of the 'old pagan religion of Western Europe, dating back to the Stone Age'.[3] The story had true romance in it and more than a glimmer of the Celtic Twilight. An ancient and mysterious religion in our very midst, what is more, a religion that was ours.

However, the work, indeed all Gardner's works, were pure fantasy.[4] None of his historical claims was either original or accurate. None of the magical practices described was authentically of witchcraft. With all the flummery of a magician more worthy of Paul Daniels than Simon Magus, Gardner had burnt some evil-smelling powders, muttered suitable words and sold the lot to an opportunistic publisher.

The claim was in the spirit of Margaret Murray. The magical rituals in *High Magic's Aid* that Gardner claimed were authentic could not be authentically those of this Witch Cult. They derived, as he indeed admitted, from S.L. 'MacGregor' Mathers's translation of *The Key of Solomon the King* and certain 'Magical MSS', in his possession.[5] Gardner took Murray, Mathers, Crowley and anything and anyone else that suited his purpose to concoct his own 'witchcraft'.[6] It was a 'witchcraft' utterly unlike the old Pagan religions of Western Europe and not a bit of it Stone Age.

Modern Witchcraft is frequently called a revival.[7] It is not a revival. It is an invention.[8] Specifically, it is an invented tradition, that is, a symbolic system of actions and beliefs that both claims to be, and seeks to demonstrate through its practice that it is, part of a continuous historical past, but which, in fact, is not.[9] J.G. Frazer, Charles Leland, Robert Graves, even Rudyard Kipling, and most especially Murray provided this past.[10] With it Gardner sought to inculcate a reverence for a female creative principle; to 're-enchant' the world; to 'return' to the magic and mystery of this imagined Golden Age.

Although much of the liturgical content was Crowley's and the matriarchal spirit Graves's, the lynch-pin of Gardner's system was Murray's. She, more than anyone else, provided that 'suitable historic past'. As we have seen, she argued that because there was a real and genuine fear of witchcraft, and free confession of its practice it must really have existed. However, she took the Christian description of witchcraft – that it was organized Devil worship – and argued that it was an organized Pagan religion, demonized and persecuted.

Following the Biblical injunction that 'thou shall not suffer a witch to live' (Exodus 22:18)[11] the Sixth Council of Paris, in 829, defined a witch as a malicious spell-caster and condemned all such to the most severe punishment. In the fifteenth century the Inquisitors Kramer and Sprenger denounced witchcraft as 'high treason against God's Majesty' and justified the torture of those accused and the death of those found guilty on account of this. James I defined witchcraft as the religion of the Devil in his *Demonologie*. In the seventeenth century Bovet stated that 'by a Witch is commonly understood a Female Agent . . . who is become Covenant with the Devil; having literally sold herself to work wickedness'. By these various accounts the witch was the very enemy of mankind, to be hunted down and destroyed, a view made law by the various witchcraft acts.[12]

'Nasty nonsense,' said Gardner, 'invented at the time of the persecutions.'[13] Such accounts he characterized as 'propaganda written by the various Churches to discourage and frighten people from having any connections with what was to them a hated rival – for witchcraft is a religion.'[14] This was exactly Murray's point: witchcraft was a full and functioning religion. However, she did not dismiss the contemporary literature on witchcraft as pure invention or propaganda, but rather read between the official lines and took at face value the accounts of the accused.

Although there was considerable log-rolling between Murray and Gardner (Murray contributed an introduction to Gardner, 1954), he did not strictly follow her.[15] Gardner refers to a supposed warning given to witches to explain their confession to diabolical involvement as simply acquiescing in the accuser's fancy to escape further torture.[16] With this he dismisses both what the accusers claimed and what the accused are recorded as saying, giving his inventiveness free reign.

However, it was, to an extent, the limitations of Gardner's originality that eventually led to his unmasking. Whilst Leland's claims can never be fully investigated, whether by design or accident, and hence hover on the brink of the believable, Gardner's sources of authority, essentially his use of Murray, but also his plagiarizing of Crowley and Mathers, bring him crashing to the ground.

When did the cracks in Gardner's elaborate edifice begin to appear? The truth is they were already there. Gardner had bought damaged goods. Although Murray's thesis found favour up until her article on the subject was published in the 1964 edition of the *Encyclopaedia Britannica* (vol. 23) it had already been subjected to extensive criticism. Prior to the publication of the book that really launched Witchcraft (*Witchcraft Today*, 1954) Gardner could have consulted several sources that cast considerable doubt on Murray's argument.[17] Certainly this was not the end of it and the evidence against her continued to mount up. Her position has now been thoroughly refuted, primarily on the grounds of unhistorical and selective use of evidence.[18]

Gardner may well have believed Murray's thesis; indeed to the untrained eye it is still compelling. That is not what is at issue here, but it provides a nice irony that he invents out of an invention. It means that Gardner either believed that someone else was a representative of this ancient witch cult, or disregarded the absence of any connection to it. By 1954, when he published *Witchcraft Today*, he had, by his own admission, already spent fifteen years as an initiated witch, had already formed his own coven, had, in short, already created enough of 'one of the ancient covens of the Witch Cult which still survive in England' to speak on its behalf.[19]

A Work of Shadows

Gardner's Witchcraft was some time in development and the version that appeared in 1954 was not the same as the one with which he was working earlier, nor was it the final article. Three separate Books of Shadows, as Gardner called the liturgical basis of Wicca, are identifiable, generally labelled Texts A, B and C.[20] The initial research carried out by Stewart and Janet Farrar, initiates of Alex Sanders's brand of Gardner's Witchcraft, traced the material back to

Text A which they assumed Gardner had derived from a coven of Witches in the New Forest as he claimed. However, the boundaries have been pushed further back by the witch-scholar Aidan Kelly, who convincingly demonstrates that this information was derived not from a working coven, but from an earlier notebook of Gardner's called 'Ye Bok of Ye Art Magical',[21] although we are still left with the question of where this material came from.

The earliest material can be dated to no later than 1948–9 because elements of it appeared in *High Magic's Aid*, which was published in 1949. A more substantial body of work existed in 1953 when he initiated Doreen Valiente (Text B). Valiente and Gardner subsequently collaborated on the production of Text C, which was the final version of what is now known as Gardnerian Witchcraft, or Gardnerianism. As Gardner claimed to have received his Witchcraft teachings from an ancient and authentic coven in the first place, it is only that earliest material that presently concerns us, for upon it rests the entirety of Gardner's claim.

Gardner's Witchcraft *c.* 1948–9 consisted of a circle-casting ceremony, a ritual called Drawing Down the Moon, another called Lift Up the Veil, three degrees of initiation and four Sabbat rituals (called November Eve, February Eve, May Eve and August Eve). It was not much. The initiatory rituals are central to Gardner's system and much emphasis was laid upon them, but as initiatory rituals they were not suitable to be worked at every meeting and when one lays them aside there was very little ceremonial left. The Sabbat rituals are extremely sketchy and largely revisit the initiation ceremony of the third degree with extensive ritual purification leading to a performance of the Great Rite.

Only the casting of the circle would be performed at every meeting. Gardner called it 'the most important thing in all their [the Witches'] ceremonies'.[22] The procedure is as follows: a triple circle is outlined with a sword or dagger (known as an Athame); salt, water and fire are consecrated; fellow practitioners are cautioned before entering the circle; the circle is sealed behind them with three pentagrams drawn in the air and the words 'Agla, Azoth, Adonai'; the ritual of the 'pentacle' is performed; the magical objective is declared; the circle is circumambulated three times; the four directions are summoned.

> **To Cast a Magic Circle**
> Having chosen a place proper, take the sickle or scimitar of Art or a Witch's Athame, and stick it into the centre, then take a cord, and loop it over the Instrument, four and one half feet, and so trace out the circumference of the circle, which must be traced either with the Sword, or the knife with the black hilt, but ever leave open a door towards the North. Make in all three circles, one within the other, and write names of power between these. (From Gardner's 'Ye Bok of ye Art Magical', c. 1947)

Every stage of this procedure, except the pentacle ritual, can be found in the *Key of Solomon the King*. The ritual that Kelly calls 'of the pentacle' is the same as Crowley's Ritual of the Pentagram, a straight borrowing from the Golden Dawn.[23] The most important ceremonial element is thus a shameless borrowing from the tradition of High Magic.

One of the principal characteristics of modern Witchcraft practice which is said to differentiate it from the High Magical model it so clearly conforms to is the use rather than the casting of the circle. In High Magic the circle is used as a protective barrier against the demonic forces summoned by the magician. In Gardner's Witchcraft, on the contrary, the circle is used not to keep anything out but to keep something in: the power raised through ritual. This one key difference has become a major point in the continued defence of Witchcraft as not just a High Magical hotch-potch.

However, a study of the symbolic meaning of the Temple in Freemasonry reveals a conceptualization very similar to that propounded by Gardner and his defenders.[24] The idea that the circle describes sacred or symbolic space is common to both systems. It can be argued, then, that the use of the circle in Witchcraft does not represent a distinctive innovation on Gardner's part (or on the part of any of his colleagues), but is another borrowing from Freemasonry. What is new and distinctive is the borrowing and mixture of two traditions: the High Magic circle and the Masonic Temple. But then all the major forerunners of Gardner – the founders of the Hermetic Order of the Golden Dawn and Crowley for instance – had been Masons as well as magicians. It does not diminish the importance of this symbolism. This is a crucial stage in the transformation of magical technique into religious ceremony. In a religious ceremony it makes no sense to keep the gods at bay and the circle must become their temple.

The ritual of Drawing Down the Moon was originally part of the May Eve Sabbat in 'Ye Bok of Ye Art Magical'. Kelly examines it separately, and with justification. He suggests that it may have been used prior to initiations and other magical workings and not just confined to a seasonal celebration.[25] This is certainly what it is now used for. The Farrars state that it 'is a central element in the holding of a coven Circle'.[26]

The High Priestess assumes what is termed the 'Goddess position', the 'Magus' kneels before her and he draws a pentagram on her body with the wand. He then invokes the goddess into the person of the High Priestess and concludes by giving her the five-fold kiss. The invocation used is a direct quote from Crowley's Gnostic Mass.[27] The five-fold kiss is of a different provenance. It does not derive from Mathers's works. In the *Key of Solomon the King* the Master kisses his disciples upon the forehead, but once only.[28] Gardner's kiss is given to the feet, knees, genitals, or genital area, nipples, and mouth, a variation on the traditionally recorded feet, knees, genitals and anus. Some say it derives from the Saracen mystery schools and was hence referred to as the Saracen Kiss,[29] although the Saracen practice actually involved breathing upon the respective part not kissing it. Comparison with the Masonic five points of fellowship – foot to foot, knee to knee, heart to heart, hand to hand, and ear to ear – is more suggestive. Knoop and Jones go so far as to argue that the Masonic practice derives from witchcraft.[30] However, it is more likely that Gardner brought it with him as with so many other Masonic elements, simply transforming the formula with a kiss.

The Witches' Kiss
Blessed be thy feet, that have brought thee in these ways.
Blessed be thy knees, that shall kneel at the sacred altar.
Blessed be thy womb, without which we would not be.
Blessed be thy breasts, formed in beauty and in strength.
Blessed be thy lips, that shall speak the sacred names.

'Listen to the words of the Great Mother, who of old was also called among men Artemis, Astarte, Dione, Melusine, Aphrodite, Cerridwen, Diana, Arianrhod, Bride, and by many other names.' Lift Up the Veil begins with a recitation of goddess names, reference to certain Spartan sacrifices, the speech of the Queen of Witcheries, and the speech of the Gracious Goddess, and ends with the speech of the Star Goddess.[31] The ritual would be performed after Drawing Down the Moon and before initiation or any other working.[32] Again Crowley's Gnostic Mass is the inspiration for most of this ritual, particularly part four, the Ceremony of the Opening of the Veil.[33] The recitation of goddess names and the Spartan reference would appear to be Gardner's. The speech of the Queen of Witcheries is copied from Leland; that of the Gracious Goddess from Crowley's *The Book of the Law*; and that of the Star Goddess is assembled from both *The Book of the Law* and the Gnostic Mass.[34]

The historian Elliot Rose subjected Gardner's material to a close textual analysis and found that it is exactly the recitation of goddess names and the Spartan reference that give away its modern composition (he is apparently oblivious of the stamp of Crowley). The blythe but illogical compression of vastly differing goddesses into the form of a Great Mother reveals the work of a comparative religionist, not of an organic religion, he argues.[35] Furthermore, it is not so much the reference to Sparta but calling it by the more recherché name Lacedaemon that alerts Rose to further authorial imposture.[36]

The First Degree of initiation begins with a warning. The initiand's courage is tested at the point of a sword, he or she is given and gives a password and is blind-folded. A further password is given and the initiand is led into the circle from behind (i.e. pushed). The circle is sealed in the usual manner and the initiand is subjected to an ordeal.[37] In fact, in style, if not quite in content, the initiation is entirely Masonic.[38] The first password is Crowleyan,[39] the second password is a kiss.[40] The sealing of the circle is simply a necessary part of having cast a circle in the first place.

In Freemasonry the ceremony of initiations proceeds with the entrance of the candidate at sword-point and his introduction to the assembly; a prayer follows, the candidate is presented to the officers of the four directions (in order north, east, south, west), declarations of intent and duty are made, the candidate swears an oath, the obligation, a sign, token and word are given by the candidate, an address is given by the Worshipful Master, and then the working tools are presented.[41]

The Second and Third Degrees follow similar lines, apart from some necessary exceptions to mark the passage deeper into the mysteries. In the Second Degree there is a curious willing of the Magus's power into the initiand. The initiand is instructed in the use of the tools that had previously only been presented. In the Third Degree the assembly partake of cakes and wine before proceeding to an act of sacralized sexual intercourse between the Magus and the High Priestess known as the Great Rite. The Magus justifies this act with a speech explaining that woman is the foremost and archetypal altar. The five-fold kiss is upgraded to an eight-fold kiss before the Magus and High Priestess consummate the ceremony in a manner whose description vividly recalls, and notably deviates from, the Masonic five points of fellowship: 'These are truly the five points of fellowship . . . feet to feet, knee to knee, groin to groin, breast to breast . . . lips to lips.'[42]

There are again considerable literary borrowings from Crowley's Gnostic Mass as well as the literal enactment of it, and from Freemasonry as we saw above.[43] However, the willing of power by the initiator into the initiand seems to be without precedent, an issue on which Kelly is strangely silent. The transference of personal power is an oddity. It establishes an apostolic succession resting upon the perceived power of the original initiator, which in this case is Gardner, rather than upon the power of the preternatural forces called upon elsewhere in the ritual.

Gardner unashamedly ransacks Crowley's Gnostic Mass, but the overall ritual procedure that Gardner uses is blatantly Masonic. Consider how Gardner's Witchcraft is structured: the working area is ritually established (a circle is cast); new candidates are initiated; the working area is ritually closed. Now compare Freemasonic structure: the lodge is 'opened'; new candidates are initiated; a charge is read; the lodge is closed.[44] The placing of Drawing Down the Moon and Lift Up the Veil (now more commonly known as The Charge of the Goddess) can be considered as equivalent to the various prayers and addresses that are included in the Masonic ceremony.

One of the most contentious issues for both Wiccans and non-Wiccans alike has been Gardner's use of the scourge in his rituals.[45] According to Gardner, the scourge functions as both an 'ordeal' and an act of purification, but others have sought ulterior motives.

Recognizing the Masonic model on which the Gardnerian initiation rituals are based, Kelly states that scourging has never been a part of Masonic ritual and that it must, therefore, be Gardner's own addition and therefore symptomatic of sexual perversity.[46] He also observes that despite similarities with the Neophyte Rite of the Golden Dawn, the use of the scourge is not part of any magical ritual that he knows of, nor is it mentioned in that great storehouse of magical lore *The Key of Solomon the King*.[47]

In fact Kelly is quite wrong on this point. The scourge is part of the magical paraphernalia of the Golden Dawn. It is specifically mentioned as part of the equipment of the Ceremony of the $5°=6°$ Grade of Adeptus Minor and the Consecration Ceremony of the Vault of the Adepti. Kelly points to structural similarities with the Neophyte rite, but states that the scourge is not used. On this point he is again wrong. The scourge is used in the Neophyte rite as part of the symbolism of the god Osiris.[48]

Given the fundamental importance of Crowley to Gardner's system we must also consider the magical use of the scourge by Crowley. Crowley clearly adopted its use from the Golden Dawn; he was, after all, an initiate of that order, and includes it in his list of magical weapons.[49] As to its actual use, we must note that in the early years of the twentieth century (approximately 1904–07) Crowley made plans for a ritual suitable for his New Aeon (that of Horus, declared in 1904) that involved both nudity and scourging.[50] Furthermore, a ritual known as the Building of the Pyramid (Ritual 671), documented by Symonds as having been practised by Crowley in 1913, involves the scourging of the buttocks. Crowley used this ritual repeatedly as the opening rite in his protracted Paris Working, his first operation of the sex magic taught by the OTO.[51]

This clearly demonstrates that scourging was known in magical ritual before Gardner and, more importantly, in the source material Gardner used to construct his own Witchcraft rituals. Significantly, scourging is connected with the sex magic of the OTO, whose Ninth Degree, the consummation of their magical system, formed the basis and content of the Great Rite in Gardner's Witchcraft. Moreover, Gardner claimed membership of the OTO, a fact plainly stated on the title page of *High Magic's Aid*. Gardner's use of the scourge is not a symptom of sexual perversity, but another pointer to the origin of his ritual material.

This point cannot be stressed enough, for upon it Kelly lays the foundation of his argument that Gardner's only innovations were in order to effect his sexual gratification, an argument that has been taken up by others and found a measure of acceptance.[52] It has been shown that both nudity and the use of the scourge derive from magical practices established independently of Gardner, but which later greatly influenced the development of his system through his wholesale incorporation of Crowleyan elements (which in turn bore the hallmark of the Golden Dawn). The only conclusion that can be drawn from this is that Kelly is engaged upon his own project of inventing Gardner.

The Derivations of Modern Gardnerian Witchcraft Practices		
Practice	Antecedents	Sources
3 Degrees of Initiation	Freemasonry	Gardner's own involvement in the Blue Lodges and the co-masonry of the Fellowship of Crotona
The Great Rite	9th degree Ordo Templi Orientis	Gardner's meeting with Crowley
	The Gnostic Mass	Crowley
Casting the Circle	Standard occult procedure	The Key of Solomon the King
Magical Weapons	Standard occult paraphernalia	Mathers, Golden Dawn, Crowley's Magick in Theory and Practice
Nudity	Stereotype of witchcraft	Numerous sources, e.g. the art of Dürer, Salvator Rosi
	La Vecchia Religione	Leland
Flagellation	Neophyte Rite of the Hermetic order of the Golden Dawn	Regardie, Gardner's meeting with Crowley
	Building the Pyramid Ritual	Crowley
	Ancient Roman Mystery Religion	Macchioro
Drawing Down the Moon	The Gnostic Mass	Crowley
Lift up the Veil	La Vecchia Religione	Leland
	The Gnostic Mass	Crowley
	The Book of the Law	Crowley

Gardner directly tackled the question of invention himself.[53] Given the blatantly plagiaristic content of his Witchcraft it might be argued that he had to. That he did so carried with it dangers: in denying certain influences he leads us directly to them.

Gardner confessed that 'I am familiar with most forms of ritual including Kabbalistic magic' and argues that 'if anyone in the last two hundred years had tried to make up a rite they would have used one of these methods or something resembling them'. However, he claimed that 'the English witches' method is entirely different'. Unfortunately for Gardner we have seen that he was right in the first place and that his latter claim was bogus.[54]

Gardner did not stop there. 'The only man I can think of,' he said, 'who could have invented the rites was the late Aleister Crowley . . . When I met him, he was most interested to hear that I was a member, and said he had been inside when he was very young.' Apparently Crowley would not reveal whether he had composed any of their rituals and Gardner reflected that in any case Witchcraft and Crowley's magick were too different to suppose that he had. Gardner should have stopped there, for in the next breath he contradicted himself. He admitted that there were 'certain expressions and certain words used which smack of Crowley'. He mused 'Possibly he borrowed things from the cult writings, or more likely someone may have borrowed expressions from him.' He had given the game away.[55]

The Invention of the Founder

If Witchcraft is an invented tradition, it must have an inventor. Even though it is still widely considered a revival, as we saw earlier, its derivative, syncretistic nature has long been recognized, as has Gardner's role. It is common now to read that he was the founder of Witchcraft. J.G. Melton, that indefatigable indexer of the religious in America, reckons him such. Witches and neo-Pagans like the writers Jones and Pennick have also declared him as such.[56]

The fact that he is seen as the founder now is only the result of the discovery of the falsity of his claims. When he was believed, he was seen as the *discoverer* of Witchcraft, not its founder. Foundation at this stage was portrayed as an historical, or even archaeological matter.

Gardner was only transmitting the secret lore.

The process of invention is twofold here: the invention of Gardner by others and Gardner's own self-invention. The likes of Kelly and Greenwood construct a sexually deviant Gardner who invented Wicca partly to satisfy his perversity. Melton and Jones and Pennick see him as the founder of a new religion. On the first count, we have demonstrated that the conclusion both Kelly and Greenwood arrive at is not the only or necessary one. On the second count, we have seen how the elements of Witchcraft were derived from various sources, but particularly from Crowley, which raises the question of whether Gardner was the founder or merely the messenger of the new Witchcraft, perhaps even that founder of a new Pagan cult as Crowley had urged Charles Stansfield Jones to be and in which office he had conspicuously failed.[57]

As to Gardner himself, he was not entirely what he seemed. At the height of his fame he was widely regarded as an academic doctor and this lent considerable weight to his claims.[58] On one level he was seen as an intellectual pioneer, discovering new truths. His tales of Witchcraft, wrapped in such fine clothes, passed into academic discourse as expert testimony before they became interesting from another angle, as expert fantasy. On another level he was seen as the gateway to this rediscovered religion; and rather than leave these decent people alone his most enthusiastic readers sought to join them through him.

It is not entirely clear when Gardner started calling himself a doctor, but the earliest reference seems to be in the membership records of the Folklore Society. In November 1950 he is listed as both MA and PhD. Shortly after he is again accorded the title in a *Sunday Pictorial* article of 29 July 1951. His reputation seems to have become more firmly cemented with the publication of *Witchcraft Today* (1954). Soon after it came out 'Dr Gardner' was being hailed as the foremost expert in his field. According to his biographer, who was at best unreliable and at worst mendacious, one Professor Varagnac of the Sorbonne based his teaching course on Gardner's work, and the Ethnographical Society supposedly bowed before his authority. Later, in 1959, a certain Dr Serge Hutin of the *Ecole pratique des hautes études* (*Sciences religieuses*) awarded him the highest accolade as 'the most qualified specialist in his field, Dr Gardner of the Isle of Man'. Even as late as 1963, the year before he died, Gardner is listed in the *Who's Who of Authors and Writers* as both DLitt and PhD.[59]

Smyth reflects that there is apparently no record of Gardner 'having attended even a kindergarten, let alone a university'. Certainly Bracelin gives no details of any higher education and all that we can be sure of is that he was largely self-taught under the erratic tuition of his wayward guardian, Josephine McCombie. Gardner himself claimed that he had been awarded an honorary doctorate from the University of Singapore some time in 1934. This seems plausible, but Valiente investigated the claim, and found it to be unsubstantiated by the university in question, which, to compound matters, had not even been in existence at that time. Gardner had also told both Andrews and Field that the University of Toulouse had conferred upon him the degree of Doctor of Literature. Again no official record of this has been found.[60]

Gardner not only sought intellectual authority for his claims, but also the authority of blood. Lineal descent from a witch was, and still is in some quarters, seen as a necessary condition of being a witch oneself. So it is that Gardner liked to relate that his family tree had near its roots a woman called Grissell Gairdner, who had been burnt as a witch at Newburgh in 1610. Furthermore, his grandfather had married a woman with a reputation as a witch and many more of his ancestors purportedly had psychic powers.

As Gardner tells the story, this lineage was crucial to his being invited to join the Witch Cult: 'Then some of these new (or old) friends said, "You belonged to us in the past. You are of our blood. Come back to where you belong." '[61] He seems to have been first publicly identified as a witch in the *Sunday Pictorial* article in which he was called a doctor.

Before founding Witchcraft, however, Gardner had had a long apprenticeship in the occult. Whilst working as a tea planter in Ceylon (now Sri Lanka), he had attended what the locals called a Magic House, the Freemasonic Sphinx Lodge, 113, I.C. This was one of the so-called Blue Lodges, which significantly only operate three degrees of initiation: Apprentice, Journeyman and Master. Gardner allegedly later went so far as to describe Witchcraft as the 'original Lodge'; and we have already seen the defining role of Masonic ritual structure in his Witchcraft. So clearly this was no casual interest; indeed, given Gardner's borrowings, we could call Freemasonry the original Witchcraft, and with greater justification.[62]

116

He became a colonial administrator, inspecting rubber plantations and later opium outlets, and finally held a post as a customs official. After he retired in 1936 he embarked upon a series of archaeological adventures, allegedly discovering the lost city of Singapura and assisting Flinders Petrie in Cyprus. Eventually settling in the New Forest area he soon became involved with the First Rosicrucian Theatre in England and joined the Fellowship of Crotona, the group responsible for the mystical theatrics, in September of 1938. The Fellowship was a branch of Co-Masonry, a form of heretical Freemasonry that admitted women into its ranks, and it was here that he claimed, in 1939, to have met authentic surviving Witches and been initiated by them into their craft.

Only one piece of corroborative evidence exists to substantiate Gardner's claim. In 1970 the occult writer Francis King presented the hearsay testimony of Louis Wilkinson. Wilkinson, a novelist who wrote under the pen-name of Louis Marlow, had corresponded with Oscar Wilde as a youth and upon making the acquaintance of Aleister Crowley contributed to his periodical *The Equinox* and crowned their friendship by reading out Crowley's wild poem, 'The Hymn to Pan' at the latter's funeral in 1947. King claimed that whilst they sat in Wilkinson's study in 1953, talking about Oscar Wilde, Swinburne and Crowley, he unexpectedly advanced the information that in his younger years Crowley had been offered initiation into the Witch Cult, but had declined on the grounds that he did not want to be 'bossed around by women'. King further claimed to have heard this same story from 'two other independent sources', which unfortunately remained nameless and therefore somewhat valueless.[63] When King challenged Wilkinson on this point, gently suggesting that Crowley may have been having a joke at his expense, Wilkinson replied that the Witch Cult was quite genuine as he himself had known several of its members 'in the late thirties or early forties . . . operating in the New Forest'.[64] Again he gives no names, nor any further details. It could even have been Gardner himself that he knew.

Despite these suggestions, Gardner's record shows only that he was admitted to a Co-Masonic organization in 1939, where he met people of a like mind and with whom he later worked Witchcraft (especially the woman he called Dafo). All of the written material that has come to light points to a pseudo-Crowleyan sect posing as Murray's Witch Cult. Given his blatant lies concerning that Witch Cult, we have no reason to take him at his word on any other point.

The huge amount of Crowleyan material in Gardner's Witchcraft would suggest a shelf groaning with Crowley's books, but whereas nowadays one can walk into almost any bookshop and take one's pick from shelves sagging under the weight of titles on occultism, magic and Witchcraft, this was not so in Gardner's day. Even in the 1950s books on such subjects were difficult to come by and then often only at a high price.[65] Crowley was not easily available in print. During his own lifetime he was not a bestseller: his sulphurous reputation saw to that. Whereas now such notoriety would earn huge amounts in publishers' advances, during the first half of the twentieth century reputable publishing houses would not sup with the Devil no matter how long the spoon. Hence Crowley brought out most of his works at his own expense; for example, he privately published his *Magick in Theory and Practice* (Book 3 of Liber IV) for subscribers only in Paris in 1929 – understandably it was not widely available. The secrets of the Golden Dawn had been leaked through his periodical *The Equinox* in the years from 1909 to 1919, but it was not until 1937–40 that Regardie published the most complete set of the rituals.[66]

Gardner published his first novel in 1939. In it he dealt with several of his abiding preoccupations – goddess worship and reincarnation – but not Witchcraft. He made no published reference to Witchcraft until 1949. What materials he did have on Witchcraft bear the unmistakable stamp of Crowley and he did not meet Crowley until 1947.[67] Much of the Crowleyan material had been published prior to that, but, as we have seen, it was not easily available. The deciding factor is the use of Ordo Templi Orientis (OTO) material, in particular the initiated understanding of the Ninth Degree that Gardner demonstrated. This could only have come from Crowley, then head of the Order, or a high-grade disciple (and we have no evidence to suggest anyone else other than Crowley).

In 1947 the stage magician and occultist, Arnold Crowther, introduced Gardner to Crowley, and although Gardner later tried to dismiss the latter as a 'charming charlatan', he was initiated by him into the OTO and granted a licence to operate a lodge of that order.[68] Crowley's diary records for 1 May, 'Dr G.B. Gardner PhD Singapore, Arnold Crowther Prof. G. a magician to tea.'[69] Gardner was also apparently trying to pass himself off as a Royal Arch Freemason, the highest Masonic degree, but no evidence exists to confirm this entitlement. Three more entries for 7,

14 and 27 May note further visits from Gardner. Whether Gardner was charming we shall never know, but he was certainly engaging in more than a little charlatanism of his own.

Crowley wrote to Gerald Yorke on 9 May asking him to send Gardner another copy of *The Equinox of the Gods* to supplement the four Gardner had already bought from Crowley, and Yorke himself lent Gardner his copy of Mathers's edition of *The Key of Solomon the King*. Gardner and Yorke had only been introduced that same year, in 1947. From these two men Gardner now had enough to write *High Magic's Aid* in 1949, and most of the material he used in the later versions of the 'Book of Shadows'. The meeting with Crowley is crucial, because he conferred upon Gardner occult authority and made available to him several of his writings that would otherwise have been difficult or impossible to obtain. Take away the material Gardner bought and borrowed from Crowley and his friends, and there is nothing left except the Leland passages. This conclusively demonstrates that Gardner wrote his earliest draft of the 'Book of Shadows', 'Ye Bok,' some time after the meeting with Crowley in 1947 and shortly before the publication of *High Magic's Aid* in 1949. His claim to have been initiated into Witchcraft in 1939 is simply a distortion of the fact that he joined the Fellowship of Crotona, because the form of Witchcraft into which he claimed to have been initiated could not have existed before 1947.

When Crowley died in 1947 there was some expectation in the Order that Gardner would succeed him as Outer Head in Europe. Gardner himself seems to have tried at least to revive the OTO in England following Crowley's demise, but found that the people on the list Crowley had given him were either abroad or otherwise living too far away.[71] With his plans to lead the OTO dashed, Gardner turned to Witchcraft, probably in late 1947 or 1948.

When dealing with the possible origins of the rituals he alludes to in *Witchcraft Today*, Gardner names several key sources; in particular he mentions Crowley, and by a series of weak devices seeks to deny the possibility that these sources actually authored the rituals. He specifically names Crowley as a possible inventor in order to refute him, but strangely leaves open the door to claims of plagiarism. Valiente had by 1953 rumbled his Crowleyan borrowings. Gardner was in a curious position because Valiente had identified the Crowleyana and he could not deny its existence without losing her and, of course, others' consent in his wider claims of Pagan survival. So he had to admit to the possibility that something of Crowley's work had crept in, whilst trying to minimize the obvious damage that such an admission could cause.

The psychology Gardner reveals leads one to re-examine his emphatic denials. The inexpert liar's first defence is to deny the very thing he has done, often before he has even been accused of it. Gardner had not met with any public criticism of the origin of the witch rituals, indeed he had Murray's enthusiastic approval, and had already privately dealt with Valiente's objections.[72] In that case, why did he feel the need to expend such apparently unnecessary time and effort in denying the direct influence of Crowley? The evidence of his own testimony is not damning, but it is more than suggestive.

Gardner claimed to have been initiated in 1939, a claim for which there are no witnesses, nor any other evidence. Moreover, he did not publicly refer to Witchcraft until 1949, when he published descriptions of fictional practices that were used in actual Witchcraft rituals for which corroborative evidence does exist. Gardner gives the earliest date and the publication of *High Magic's Aid* in 1949 fixes the latest, but internal evidence points to the period from 1947, his meeting with Crowley, to 1949 as being the birth of modern Witchcraft.

If there was a New Forest coven that initiated Gardner, as some still insist,[73] then it had no ritual structure, no liturgical content, nothing at all of a pre-Murrayite, non-Masonic and un-Crowleyan nature that found its way into the earliest known drafts of Gardner's Witchcraft. And even supposing that there may have been a New Forest coven, Gardner still invented, or was party to the invention, of modern Witchcraft.

The Craft of Reinvention

The revelation of Gardner as false founder did not lead to the demise of Witchcraft, as one might expect, but surprisingly to its even greater proliferation. The elimination of the founder led to the creation of multiple founders. In the 'economy' of religion the break-up of Gardner's monopoly led to the establishment of a competitive free market of religious entrepreneurs. But it was not just Gardner's unmasking that allowed such free reign – on its own it would seem to be entirely destructive – but also the fact that he became a role model. The falsity of his claims was ignored in favour of the spirit of his creativity. Undoubtedly Gardner's exposure met something in the *Zeitgeist* that allowed Witchcraft to survive and increase. As the first signs of his fraud began to emerge in the early 1970s, Witchcraft found itself being exported to the USA.

The disintegration of Gardner's claims met the anti-authoritarian, anti-hierarchical ethos of the hippy movement: the pursuit of new spiritualities,[74] the desire for direct experience and the demand to do it for oneself. However, this development was not a smooth one. Charismatic leaders continued to arise and claim Gardner's mantle, either reiterating his claims or propounding more 'authentic' ones of their own. Because Gardner claimed to have been initiated by authentic Witches, Murray's Pagan survivals, even though he had in fact invented his own Witchcraft, he left the door open for others to make similar claims, people such as Robert Cochrane and Alex Sanders.

Today's Witches are acutely aware of the religious freedom of their tradition. As one put it: 'Our religion provides no supportive underpinnings for arbitrary rules.'[75] When the Farrars published their reconstruction of the Gardner/Valiente 'Book of Shadows' (Text C) they went out of their way to stress that they were 'not setting up the definitive Gardnerian Book of Shadows as Holy Writ'. In fact they admitted that they had 'departed from the original' where they thought necessary and denied that the Gardnerian system was superior to any other modern Witchcraft rituals, adding only that they found it worked.[76]

One feminist neo-Pagan argues: 'History is, for us, only a source of inspiration, to be selectively drawn on like all other sources.'[77] Given the collapse of Gardner's suitable historic past, history *can* only be a source of inspiration, since the historical facts are undeniably damning. Margot Adler takes a similar line. With a pragmatic 'so be it' in the face of a discontinuous history she more aggressively asserts: 'It's not such a bad fate to be a provider of positive visions in a time of difficulty and darkness.'[78] Of course she is right. We should not use historical accuracy to attack the religious claims being made, but nor should we condone a wilful distortion of the past.

Miriam Simos, more generally known to the world as Starhawk, makes the absence of that historical connection the centrepoint of Witchcraft: 'Witchcraft . . . is not based on dogma or a set of beliefs, nor on scriptures or a sacred book revealed by a great man. Witchcraft takes its teachings from nature, and reads inspiration in the movements of the sun, moon, and stars, the flight of birds, the slow growth of trees, and the cycles of the seasons.'[79]

It is interesting in a religion without dogma, that one can be as prescriptive as Starhawk. That aside, note in particular the mention of a 'sacred book revealed by a great man' – that was exactly what Gardner was seeking to achieve. The 'Book of Shadows' was his intended sacred book and it was his intention that every Witch should make a copy of it. The form of revelation, however, was clearly different from the usual pattern, since the book itself, or at least the teachings within it, were supposedly given to Gardner by other Witches. He was setting himself up as a connection with the past, not specifically, nor directly, with a deity.

Inventiveness or creativity is not only celebrated at the personal level, but is worshipped as a divine principle. We read that witches seek to 'attune themselves to the creative forces of the Cosmos'. Again it is a 'religion which worships the God and Goddess as the ultimate creative polarity'. Starhawk raises the theme of invention itself as a spiritual principle symptomatic of the tradition's connection with the divine: 'It is a religion of connection with the Goddess . . . Because the Goddess is here, She is eternally inspirational. And so Witchcraft is eternally reinvented.'[80]

Kelly echoes the sentiment when he says: 'The Craft is a religion dedicated to creativity, because it is a religion we are creating for ourselves continually.'[81] Judith Harrow sees this as eminently practical: 'Selecting what's usable from tradition may be perfectly legitimate when constructing a nurturant spiritual practice for today's needs and today's consciousness.'[82]

The Pagan academic Dennis Carpenter also argues that it is the inspirational value of Gardner's historical claims rather than their veracity that is important. Carpenter goes so far as to dismiss the problem as insignificant, thus failing to see its defining role in the development of Witchcraft.[83] Witchcraft's historical claims can only be inspirational because they are historically false.

Carpenter makes some startling claims about the uniqueness and particular appropriateness of Witchcraft and neo-Paganism to current conditions. Specifically, he sees in Witchcraft's present character the shape of post-modernism. It should be pointed out that he uses a single description of post-modernism that is particularly suited to his ends, that of Griffin. That aside, and more relevant for our own concerns here, is the fact that he ignores the possibility that it has been post-modernism that has shaped Witchcraft, so that Witchcraft's unique appropriateness to post-modernism is no surprise. The single most important element in his argument is that Witchcraft emphasizes personal experience instead of textual or centralized religious authority. It is the argument here that this is the only course open to Witchcraft in the wake of Gardner's exposure, since he attempted to offer both an authoritative text and himself as the link with the authentic religion. The importance of the collapse of his project cannot be underestimated in the role it has played in defining Witchcraft as it is now.[84]

Orion says that the fundamental characteristic of all neo-Pagan traditions, Witchcraft included, was creativity, and Carpenter echoes this sentiment. He goes further to suggest that it is the creative freedom offered by neo-Paganism that draws people to it.[85] If this is the case, then, by the strangest twist of fate, the collapse of the Gardnerian project has been one of the most important – perhaps the most important – reason, not only for the survival but for the success of Witchcraft.

Gardner failed to pass off his crude forgery as the authentic Witchcraft, but, paradoxically, was more successful in creating a religious movement than he could have possibly imagined. Divested of his pretensions he fulfils a vital role. From discoverer to founder and finally to liberator, Gardner is seen as having freed Witchcraft from what it was supposed to be and made it what anyone wants it to be. The archetypal power of the creative inventor proves the inspiration and direction of Witchcraft: 'Most pagans will pick 'n' mix from various traditions . . . In taking what we choose from different traditions we are following in the footsteps of Gardner.'[86] Gardner succeeded in making Witchcraft no longer what we thought it was, but it is not now what Gardner meant it to be.

6. OUT OF THE CAULDRON, INTO THE FIRE: THE GROWTH AND DEVELOPMENT OF WICCA

Out of the seething cauldron of Gardner's fertile imagination, shameless plagiarism, energy and ambition came the most radical and fastest-growing religion of the twentieth and now the twenty-first centuries. Against patriarchal monotheism, Gardner posed a ditheism of sexual equality, of God and Goddess on an equal footing. Against a church of clergy and laity, Gardner posed a circle of initiates. Against conventional mores they eschewed 'Sunday best' and priestly robes to worship their gods unclothed. They took control of their lives through magic and attuned themselves to the natural world through ritual. The fire of Gardner's inspiration rapidly spread through his books, newspaper articles and by word of mouth to touch an increasingly wide group of people. However, that fire also burnt Gardner.

Having seen how the framework for a new vision of Witchcraft was established in the nineteenth century and how this was used by Gerald Gardner to invent a magico-religion upon Masonic lines, we shall next examine how this new Witchcraft was taken up and developed by others, and how it spread out from its base in England to reach the USA and a new set of emergent, radical ideas.

Up until the 1950s only two other names were associated with Gardner and Witchcraft: Old Dorothy Clutterbuck, his supposed initiator into the Craft; and Dafo, who acted as Maiden and succeeded Clutterbuck in the office of High Priestess. Whilst Old Dorothy Clutterbuck, otherwise known to the community as Mrs Fordham, was a resident of the New Forest area, the record she has left of her life, in her own diaries and in public records, is not only silent on the subject of Witchcraft, but suggests the life of a devout Christian and pillar of the community which flatly contradicts Gardner's portrayal of her as the High Priestess of a coven of Witches. Dafo, on the other hand, was certainly involved: eye-witness testimony from at least one other source (Doreen Valiente) as well as statements made in interviews (with the historian Hutton) confirm her existence and role in modern Witchcraft. Several other members of the group have been suggested: Dolores North, Gregory Watson McGregor Reid, the Revd. J. Ward, Charles Seymour, Christine Hartley, Mabel Besant-Scott and George Sullivan.[1] Whilst several of these people were involved with the first Rosicrucian Theatre, of which Gardner was a member, there is no other evidence to suggest that they practised any form of Witchcraft. By the early 1950s only another eight to ten people were reported as being involved and their main interest seems to have been nudism rather than Witchcraft. Their names have gone unrecorded, and none of them has come forward to testify to their involvement. Whilst Seymour and Hartley were undoubtedly interested in Witchcraft, as testified in their writings, and would produce some remarkable works on the subject that have only recently received the attention they deserve, none of the people allegedly involved in the early stages left any noticeable imprint.

It has been suggested that Reid gave Gardner the idea for the Sabbat structure, but then he could easily have taken that from Murray. It has also been suggested that Dolores North typed out the first draft of *High Magic's Aid*, but that in itself does not indicate that she influenced Gardner. Instead, it was someone from outside this little group of occultist friends who had the greatest impact on the development of Witchcraft, a woman whose influence was so great in fact that she has been credited as the Mother of Modern Witchcraft.

The Mother of Modern Witchcraft

Mother darksome and divine,
Mine the scourge and mine the kiss.
Five-point star of life and bliss,
Here I charge ye in this sign.[2]

A plain, owlishly bespectacled woman with a slight stoop and a friendly twinkle in her eye wrote to Cecil Williamson in 1952, the proprietor of the Witches' Mill Museum of Magic and Witchcraft asking for more information on the Old Religion. She was Doreen Valiente, thirty years old, with a lifelong interest in the occult, and living in the seaside resort of Bournemoth. Williamson passed the letter to Gerald Gardner, then ensconced as his resident witch, and so began one of the greatest creative partnerships in the history of modern Witchcraft.[3]

After a brief correspondence she and Gardner met in the Christchurch home of Gardner's High Priestess, the woman he only ever referred to by her Craft name, Dafo.[4] Valiente recalled that she had misgivings about initiation into Witchcraft, fearing she would be required to sell her soul to the Devil. She decided to go ahead anyway. 'To be willing to sell one's soul to the Devil,' she said, 'was a state of mind that living in Bournemouth readily induced.' When she came face to face with Gardner, at least some of her doubts evaporated: 'I realised that this man was no time-wasting pretender to occult knowledge', although she still asked herself, 'Did they go in for the sort of thing I had read about in novels by Dennis Wheatley, where a materialization of Satan himself presided over a blood-stained altar?' Far from being sinister, however, Gardner and Dafo appeared 'kind and intelligent'. Valiente was given a copy of Gardner's *High Magic's Aid* and allowed to make up her own mind.[5]

Returning to Dafo's home the following summer, 1953, Valiente was initiated into Wicca. She did not tell either her husband or her mother: Witchcraft was taboo. The ritual was undoubtedly a little out of the ordinary:

> In my mind's eye, I can see him [Gardner] now, standing by our improvised altar in that candlelit room. He was tall, stark naked, with wild white hair, a sun-tanned body, and arms which bore tattoos and a heavy bronze bracelet. In one hand he brandished 'Old Dorothy's' sword while in the other he held the handwritten 'Book of Shadows', as he read the ritual by which I was formally made a priestess and witch.'[6]

Later in the year she met the rest of the coven in Gardner's North London flat, about eight or ten others, she was not quite sure.

Soon Valiente was working as Gardner's *de facto* High Priestess. She immediately spotted his numerous borrowings, especially his excessive use of Crowley, but she apparently believed his justification, that the coven had passed only fragmentary rituals on to him, which he had found it necessary to pad out with Crowley and any of the other sources she was sharp enough to spot. She therefore accepted his central claim, that he was the messenger of the survivors of the ancient pagan religion of Europe. Valiente said:

> People may well wonder why, having traced Gerald's rituals to their component parts as having been derived from the works of Margaret Murray, Charles Godfrey Leland, Rudyard Kipling, Aleister Crowley, the *Key of Solomon* and the rituals of Freemasonry, I continued to believe that they were descended from an old witch coven in the New Forest. The reason is that underlying all these I found a basic structure which was not from Crowley or Margaret Murray or any of the other sources mentioned.[7]

Unfortunately we have conclusively seen that there was no underlying structure that could not be traced to these other sources. One can only think that their composite nature and Valiente's own lack of experience in other mystical or magical organizations prior to joining Gardner blinded her to this truth.

Although she never called herself the Mother of Modern Witchcraft, Valiente had good cause to do so. Whilst she went along with Gardner's explanation for the derivative and composite nature of his Craft she was never entirely comfortable with it, especially the use of Crowley. Crowley had never enjoyed a favourable press, but with the publication in 1951 of John Symonds's biography *The Great Beast*, his reputation was more sulphurous than ever, and Valiente felt sure this would both detract from their Witchcraft and deter people from joining it. With Gardner's grudging permission she undertook to write Crowley out of Witchcraft.

Her best and most widely known additions to the Gardnerian corpus are 'The Charge of the Goddess' and 'The Witches' Rune'. The Charge is a ritual address delivered by the High Priest and High Priestess during the key ceremony of Drawing Down the Moon, whilst the Rune is a more multi-purpose chant to raise 'the power'. Derived from the Old Norse *rún* meaning 'whisper', 'secret counsel', 'mystery,' the Rune begins with the nonsensical, but evocative chant, *Eko, Eko Azarak*, an invention of Crowley's friend J.F.C. Fuller,[8] before entering the more familiar grounds of Valientean verse with the much quoted line, 'Darksome night and shining moon'.[9] It neatly encapsulates the casting of the circle and the invocation of the God and Goddess, using the *Eko* chant again as a finale to whip the practitioners into a magical frenzy. The Charge is somewhat longer and more involved, essentially a rewriting of Gardner's own composition and hence still highly derivative of Crowley and Leland; Valiente was just more skilful at burying the borrowings.

With a revised 'Book of Shadows' ready for a larger audience, Gardner sought out journalists and writers, eager to spread the message. What followed was a series of hostile newspaper articles, clearly revelling in the Satanic stereotype of Witchcraft to boost their circulation. In 1955 a story under the headline 'This Man's Whitewash is Dangerous. Witchcraft is No Fun' proceeded to treat Gardner most unchivalrously:

> Dr Gerald Brouseau Gardner is an authority on witchcraft. It is through him that many people get their first mistaken ideas about witchcraft. He is a self-confessed witch and a practising devotee of a witch coven in Britain. But he is also a white-washer of witchcraft. He puts around the . . . dangerous idea that witchcraft is not evil. He seems to overlook the fact that what may begin as an innocent dabble in search of excitement may lead eventually to devil worship.[10]

More of the same followed in 1956, with the headlines screaming tales of black magic and murder. The press had the bit between its teeth and went off in a hundred different directions, leaving poor Gardner at the starting line. Whilst people like Jack Bracelin (putative author of Gardner's biography) argued that it was just such negative headlines that drew him into the Craft, in an attempt to find the truth, others thought such malicious lies could only do them and their cause irrevocable harm.

Dismayed by Gardner's increasingly reckless attempts to gain publicity for the Craft, Valiente and some others (as is usual, we are not given their names, except for a gentleman called Ned) drafted a document entitled 'Proposed Rules for the Craft', whose thirteen proposals were essentially intended to require adherence to the oath of secrecy that all the Gardnerians had taken as part of their initiation. Gardner, evidently riled by the mutiny of his High Priestess, responded with a document of his own, the 'Laws of the Craft'. He resorted to his old trick of invoking ancient authority and instead of admitting his authorship of the Laws palmed them off as belonging to the original Witch Cult. As Valiente tells the story, she was only trying to protect the Craft, but she was also trying to bind Gardner. They were struggling for power and in the process ripping the coven apart.

Gardner refused to be caged and Valiente and her followers parted company: 'We had had enough,' she said, 'of the Gospel according to St Gerald.'[11] So in 1957 she went on to form her own coven. She met Gardner again and was reconciled, but the two never worked magic together again, and the Father of Witchcraft died whilst cruising in the Mediterranean in February 1964. Although the press continued to hound the Wiccans, the years following 1957 seem to have been quiet ones for Valiente, until in August 1964 her magical career took a new and dramatic direction. when she met a man who claimed to be a real, traditional (as opposed to Gardnerian) Witch, a man who called himself Robert Cochrane.

Doreen Valiente

Born Doreen Dominy in 1922 in London, Valiente claimed that she began to experience psychic episodes as a young child and that by her late teens she was a practising clairvoyant. These early experiences led to a lifelong interest in the occult. By day she worked as a humble secretary, by night she immersed herself in the mysteries through the writings of Aleister Crowley, Helena 'Madame' Blavatsky and Israel Regardie. From her pen came several works on Witchcraft beginning with *Where Witches Live* in 1962, to be followed by *An ABC of Witchcraft* in 1973, *Natural Magic* in 1975 and *Witchcraft for Tomorrow in* 1978. Her next work, *The Rebirth of Witchcraft* (1989), attempted to trace 'the history of contemporary Wicca from its shadowy roots at the turn of the century to the present day'. She also contributed the introduction to Evan John Jones's book *Witchcraft, A Tradition Renewed*, which came out in 1990. She died on 1 September 1999, at the age of 77. Stewart Farrar, himself a major figure in Witchcraft, said, 'There are few who had met her who did not find her unassuming, modest, and unpretentious.'[12] The manuscript for an unpublished novel called *The Witches' Ball* was discovered amongst her papers in 2001.

Britain's Number One Witch

With the death of Gardner the leadership of the Witchcraft move-ment fell vacant. There was no lack of applicants for the post, however Gardner had all but destroyed Wicca and the pretenders to his throne claimed a different descent, a more traditional and hered-itary, and hence a more authentic, descent. Valiente herself was more of a Captain's no. 2, the quintessential right-hand man, even if a little mutinous at times, and despite her contribution to Wicca she did not attempt to lead the movement. Instead she sought out another leader to follow.

To Valiente, Robert Cochrane seemed tall, handsome and of high intelligence. In 1964, when they met, he was still only around twenty-eight years of age. She later described him as 'perhaps the most powerful and gifted personality to have appeared in modern witchcraft'.[13] However, his career was brief and his contribution erratic, factors that have generally kept him out of the history of modern Witchcraft. Even if it has been largely overlooked his role was nonetheless important.

Cochrane claimed to be a real, traditional Witch. His practices, he said, did not come from Gardner, but had been passed down to him by a relative. Unlike Gardner his group did not worship naked, but wore hooded black robes, did not use the scourge to purify or work up magi-cal energy, and used a forked staff, like an old walker's thumb-stick, which they called a 'stang', as the central ritual implement. Like Gardner they observed the eight annual Sabbats and full-moon Esbats, and they worshipped a god and goddess. Like Gardner they also invoked the Watchtowers, or Four Castles, as part of the circle-casting ceremony, but transposed the usual elemental attribution of air in the east, fire in the south, water in the west and earth in the north to fire in the east, earth in the south, water in the west and air in the north.[14] Since her disillusionment with Gardner, Valiente had been searching for a more genuine Witchcraft and here, in the form of this charismatic young man, she had found it.

After a varied life as a bargee and blacksmith, Cochrane had settled down in the Thames Valley as a designer in a large corporation. His former career was partly reflected in the name he chose for his group, the Clan of Tubal Cain: a clan, because he thought the word 'coven' too Gardnerian; and of 'Tubal Cain' because he had been the original blacksmith, but more probably because he was associated with witch-craft in *The White Goddess* by Robert Graves, a work that greatly influenced Cochrane's approach.[15] Graves describes Tubal Cain as a Kenite goat god in a discussion of the poem 'The Coal Black Smith', Scottish witchcraft and the association between horned gods and smithing.[16] When Valiente met him Cochrane's coven consisted of his wife and three other men, one of whom was undoubtedly Evan John Jones (who later wrote a book on Witchcraft drawing heavily on Cochrane's ideas and with an introduction contributed by Valiente). Cochrane took the role of Magister, as the high priest was called, his wife that of Maid, and one of the other men functioned as Summoner, the officer responsible for calling group meetings, organization and recruitment.[17] Later they were joined by two more women before events overcame them.

How Tubal Cain Got Into Witchcraft
Cochrane was deeply influenced by his reading of Graves's *The White Goddess* where it is argued that the traditional verse known as 'The Coal Black Smith' was sung during the witches' Sabbat. Graves went even further to assert that 'the association of smiths and horned gods is as ancient as Tubal Cain, the Kenite Goat-god.'[18] Tubal Cain thus became the most ancient horned god and an irresistible deity for the young Cochrane.

'The Coal Black Smith' (first verse)

> *I shall go into a hare*
> *With sorrow and sighing and mickle care,*
> *And I shall go in the Devil's name*
> *Aye, till I come home again.*[19]

Cochrane was antagonistic to Gardner and Gardnerians in general, although both Valiente and his main supporter in *Pentagram*, a man called Tailesin, were Gardnerian initiates. He lambasted 'modern Witchcraft' for being 'a secure and naive belief that Nature is always good and kind', and 'a heap of musty nonsense, half-baked theology and philosophy' that had become an 'escape hatch' and 'funk-hole' for those unwilling or unable to face the realities of the twentieth century. Instead he championed the 'mysteries' contained in folklore and legend, a fluid tradition of experience not tied to any dogma or liturgy. He called for revolution within the Craft and social engagement with the problems of the day.[20]

His unique approach to the Craft was publicized in Justine Glass's book *Witchcraft, The Sixth Sense – and Us* (1965). Unfortunately, he took the opportunity to gull a credulous writer and much of the book's content is suspect, if not actually worthless. Valiente charitably believed that Cochrane was only pulling Glass's leg,[21] but a more objective eye can discern a conscious attempt to fabricate claims for the authenticity of his particular brand of Witchcraft. One example will suffice: the photograph of a supposed witch heirloom in Glass's book, a copper plate bearing the date 1724, which Cochrane claimed had been handed down through his family for generations, had in fact been bought for him by Valiente in a Brighton junk shop.

Despite such clear evidence of charlatanism and a reputation for being awkward and deliberately mystifying (what Cochrane called his 'grey magic', a sort of psychological technique to put people at a disadvantage), Cochrane was renowned for the effectiveness of his magical ritual. Jones later waxed lyrical that during his ceremonies 'we all knew what it felt like to be one of "Diana's darling crew" '. Valiente described how during a Hallowe'en (Samhain) Sabbat held on the Sussex Downs, as they danced within a circle marked out with ash, the four cardinal points lit by lanterns, 'we felt that we were not alone on those wild hills . . . It seemed to me that the circle was growing lighter. A kind of green fire seemed to be spreading and sparkling over the ground.'[22]

In 1964 one of Cochrane's colleagues, a 36-year-old press relations consultant calling himself by the pseudonym of John Math, founded the Witchcraft Research Association.[23] The launch dinner on 3 October was attended by over fifty people and Valiente gave the opening address, in which she called for unity amongst Britain's Witches. However, Cochrane and his followers used the Association and its periodical *Pentagram* to wage war on Gardnerians and Gardnerianism. Their vitriolic campaign alienated the rest of the Witchcraft community and what had every mark of a power bid on Cochrane's part backfired. The *Pentagram* folded after six issues and the Association dissolved soon after.

Cochrane's meteoric career now came crashing down to earth and all his dazzling ritual skills were not enough to save him. Despite the newspapers constantly sniffing round for salacious gossip and the whiff of scandal, and a largely unsympathetic, if not antagonistic, public, Cochrane's destruction was his own fault. First came the break-up of the Clan. Cochrane began by ejecting Valiente from the group after she dared challenge his authority (something she always seemed to manage to do). Cochrane's failed war on Gardnerianism and the internal power struggle with Valiente weakened his standing in the group. The loss of Valiente diminished it, but it was not yet destroyed – although it soon would be. He formed a liaison with one of the other women in the Clan, according to Valiente expecting that his wife would submissively accept the arrangement. She did not, however and, leaving him, filed for divorce. The Clan was now without a High Priestess and, so Valiente thought, the real source of its magical power (although this view plainly contradicted her earlier estimation of Cochrane's abilities).[24]

Cochrane's spiral of decline had yet further to go. He turned to drugs, not the usual kind of recreational substances that were then popular like cannabis and LSD, but the intoxicating poisons long associated with witchcraft: the fairy toadstool, fly agaric (*Amanita muscaria*), and deadly nightshade. He became clinically depressed, took sick leave from his employers and was prescribed anti-depressant drugs by his doctor. He began telling his followers that he would commit ritual suicide at Midsummer that year, 1966. However, his threats were no longer being taken seriously, as even the once gullible Justine Glass remarked, 'It's just Robert talking.'[25] His unconscious body was found the next morning. He was taken into hospital in a coma and never regained consciousness. He had consumed a lethal cocktail of sleeping pills and deadly nightshade.

Cochrane kept alive the idea that there was an authentic Witchcraft tradition surviving in Britain, although what is known of his claims and practices do not suggest that this was the case. His particular ritual innovations created a more 'English' Witchcraft, prudishly donning robes, but also a more 'sixties' Witchcraft, experimenting with drugs and pushing at the doors of perception. His legacy is still alive today both in the United Kingdom and the USA. In the UK there is still a Clan of Tubal Cain, although not, of course, the original one, and another group called Regency. In the USA Cochrane lives on in the 1734 Tradition, a non-profit religious organization registered in California and founded by Joseph Wilson.[26]

In contrast to Cochrane's low profile as a Witch, Britain was home to another, less publicity shy, individual. She was Sybil Leek, the owner of an antique shop in the picturesque village of Burley in the New Forest.[27] In 1963 at the age of forty, this rather rotund woman announced to the world that she was a witch and the High Priestess of a local coven. The press immediately pounced on the story.

Leek claimed to be able to trace a long line of esoteric ancestors: hereditary witches on her mother's side back to 1134 including the mildly famous Molly Leigh, who died in 1663; and on her father's side occultists in some close association with the royal families of tsarist Russia; all, of course, with profound psychic abilities. She professed to have an IQ of 164, and apparently demonstrated an early capacity for writing. However, her schooling was brief. Having been taught at home by her grandmother she was, at the age of twelve, required to attend the local school, which she left at sixteen.

She claimed to have met Aleister Crowley at the age of nine and reported that he was a frequent visitor to her house. He would take her out climbing and recite his poetry, which proved a powerful stimulus for her to write her own. He taught her the power of words and of words of power, and of sound in its manifold magical combinations. He told her grandmother that young Sybil would in due course continue where he had left off. Close scrutiny of Crowley's diaries reveals no evidence of an acquaintance with the Leek family, or tutelage of their daughter. If Crowley had actually met everyone who claimed his acquaintance his life would have been one constant promotional tour (some might say that it was, but no matter, the claims are clearly absurd).

At fifteen Leek fell in love with a 39-year-old pianist and conductor, and at sixteen she married him. For two years they travelled Britain and Europe together, then he died suddenly and Leek returned home again. Some time shortly afterwards she claimed, her grandmother took her to Gorge du Loup, near Nice in the south of France, to be initiated into Witchcraft.[28] An elderly Russian aunt who was High Priestess of the coven had died and Leek was to be her replacement. But instead she returned to England, to a village called

Burley to be precise, that lay in the heart of the New Forest, where she apparently 'lived among the Gypsies'.[29] Here she joined the venerable Horsa coven, which was said to have been extant for 700 years. Eventually she was honoured as its High Priestess. She also ran three antique shops, married a man named Brian and gave birth to two sons, Stephen and Julian, who were said to be inheritors of the family's psychic gift.

The Horsa Coven

We of the Horsa Coven have a long history – both as a group and individually. Everyone is dedicated to witchcraft and the Old Religion, everyone has a flair for healing and we are all determined to use our powers for good and to deflect some of the evil which Black Magic tries to create throughout the world. If we can remain true to these basic ideals, so rooted in tradition, then we are doing our duty.[30]

Following Leek's approximate dating, she would have been involved with the Horsa coven during the 1940s and worked with them for some twelve years. Given her penchant for publicity and her positive love of the limelight it is unclear why she waited until the 1960s before she revealed her involvement. Whilst it has been suggested (by Grace Kemelek, about whom more later) that the Horsa coven was the one that originally initiated Gerald Gardner, we have demonstrated the origin of the Gardnerian material and can confidently discount this speculation. There is no evidence for the existence of the coven, nor the French connection, other than Leek's own word, which in itself has been shown to be unreliable. Whilst we cannot entirely disprove the existence of the Horsa or the French group – it is in the nature of such claims of membership of secret societies that they can rarely be absolutely disproved – we cannot accept Leek at her word. Given the Gardnerian content of her brand of Witchcraft, including the use of the Charge, we can only surmise that it is post-Gardner and of Gardnerian origin. She was simply able to exploit Gardner's claim that there had been a New Forest coven in existence prior to him (and hence his subsequent invention of Wicca) to invent one of her own which would then appear to be supported by Gardner's earlier claim (not one to do things by halves she actually invented four covens operating in the New Forest area).

According to the story, it was an uncanny experience in the 1950s that confirmed in Leek's mind that her task here on earth was to evangelize Witchcraft. Whilst walking alone through the forest one fine spring day she was unexpectedly encompassed in bright blue light, and peace and purpose were infused into her. The decision to spread the word, so to speak, brought the media like a cloud of gnats, the hatred and suspicion of her neighbours and the ruin of her successful antique business. Effectively drummed out of town, her landlord refused to renew her tenancy unless she publicly denounced Witchcraft. She fled to America with her family and her familiar, a jackdaw called Mr Jackson Hotfoot, lock, stock and barrel. She had become, according to one newspaper headline, 'Britain's Number One Witch' and Britain clearly did not want her.

The Leeks arrived in New York, but Sybil found it too depressing and they moved to more congenial California and settled in Los Angeles. Here she met Crowley's erstwhile secretary, Israel Regardie. She found work giving astrological predictions, often to celebrities and others in the public eye, eventually becoming the editor and publisher of her own astrological journal. In 1968 the publication of her first book, *Diary of a Witch*, brought a huge response from the public. She travelled the country lecturing, appearing on the media circuit, becoming a celebrity and, protecting her brand name, became Sybil Leek Inc.

Whilst she did not directly oppose any of the other claims of authenticity then being made, she did seek to assert the dominance of her own position: 'The heartbeat of witchcraft must always reside in the old established covens, such as Horsa.'[31] The coven comprised thirteen people, six men and six women, after the Murrayite model, led by a High Priestess, after the Gardnerian model. They invoked the four Watchtowers, consecrated water and salt, used the Athame, and initiated with binding and oaths at knife-point: all familiar from Gardner. Whilst Leek taught the Gardnerian theology of God and Goddess, she subsumed these under a monotheistic doctrine: 'Witchcraft, as any religion, involves the acceptance of certain tenets which are based on faith and acceptance of a Supreme Being, a God without a name.'[32]

Leek wrote over sixty books on subjects from astrology to phrenology and Witchcraft, as well as a regular magazine column. She even became something of a 'spokeswitch' for the Time-Life Books series on the occult. Careful never to 'preach' Witchcraft, she sought to explain its holistic philosophy and stressed its difference from Satanism. Frowning upon ritual nudity or the use of drugs, she nevertheless believed in cursing, which set her apart from most other neo-Pagan Witches, then and since. Reincarnation proved a popular theme, upon which she discoursed often, reputedly guided in this by the spirit of H.P. Blavatsky. Other than these slight differences, she made no contribution to the theology or practice of Witchcraft, directing her energies instead to the promulgation and public acceptance of the Gardnerian party line, minus those elements she did not agree with. Like Cochrane she tried to undermine Gardnerianism by claiming older, more traditional origins, but like the claims of Gardner himself they simply had no foundation in verifiable fact. She is almost forgotten today, perhaps because, just as she was declared 'Britain's Number One Witch', she was forced to abandon the throne of the Witchcraft movement and flee the UK. But that throne would not be without its pretenders.

King of the Witches

Alex Sanders was born in Manchester in 1926 to humble parents, the eldest of six children. His father was a music-hall entertainer and drunkard. His grandmother, Mary Biby, was by all accounts a rather unusual woman and it was she who by Sanders's own account introduced him to the Craft. At the age of seven he found her standing naked within a chalk circle drawn upon the kitchen floor whereupon she revealed herself as an hereditary Witch and initiated him forthwith. On her orders he removed his clothes, entered the circle and put his head between his knees. Taking a knife she nicked his scrotum, drawing blood, and declared him 'one of the clan'.[33]

Sworn to secrecy, his instruction in Witchcraft followed. His grandmother lent him her 'Book of Shadows' and the young Sanders diligently copied out the spells and rituals therein. She also told him that he was descended from a medieval King of the Witches, the Welsh chieftain Owain Glyn Dwr (a national hero of the Welsh, Glyn

Dwr has no known connection with Witchcraft).[34] At this time he also discovered a psychic gift of clairvoyance and an ability to heal by laying on hands.[35]

Sanders also said that at the age of ten he had been taken to see a man who was introduced to him as Mr Alexander, whom he later discovered to have been the ubiquitous Aleister Crowley. Crowley then supposedly performed the Rites of Horus with the boy.[36] If he did, Crowley makes no mention of it, nor do any of his numerous biographers.[37] The pattern is becoming clear: early initiation, usually by a grandmother, and a connection with Aleister Crowley. It seems quite common for the more unscrupulous occultists to contrive some association with Crowley as a stamp of their authenticity.

In his later youth Sanders worked as an analytical chemist in a Mancunian laboratory. Here he met a 19-year-old girl, Doreen, three years his junior and made her his bride. From their union came two children, Paul and Janice. The marriage crumbled in five years; Doreen took the children and left. Sanders became a drifter, taking casual and poorly paid employment, drinking and having casual relations with partners of both sexes. Having fallen into the gutter, and with no apparent means of escape, he decided to take the 'left-hand path' on the spiritual road and put his powers and training to the accumulation of riches. He prostrated himself before the Devil and implored the old gentleman to grant him 'wealth beyond measure'. He also dabbled with the Sacred Magic of Abramelin the Mage, which divulges numerous recipes for the construction and consecration of talismans to bring about almost anything one might desire. He claimed that by these methods he succeeded in attracting a number of wealthy people into his personal orbit and accumulated the riches he desired.[38]

However, the left-hand path was soon to come to a dead end. His younger sister Joan developed cancer and died, his then girlfriend committed suicide, and the money began to disappear just as fast as it had come. Sanders was convinced that he was paying the price for working black magic, a price he had always thought he would one day have to pay. According to the story told by his later partner, Sanders decided to put his evil ways behind him and devote himself to the furtherance of Witchcraft, although his subsequent career shows little deviation from the course of self-seeking and destructive ambition.[39]

Sanders proceeded to form his own coven and thrust himself into the media spotlight first with the *Manchester Evening News* in a story headed 'Amazing Black Magic Rites on Cheshire Hillside' (15 September 1962), later with a record and stage act. He thus attracted more followers, and by 1965 he claimed a following of 1,623 initiates organized in a hundred covens across the land. This loyal body urged their guru to accept the mantle of the kingship of Witchcraft. Sanders claimed that a council of Witchcraft elders elected him King of the Witches in recognition of his efforts to expand the Craft.[40]

He met Maxine Morris (whose story will be told separately below) in the 1960s, initiated her into the Craft in spite of (or perhaps because of) her Roman Catholicism and married her after the fashion of Witches by a ceremony of handfasting (a civil ceremony followed in 1967). She was promptly elevated in her new vocation to become his High Priestess. The couple established themselves in a basement flat in London's Notting Hill Gate, from where they ran their coven and taught classes in Witchcraft. Followers accumulated and a daughter, Maya, was born in 1967. A son, Victor, followed in 1972. Their relationship was under enormous strain, however, brought about by Sanders's increasing lust for young men and undiminished pursuit of fame, and in 1973 they divorced.[41]

Sanders left London and moved to Bexhill. His notoriety ensured occasional mentions in the press, but his day was over. In 1982 he married again, this time to a wealthy divorcee. It did not last, however. She left in a blaze of scandal, claiming that he had squandered the divorce settlement of £50,000 from her previous marriage and had been an unsatisfying lover, more concerned with the affections of young men than her own.[42]

In 1987 he was diagnosed with lung cancer. By 30 April, the date of the Pagan festival of Beltane, 1988, he was dead. Two of his oldest friends, Nigel Bourne and his wife Selidy Bates, arranged the funeral service at Hastings crematorium. A crowd of some hundred people turned up for his interment. A tape was played to the assembly, appointing his son Victor as his successor. Victor, however, had not the least intention of taking up his father's tarnished crown, and had emigrated to the United States. The Council of Witchcraft Elders, a body purporting to have 100,000 members in Britain, announced that there would be no successor to Sanders's empty throne.[43]

The Magical Adventures of Alex Sanders

Michael, the Magical Child. One of Sanders's more extraordinary claims was to have a produced a magical child called Michael. Like many ordinary offspring Michael went through a turbulent adolescence, which Sanders used to excuse his own bad behaviour, before growing up to become a useful familiar spirit and spiritual guide through mediumistic trances.

Spirit Guides. Sanders's other contacts with the spirit world included a Native American called Red Feather and an entity calling itself Nick Demdike and claiming to be a victim of the witch trials of Lancaster in the seventeenth century.[44]

Healing Hands. Cancer, cystitis, drug addiction, unwanted pregnancies, even warts – Sanders claimed to be able to charm all these problems away either by directly laying on his hands, or by simply pointing at the problem and commanding it to go.

For all his media flair and popular following Sanders was a fraud. He passed off the writings of other people as his own, or as inherited by him, notably those of his forerunner Gerald Gardner and Gardner's High Priestess Doreen Valiente. He also liberally plagiarized the works of Eliphas Levi and the Austrian occultist Franz Bardon. His claims of the extent of his Witch kingdom are also highly suspect, if not laughable. His only published work on Witchcraft, *The Alex Sanders Lectures*, is a slight book and of little value.[45]

His tales of early initiation at the hands of his grandmother and of a line of ancestors well versed in Witchcraft is dubious to say the least. Patricia Crowther claimed that Sanders had written to her in 1961 after seeing her on the television, begging to be initiated into one of her covens: 'To be a witch is what I have always wanted and yet I have never been able to contact anyone who could help me . . .'[46] She invited him to attend an interview, and he also attended one of her coven meetings. Crowther took a dislike to him when he boasted of how he might, at any time, make the front page of the *Manchester Evening News*, and turned him down.

Failing to ingratiate himself with Crowther, Sanders apparently turned to Gardner instead and badgered the old man at his Isle of Man home only eighteen months before he died. He achieved some measure of success and was allowed to copy out several passages from Gardner's 'Book of Shadows'. Still he was uninitiated; his wife Maxine claimed that it was one of Crowther's coven maidens who finally fulfilled his desire.[47]

His contribution to the development of modern Witchcraft is undeniable, but it has not always been welcome or beneficial. The academic and Wiccan High Priest, Alan Wharton, accused Sanders of being a 'menace to society' who had 'no true knowledge of witchcraft and created more damage to the newly emerging craft than any person I have ever known'.[48]

Unperturbed by the obvious holes in Sanders's character and the heavy creaking emanating from his 'Alexandrianism', many such covens still exist. The tradition exported well to North America, but was never to become as popular as Gardner's original. In the USA all the Alexandrian covens cut their ties with Sanders from the 1980s. His brew found greater favour amongst the Canadians, where it was apparently more firmly established before Sanders's plummet from credibility. By the time he died in 1988 his approach to initiation had produced a larger following than Gardner had been able to achieve and brought into Witchcraft's orbit individuals of great talent whose later work would lead to its further development and proliferation.[49]

The woman who became famed as Alex Sanders's Witch Queen took an initial dislike to the diminutive, prematurely balding man. She first met him when he was a regular visitor to the house to see her mother, May Morris, a firm Roman Catholic with a taste for parlour occultism. Maxine, although only sixteen at the time, had already been deeply involved with the occult, or so she claimed.[50]

A young woman visitor to her mother's house had fascinated the girl. She was a member of a highly secret order of magical adepts following some sort of Egyptian tradition. She took Maxine to an underground cavern in Cheshire, where she was initiated into the Order, or abused by it – Maxine herself seems a little unsure on this. Deep in the proverbial bowls of the earth, by the light of the flickering torchlight, robed strangers stripped her, anointed her body with perfumed oils, robed her and laid her out upon an altar of the living rock. She compared what followed to her experiences with LSD; the narcotic substances smeared over her body transported her into a deep trance in which she travelled on the astral plane for what seemed like days. The strange young woman took her home again afterwards, and her mother was none the wiser.[51] Needless to say the adventure is entirely unsupported by any other evidence, and rests completely upon Maxine's word. What seems curious is that having allowed this group to initiate her under conditions in which she must have trusted them absolutely (how many people would strip off in a torch-lit cave on command?) she reported no further involvement with them, nor gave any reason why this was so.

Sanders's attraction grew by degrees; it seems that it was the mystery of Witchcraft that he kept hinting at that she found most alluring. Her mother refused to grant permission for the girl's involvement. An argument and an eventual split between them ensued; Maxine moved out and into a place of her own. Now willingly at Sanders's mercy she gave herself to the initiation with only a little trepidation. The First Degree rites of initiation into his coven stipulated that all participants should be naked and that the aspirants, Maxine and a boy called Paul, should be bound with cords, hand and foot. The assembly danced and chanted, dreadful oaths of allegiance to the Craft were sworn and the new recruits were welcomed into the group with the five-fold kiss upon feet, knees, genitalia, breasts and lips.

The Second and Third Degrees swiftly followed. The pair were again stripped and tied up, more terrible oaths were sworn, Maxine was renamed Veda and ritually 'purified' by forty lashes on her naked buttocks. She then scourged Sanders thrice forty with the whip, to his evident delight, though given his frailty she thought he might not stand it. Next came the Great Rite, with increased chanting, more flagellation and incense more pungent still. Maxine lay upon the floor, limbs stretched out to the edge of the magic circle, with Paul kneeling between her legs. She was covered with a veil, which, with Paul now lying atop her prone body, was slowly drawn away. The fertility rite, now thought of as bringing about the fertility of mind rather than field, was thus performed, symbolically at least; she claims that no sexual intercourse took place.[52]

The ceremony lasted three hours in all. At its conclusion Maxine was robed in white linen made heavy with the weight of seed pearls strewn upon it, cloaked in black velvet, crowned with silver in which a moon-shaped stone had been set and proclaimed High Priestess and Witch Queen. And she was still only sixteen. However, her role was a passive one. At Sanders's public lectures she was required only to sit on the podium regaled in her finery: 'All I want you to do,' Sanders told her, 'is sit there and look beautiful and represent the goddess.'[53]

Sanders, as Stewart Farrar said, 'was a born showman', and duly set about creating as big a media splash as possible. Maxine, although she apparently willingly went along with him, later regretted that her Craft had been 'cheapened and devalued by sensational publicity'. For her that publicity was often personally embarrassing, such as when newspapermen would be tipped off about open-air ceremonies – she ruefully reported having the most photographed posterior in Britain.[54]

After her divorce from Sanders in 1973 she briefly turned away from Witchcraft and joined the semi-occult Liberal Catholic Church. Today she runs a coven from her London home. It has spread across the country, and she is nominally the spiritual head of the Alexandrian tradition of Witchcraft. She continues to teach people in the ways of the Craft and despite such extraordinary beginnings has become a much respected figure on the occult scene and one of very few people who could be considered an elder of Witchcraft.[55]

We have seen how every successor to Gardner claimed separate authenticity, but that like Gardner they rooted that claim in unprovable traditional grounds. It must have been obvious to everyone who came across the Gardnerian material, not just Valiente, that it was a fake. It was not a hoax, because Gardner meant it with all seriousness, he wanted it to be true and simply did not let the fact that it was not stop him. We could, therefore, oxymoronically and paradoxically, call it a genuine fake. Like Gardner his successors also wanted it to be true and would not let the truth stop them, something born out by the fact that their supposedly different witchcrafts differed from Gardner's in no significant degree. It has been said that one should never let the truth get in the way of a good story. We can now apply that theologically: never let the truth get in the way of a good religion.

Witchcraft Goes West

The situation in England was moribund. The media had seized upon the most flamboyant and extrovert characters on the Witchcraft scene, exposed them to the outrage of the public, and effectively destroyed them (an end many of their erstwhile victims actively although unwittingly sought). Wicca itself was fragmented and consumed by numerous, ruinous internecine battles. It was largely those who fled England who ensured the Craft's survival and greater development.

Although they were not without their effect, as we have seen, Gardner's writings could hardly be considered national let alone international bestsellers, so it was largely down to missionaries to spread his message abroad, and in particular to one man, Raymond Buckland.

Born in London on 31 August 1934 of a Gypsy father and an English mother, and therefore technically a *poshrat*, the young Buckland was raised in the Church of England. At the age of twelve an uncle with an interest in spiritualism spirited him away and gave the innocent Christian a taste for the occult. The young man started upon a career in aviation, serving with the Royal Air Force from 1957 to 1959 and, after emigrating to America in 1962, joined the British Overseas Airways Corporation (now British Airways). Like so many others, reading Margaret Murray's *The Witch-Cult in Western Europe* and Gerald Gardner's *Witchcraft Today* decided him upon a spiritual career in Witchcraft. He started up a correspondence with Gardner, meeting him shortly before the old man's death in 1964. At the same time Gardner's High Priestess, Lady Olwen (Monique Wilson), initiated him into the Craft.[56]

He went back to the USA and with his wife Rosemary established the first Gardnerian coven there. The time was ripe for it, but they proceeded cautiously, for which, in the impatient New World, they were greatly criticized. Buckland was keen to keep a low profile, withholding his name and address from the media. But the media, like a hound that's caught the scent, were reluctant to let go and inevitably his real identity was made public, throwing him involuntarily into the limelight as a spokesman for the Craft.[57]

Inspired by Gardner's Museum of Witchcraft on the Isle of Man,[58] Buckland began a little collection of his own, which grew and continued to grow until the cabinet display became a basement jumble, then a building all to its self. He began writing too. In 1969 his first publication appeared, *A Pocket Guide to the Supernatural*. Hot on its heels in 1970 came *Witchcraft Ancient and Modern, Practical Candleburning Rituals*, and a facetious *jeu de sprite*, *Mu Revealed*, published under the anagramatic pseudonym Tony Earll, which re-arranged spells 'not really'. In the grip of the *cacoethes scribendi* the next year saw the publication of *Witchcraft from the Inside*. Sated for the moment it was three years before he was next in print with *The Tree: The Complete Book of Saxon Witchcraft*, and *Here is the Occult*. In 1975 followed *Amazing Secrets of the Psychic World*, in 1977 *Anatomy of the Occult*, in 1978 *The Magic of Chant-o-Matics*, in 1983 *Practical Colour Magic*, and in 1986 his eleventh book and definitive statement on Witchcraft, *Buckland's Complete Book of Witchcraft*, which some felt revealed too much. In addition he contributed articles on Witchcraft to numerous magazines and newspapers, lectured at universities and appeared on television talk shows. A book on Gypsies lurks amongst his corpus, as do several screenplays and novels. His fiction ranges from comedy to mystery to Tolkienesque fantasy, but steers clear of the occult.

From retiring proselyte he was rapidly transformed into a tireless popularizer. Not only was he telling people how to do it and spreading the word through every medium available to him, but also showing them how to do it. He and his wife set up a workshop and study group for the committed but unknowledgeable, entitled 'Basics of Wicca'.

Hollywood was quick to utilize this high-profile, prolific witch. Orson Welles employed him as technical adviser to *Necromancy* and a stage production of *Macbeth*, and the director William Friedkin took his counsel for the making of *The Exorcist*.

Meanwhile his personal affairs were far from smooth. In 1973 he and Rosemary split up. They relinquished control of their coven to two Long Islanders, Theos and Phoenix. Buckland moved to New England, met Joan Helen Taylor and married her – a sound match for a decade, before another divorce. He was not long unwed, however, soon marrying Tara Cochran.[59]

Perhaps unsurprisingly, his spiritual affairs were also in turmoil. Gardnerianism no longer met his religious needs and, more, he was disgusted by those who used it for their self-aggrandisement. So, in late 1973 or early 1974, he formed his own tradition, Seax-Wica. Based upon Saxon culture, this new tradition was of a more democratic spirit than Gardner's. With Joan he moved to Virginia, establishing the Seax-Wica Seminary, a correspondence school, there. At its peak it claimed over a thousand students, but interest and enthusiasm could not overcome the Bucklands' lack of funds and plans to establish a permanent campus were abandoned.[60]

Buckland and Tara relocated to San Diego in 1984. The seminary correspondence course was wound down and Buckland retired from his high-flying career as Witchcraft's spokesman. With his Seax-Wica firmly established worldwide, he and Tara removed themselves to practise their Craft in solitude. Whilst Sybil Leek had merely posed as a traditional witch and supposed member of the bogus Horsa coven, Buckland had brought Gardnerianism to the USA and established a line of apostolic succession there, something that Leek could never do, but like Valiente and others he had felt a need to reappraise Gardner's Witchcraft and developed a powerful and influential tradition more suited to his time.

Almost three hundred years after the horrors of the Salem witch trials of 1692, Witchcraft returned to Salem in the form of Laurie Cabot. Although born in Wewoka, Oklahoma (on 6 March 1933), she became the Official Witch of Salem, the founder of her own tradition, Witchcraft as a Science. In 1973 she inaugurated the annual Witches' Ball in Salem, in 1986 she started the Witches' League of Public Awareness, and in 1988 she founded the Temple of Isis (an affiliate of the National Alliance of Pantheists).

The story, as Cabot tells it, began when she was fourteen and browsing the library shelves for books on comparative religion, something that attracted the attention of a local Witch. Keeping her identity secret, the woman encouraged her to look beyond Christianity for the answers. Eventually she revealed herself as a Witch and introduced her to her two compatriots, who together initiated Cabot at the age of sixteen.

After high school Cabot gave up her plans to attend Smith College and instead became a dancer in the Latin Quarter of Boston. After two failed marriages, and with two young children in tow, she vowed to live as a Witch and always to go about publicly in the traditional appearance of a witch, which she took to be long black robes, a pentagram medallion and heavy black eye-liner – a striking if arbitrary costume.

Salem was not Cabot's choice; a friend persuaded her to move there and so she did. Together they bought a house that Cabot convinced herself had been built by her father in a previous incarnation. However, she was evidently not much taken with his handiwork and after a year moved to other lodgings. She opened the Witch Shop in Salem, a bold move but an unsuccessful one: the shop soon closed for lack of business. However, another shop, Crow Haven Corner, proved more popular.

In 1971 Cabot began her campaign to be named Salem's Official Witch. Her initial petitions fell on unsympathetic ears. The Mayor thought such a suggestion was thoroughly improper. It was six years before she was granted leave to call herself the Official Witch of Salem by the Governor of Massachusetts and future presidential candidate, Michael Dukakis.

Dealings with officialdom evidently nurtured a germ of political ambition in her, as in 1987 she stood for the position of Salem's mayor. Derogatory remarks allegedly made by one of the other contenders perhaps decided her. Her campaign was much supported and gleefully covered by the sensation-seeking media. However, she unexpectedly withdrew from the running at the last moment.

In 1988 she established the Temple of Isis, affiliated to the National Alliance of Pantheists. They also ordained her as a priest able to perform legally the ceremony of marriage. She continues to represent Witchcraft in her very public and idiosyncratic manner, to fight for the rights of witches and to give psychic counselling, or tell fortunes as it used to be described.[61]

Not every development in America was an offshoot of Gardnerianism. Whilst every aspiring King of the Witches claimed traditional authenticity for his cobbled-together Gardnerianism, one new tradition emerged that genuinely appeared to be of a different pedigree.

At the age of nine Victor Anderson[62] was initiated into the Craft by a small nude woman of advanced years whom he discovered sitting in the centre of a circle. He took off his clothes and was sexually initiated by her. A vision followed in which the old woman, now become the Goddess, led him by the hand through pitch-black nothingness to a wild jungle under a starry sky and green moon. The Horned God, a powerfully built man, his penis erect and swaying before him, but with an air of effeminacy and a blue flame issuing from his head, approached them. He apparently communicated with this and other beings before the vision broke up and he again found himself sitting in the circle. The old woman taught him the ritual use of herbs and washed him with butter, salt and oil before he dressed and went home.[63]

Henceforth he was part of a coven more traditional than the various modern traditions now being touted, but also less fully developed. The coven practised what Anderson described as a 'devotional science', devoid of a complex theology. It involved the simple emphasis on a life lived in harmony with nature, a nature governed by the 'Old Gods' and the 'Old Powers'.[64]

The appearance of Gardner's *Witchcraft Today* inspired Anderson to form his own coven. One of his first initiates was 13-year-old Gwydion Pendderwen.[65] Anderson schooled him in Witchcraft, Celtic folklore and various magical systems such as the Huna, Haitian and West African strands of Voodoo. Together they founded the Faery Tradition. Pendderwen wrote much of its liturgical material, but after visiting Alex Sanders and Stewart Farrar in the UK during the 1970s chose to incorporate a good deal of Alexandrian material into their tradition.[66]

Pendderwen went on to found Nemeton and Forever Forests. Nemeton (Welsh meaning 'sacred grove') came about after he joined the Society for Creative Anachronism and became Court Bard to the society's Kingdom of the West. With a fellow society member and initiate of the Faery Tradition, Alison Harlow, Pendderwen established it in 1970, initially as a networking service for neo-Pagans. After a visionary experience in Ireland, he returned to the USA and retired to live as a hermit in a cabin at Annwfn in Mendocino County. Without electricity and with only a cat for company he learned carpentry and gardening, and pursued with vigour his artistic intent. Now identifying with the Green Man, he started holding tree plantings on his own and some nearby land each winter. This developed into Forever Forests in 1977, a movement to sponsor tree plantings and promote ecological awareness as part of a magical process to re-establish harmony between man and Mother Earth.[67]

In 1980 he came out of seclusion to perform in the first Pagan Spirit Gathering. For the next two years he was busy with tree plantings, organizing Pagan events, raising sponsorship and protesting against nuclear weapons. This latter move resulted in his being arrested for civil disobedience along with members of Reclaiming during a demonstration at the Lawrence Livermore Laboratory in California. His desire to establish an extended family at Annwfn was defeated by personal differences and a shortage of funds. Before he could try again he was killed in a car accident in the autumn of 1982. Much of his poetry, rituals and other writings remains unpublished.[68]

The USA also saw the development of a radical new interpretation of Witchcraft. As sisters started doing it for themselves, amongst those who burnt their bras were those who unsheathed their

Athames. Zsusanna Budapest, a lesbian separatist and founder and leader of the feminist branch of witchcraft, Dianic Wicca, was to change the landscape of Witchcraft forever.[69]

Originally from Hungary, she had fled the country after the unsuccessful uprising of 1956, and eventually found her way to the USA. Whilst living in Hollywood she first became acquainted with the feminist movement. After attending a commemorative rally to mark the anniversary of women's right to vote she was inspired to work at a local women's centre and began to feel the need for a woman-centred theology, a spiritual feminism to complement the political, but not merely as a complement. Religion in her opinion is the 'supreme politics' because it suffuses every other sphere of activity.[70] With six friends she established the Susan B. Anthony coven in 1971 at the Winter Solstice.

The coven took its name from a prominent American suffragette and marked the beginning of feminist Witchcraft in general and Budapest's own brand of Dianic Wicca in particular. By 1976 the coven had expanded to a core of some twenty to thirty women with up to 300 taking part in some of their activities. Starhawk was among the coven's more notable members. Across the USA, in at least five other states, affiliated groups sprang up. In Los Angeles a bookshop was opened, the Feminist Wicca, to spread the message selling her self-published textbook on things Dianic, *The Feminist Book of Lights and Shadows*. A two-volume work followed, *The Holy Book of Women's Mysteries*. However, in the early 1980s air pollution in Los Angeles forced her out of the city. The bookshop closed and the coven passed out of her control.

Breathing the purer airs of Oakland, Budapest started another coven, the Laughing Goddess, but it soon collapsed through want of solidarity and the discouraged Budapest decided neither to form nor to join any more covens. She did, however, continue to lecture on the subject and to teach the techniques of ritual to those who cared to know them. She hosted a local radio show, became director of the Women's Spirituality Forum in Oakland, presented the cable television programme *Thirteenth Heaven*, and took to organizing annual events, conferences, camps and retreats.[71]

Budapest's most important recruit was a young woman in her twenties called Miriam Simos. Born in 1951 to Jewish parents, Simos's early high school career in political activism led her to seek out a feminist spirituality. What she found was Budapest's Susan B. Anthony coven. She renounced her Judaism and became a practising Witch, adopting the Craft name of Starhawk as a public and visible sign of her religious stance. After Budapest's coven broke up Starhawk practised the Craft solitarily for many years, deriving much of her own knowledge from meditation and dream, before setting up the Compost coven. This group was formed from the body of students who attended her classes in Witchcraft given at the Bay Area Centre for Alternative Education. Starhawk, of course, became the coven's High Priestess.

Some time later she was initiated into the Faery Tradition and formed another coven, although this time all-female, called Honeysuckle, based upon this tradition. During this period she wrote her most popular work, *The Spiral Dance: A Rebirth of the Ancient Religion of the Great Goddess*, a feminist book based on the Faery Tradition.

In San Francisco she founded Reclaiming, a feminist collective giving private tuition in Witchcraft and public demonstrations. The Reclaiming group has also publicly demonstrated against nuclear weapons and in one incident several of the group were arrested. Starhawk cemented her public profile as the leading feminist Witch with the publication of *Dreaming the Dark* in 1982 and *Truth or Dare: Encounters of Power, Authority and Mystery* in 1987. She continues her work with the collective as well as lecturing and holding workshops internationally on the subject of Witchcraft.[72]

There were other individuals and other groups pushing Witchcraft forward, notably Yvonne and Gavin Frost's Church and School of Wicca, Mary Nesnick's Algard Wicca and George Patterson's so-called Georgianism, but there was to be little in the way of major innovation. The Gardnerian model, transfigured through Alexandrianism and myriad other 'isms', had become the template for Witchcraft.

Witchcraft is now well and truly out of the cauldron. The pioneering work of Valiente, Leek, Sanders and Buckland in devising new forms of the Craft or in bringing it to greater attention has established Gardner's original Wicca as a worldwide religion. The additions of Budapest and Starhawk have widened its appeal and infused it with more radical political ideas, giving it an active social dimension. Despite the in-fighting of Cochrane and the antagonistic feminist separatism of others, Witchcraft is now in a stronger position than ever before.

But it is also still in the fire. It is still being forged, still growing and changing; and it is still subject to the heat of controversy, disapproval and even persecution. So far we have largely concerned ourselves with its history, but to understand what the future might hold for the Craft we must examine it more closely. We must ask, who the Witches are, what they do, and why they do it. As Christianity in the West wanes, and new faiths rise to eclipse it, what will be the fate of Witchcraft?

PART THREE

EMPIRE OF SHADOWS

WITCHCRAFT IN THE WORLD TODAY

7. THE SOCIETY OF WITCHES: THE NEW FACE AND FORM OF WITCHCRAFT

The witches are abroad, and hurtle swiftly aloft, a hideous covey, borne headlong on the skirling blast. To some peak of the Brocken or lonely Cevennes they haste, to the orgies of the Sabbat, the infernal Sacraments, the dance of Acheron, the sweet and fearful fantasy of evil. In delirious tones they are yelling foul mysterious words as they go: 'Har! Har! Har! Altri! Altri!'[1]

On a broomstick of pictures and words we have travelled through the history of Witchcraft. We have seen how the witch has fallen from the celestial sphere, from her position as goddess and priestess, to become an anti-Christian creation, an agent of the Devil bent on the destruction of mankind. And we have seen how Witchcraft has risen again through the efforts of more enlightened thinkers to become a religion in its own right, perhaps not the same religion, or facet of religion, as it was before, but nonetheless, a valid and genuine expression of the spiritual quest.

Now it is time to examine who today's Witches are. It is time to shake the wand of serious, scientific research, of statistical analysis, at the stereotypes that still haunt the perception of Witchcraft. It is time to dispel the sweet and fearful fantasy of evil.

Portrait of a Witch

Red-rimmed eyes, hooked, green nose with a hairy wart, a shock of unkempt hair protruding beneath a tall black pointed hat·– that is what we all knew witches looked like when we were children. Growing older we came to realize that this bedtime bogey was a fiction, but there was nothing to fill its place. Most people dismiss the idea of witches altogether, simply a fiction like their fantastic portrait. Some people, sadly, continue to think of them as something monstrous, inhabiting the borderlands of reality. Some people, happily, know what a witch looks like by looking in a mirror.

We have already met many of the people responsible for inventing, developing and advancing the modern religion of Witchcraft, individuals every one, as different from each other as they were of like mind in their adherence to Witchcraft. Now it is time to consider who Witches are as a group, so that we may see the forest and not just the trees. Our portrait will not just have a single sitter.

With the popular image of the witch burned into the consciousness of the reading public, Gardner was presented with a considerable obstacle in the effective promotion of his new Witchcraft religion. Who in their right minds would want to be thought a warty, old hag? So before he had anything at all of what could be called a 'following', he set about repainting the portrait of the witch.

It was certainly a much more flattering portrait than the stereotype. Gardner's witch was young, intelligent, adventurous, in the phraseology of the time one of the 'bright young things'.[2] Whilst elsewhere he had been happy to repeat freely the theories and opinions of others, he left Murray and Leland on the shelf in this regard.[3] Murray's witches were uninformed backwoodsmen and Leland's were thieves and harlots.[4]

Social studies of modern Witches support Gardner, although the 'intelligent classes' that Gardner referred to are not the usual socioeconomic categories used by the sociologist. Nonetheless, most of the evidence demonstrates a higher than average educational attainment amongst Witches, supporting his claim that they are intelligent.

In the UK the Sorcerer's Apprentice, an occult supplies shop in

Leeds, conducted research into its customer base.[5] They found that occultists, including Witches, have a higher educational attainment than the average. Unfortunately, they declined to indicate what the national average is, or even to demonstrate an awareness of what it is. However, more than a third of those surveyed had gone on to some form of higher education, with a fifth having gone on to university.[6] The anthropologist Tanya Luhrmann also found a large number of graduates amongst her study group and overall a higher than average intelligence.[7] However, she subjectively measured their intelligence, and largely inferred it from their education. The sociologist Michael York also found neo-Pagans and Witches to be well educated.[8] Of those he sampled, over a third were graduates.[9] My own, more recent, research supports this trend. I found that of those Pagans and Witches I interviewed just over a quarter had a degree.[10]

As regards the intelligence of American Pagans, the evidence, though relatively slight, is more congruent. G.G. Scott found a high level of educational attainment amongst her Witches.[11] She estimated that half of those she studied were graduates, including a few who held doctorates. The other half had at least a high school diploma and a few had experience of college education. Unfortunately, she was not precise as to the exact numbers. The second largest group of Pagans surveyed by Margot Adler consisted of sixteen college and graduate students, or 8.2 per cent of the whole.[12] However, her method only picked up those who were still students and hid the actual number of graduates in her survey. Although there are clearly flaws in the methodology employed, the findings would suggest a comparable picture to that in the UK.

Whilst it appears that Witches are indeed 'bright', are they also 'young things'? At least one American commentator has observed that 'crones are out'[13] and the large entertainment market catering to the 'teen witch' phenomenon, from *Sabrina the Teenage Witch* to *Charmed* would suggest a general perception that today's Witches are young. However, sober academic research presents a different picture. Researchers have consistently found few 'young things' and quite a number of middle-aged ones. Most of those involved in Witchcraft are in their thirties and forties.

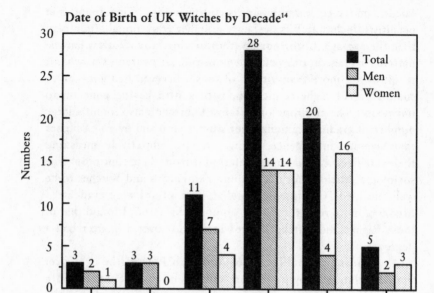

Date of Birth of UK Witches by Decade[14]

In the UK, almost half of the neo-Pagans York surveyed were aged between thirty and forty-nine.[15] Greenwood gave no precise figures, only an age range from early twenties to mid-forties amongst the three covens she studied.[16] The Pagan psychologist Vivianne Crowley similarly only gave an age range, this time from twenty-six to forty-five amongst applicants to her study group.[17] The writer Anthony Kemp, better known for his military history, could only say that most of the Witches he met were in their thirties.[18] In my own research I addressed this issue directly and discovered that the average age of Witches was forty-five.[19]

In the USA, the *Green Egg* magazine survey of 1991 found that the largest single group of its readers, just over a fifth, were aged between thirty-one and thirty-five, and that almost the same number again were aged between thirty-six and forty.[20] Richard Kyle gave the range 'teens to early thirties' for Witches in general.[21] Sociologist Helen A. Berger found neo-Pagans in New England to vary in age from twenty to forty-five, but she failed to break this down into exact proportions.[22] In Canada, Shelley Rabinovitch found more than half of the neo-Pagans she interviewed were over thirty.[23]

There is of course some problem in comparing these figures, not least the cultural divide between America and Britain, but more importantly what was being measured. *Green Egg* is talking about its readers, the Sorcerer's Apprentice about its customers, in the main, most of them occultists – Luhrmann about magicians, Adler and Rabinovitch about neo-Pagans in general, York about neo-Pagans and Witches, Crowley about applicants to a study group who may or may not be Witches. Only Scott, Kyle, Greenwood and I are talking specifically about Witches. Whilst there is some overlap between these groups it has to be borne in mind that they are not strictly synonymous.

Without doubt, however, these modern Witches are not the 'secret, black and midnight hags' of Shakespeare's imagining, nor Murray's ignorant peasants, nor Leland's wicked outcasts. Although they are not exactly Gardner's 'bright young things', they are nonetheless bright, but largely middle-aged.

Gardner classified his Witches as belonging to in what he called the 'intelligent classes', and whilst we have seen that they are intelligent this does not constitute a class. So what class, if any, do Witches belong to? Class can be measured in a number of different ways, chiefly by occupation and by income.

Witches are found in almost every occupation one can think of, from international financier to receptionist, and from teacher to painter and decorator. However, my most recent research reveals a distinct pattern to the sorts of jobs Witches are most likely to do. Working male Witches were found to be most often employed in skilled and semi-skilled jobs. Female Witches generally held higher-status jobs in management or were the owners of their own businesses, although the greatest number of working female Witches were in the health care professions.[24]

In the UK, I found that most of the men studied were unemployed, otherwise unwaged or retired, including one former international banker. Very few of the women were retired, which reflected the general age difference between men and women in the sample. As for female unemployment, again very few of the women were actually unemployed or unwaged, but they were more likely to be students or staying at home as a full-time parent or home-maker. None of the men were in the parent/home-maker category and only one was a student.[25]

Occupation of UK Witches

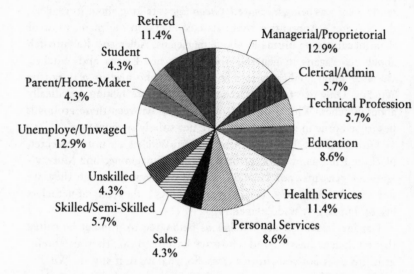

Retired
11.4%

Student
4.3%

Parent/Home-Maker
4.3%

Unemploye/Unwaged
12.9%

Unskilled
4.3%

Skilled/Semi-Skilled
5.7%

Sales
4.3%

Managerial/Proprietorial
12.9%

Clerical/Admin
5.7%

Technical Profession
5.7%

Education
8.6%

Health Services
11.4%

Personal Services
8.6%

In general, the female Witches had the better jobs: more of them were in management or were the proprietors of their own businesses than the men. Two-thirds of all managers/proprietors were women. Several were directors of their own companies, the largest of them employing twenty people. However, the largest number of women were in the health care profession. They constituted almost everyone in this occupational group. We find mostly nurses and therapists (a hypnotherapist and a Kleinian psychotherapist), but no doctors or consultants.[26]

Moreover, most of the unskilled workers were women, as were most of those working in education, most of those in personal services and all of those in sales. The number of female Witches in these categories was low, however. For example, only about one in twenty female Witches was employed as an unskilled worker and only about one in twelve was employed in sales. In addition, roughly one in twenty female Witches was employed in a clerical or administrative position.[27]

The single largest group of male Witches in employment was in the skilled or semi-skilled category; indeed everyone in this category was male. One in eight of all male Witches was a skilled or semi-skilled worker. In contrast to women very few men were in health care, but

An ancient Greek ritual scene dating from the nineteenth century (private collection). A sacred fire burns on the tripod as the new initiate of long-forgotten mysteries receives gifts from the Priestess

The dramatic rock outcrop of Externsteine, Horn-Bad Meinberg, North Rhine-Westphalia, Germany, once the reputed former haunt of the prophetess Veleda and now a magnet for modern Pagans. At the top of the highest peak a temple was anciently carved out of the rock with its window sited on the first rays of the rising sun at the Summer Solstice

A Druid's sickle (private collection). The sickle has become an immediately recognizable symbol of druidry because of its key role in cutting the sacred mistletoe

Lucifer beginning to reign over the souls of sinners in a drawing by John Baptist Medina for John Milton's *Paradise Lost*, London, 1688. When Lucifer fell from Heaven, Paganism fell with him, at least in Christian eyes. The Church's demonization of Pagan practices created a heretical religion of the Devil: Witchcraft

Four Scenes from R.P. Guaccius'
Compendium Maleficarum, Milan,
1626, showing supposed elements of
the Witches' diabolical religion:

baptism

receiving the Devil's mark

the obscene kiss (*osculum infame*)

exchanging a white book (the Bible)
for the Devil's black book

Witches concocting an ointment to be used for flying to the Sabbath. By Hans
Baldung Grien, Strassburg, 1514

Two Dominican monks burned at the stake by order of the Inquisition for allegedly signing pacts with the Devil. From the *Histoire veritable de quatre Iacopins*, Geneva, 1549

Was Aleister Crowley the real father of modern Witchcraft? The numerous borrowings from the works of Crowley in Gerald Gardner's Wicca are unmistakable, but just what role did he play in founding this new religion?

The mother of modern Witchcraft, Doreen Valiente did much to rewrite Gerald Gardner's ritual material, adding more poetic style and removing some of the more obvious borrowings from Aleister Crowley

'The Witches ride to the Brocken's top' (Goethe, *Faust*, Scene XXI). The typical stereotype of the Witch as a broomstick-mounted hag is portrayed here captured *en masse* hanging from a shop display on the infamous Brocken, legendary scene of the Witches' Walpurgisnacht revels in the Harz Mountains, Germany

A modern Witch's altar. Arranged around a contemporary, flowing representation of the Goddess can be seen a leather-bound book of shadows, white candles, iron cauldron, silver chalice, sickle, athame, brass bell, and the gold disc of a pentacle

A Witch invokes. The cauldron and broomstick play important symbolic roles for the modern Witch. Here the broomstick has been used to purify the ritual space before a burnt offering of herbs is made in the cauldron

Faust from the title page to Christopher Marlowe's *The Tragicall Historie of the Life and Death of Doctor Faustus* published by John Wright in London, 1631. The Faust stories were originally Christian morality tales warning that magic can only be practised by entering into a pact with the Devil. Today's Witches, however, although they practise magic, sign no pacts

A modern wood-carving set amongst the daffodils in the grounds of Shambellie House, Dumfries and Galloway, Scotland. Carved from an old tree stump this humble little figure seems to rise out of the earth with the spring flowers, perhaps suggesting the return of the old gods

they were more likely than women to be in the technical professions: computer consultancy, science technicians and supervisory roles in engineering; in fact, three-quarters of all Witches working in the technical professions were male. However, the numbers were not great, only something approaching one in ten male Witches, or about one in forty females had jobs in this sector. Few of the total sample were involved with computers, a finding borne out by Crowley, but in contrast to the profile presented by Adler.[28]

Adler's survey of American Pagans found that a significant proportion of her respondents, 21 out of 195, or 10.8 per cent, were involved with computers as programmers, systems analysts or software developers – something Adler makes much of. None of her respondents was involved in unskilled work and few in semi-skilled occupations. Luhrmann found, as Adler had, that people working in the computer industry predominated, although she does not provide any statistical evidence for this observation. The Sorcerer's Apprentice also indicated that computer programmers and operators had made up a significant, if unspecified, proportion of the occultists surveyed. However, two more recent studies in the UK paint a different picture. Greenwood's Witches typically held down professional positions in health care as laboratory assistants or nurses, in social work and in teaching. Crowley found that of the 111 subjects she surveyed only 5 per cent were involved in computing, the third smallest occupational group. Crowley uses this to refute Adler yet she does not consider cultural or, given the age of Adler's figures, historical differences. Nor does she consider the possible bias of her own sample, drawn as it is from her files of applicants to an unnamed course that she runs.[29]

In the USA, J.G. Melton declared that American Pagans were 'white-collar, middle-class professionals', although this is contradicted by more detailed research carried out by Scott. She found that the Witches she studied were 'from lower-income backgrounds', or as a matter of choice had 'rejected middle-income status' to take 'lower-level skilled and unskilled jobs'. Luhrmann attempted to explain this away by pointing to their low-paid but still 'middle class' occupations in charity, the arts and crafts.[30]

In the UK, Luhrmann also states that the Witches she studied were largely middle class, although she based this conclusion not on their socioeconomic status but on their 'temperamental cast'. This she describes as being 'imaginative, self-absorbed, reasonably intellectual, spiritually inclined . . . emotionally intense' and possibly 'rebellious . . . interested in power . . . dreamy or socially ill at ease'. If this is a description of the middle-class psyche it is not one that most people would readily recognize. Additionally, this description was not received uncritically by the community she described. A reviewer in *The Cauldron* opined that she 'misrepresents its [magic and Witchcraft's] practitioners as dreamy, middle-class romantics'.[31]

The Sorcerer's Apprentice found that their customers largely pursued middle-class occupations. Prominent amongst these were journalism and other forms of professional writing, the Civil Service, management and science. However, no actual figures were given as to the occupational structure of the sample; the author simply states that 'the percentage of skilled and professional careers is phenomenally higher than the national average'.[32] These findings leave much to be desired and any support that they lend to Luhrmann is seriously circumscribed.

Given the wide range of jobs Witches do it is unsurprising that we also see a wide range of incomes. During my research in the UK I found that income ranged from under £5,000 to over £40,000 with an average of just under £18,000, a few thousand pounds short of the national average.[33]

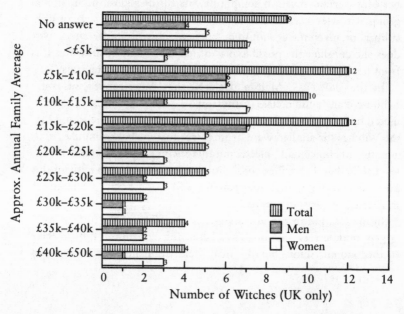

Witchcraft Earnings in the UK

Other research bears this out. In contrast to both the Sorcerer's Apprentice and Luhrmann, York found low levels of income amongst his neo-Pagan/Witchcraft subject group. Just over a third, the single largest group of those he studied, earned between £5,000 and £10,000. The second largest group of people, almost a fifth of those asked, earned less than this. Overall, almost three-quarters had an income of £15,000 or under.[34]

York also asked his subjects what their family's financial status had been during their childhood and gave four categories: poor, lower-middle, upper-middle and wealthy. Just under half described their family's social class as lower-middle. A little over a fifth described it as upper-middle, a little under a fifth as poor and only about one twentieth as wealthy.[35]

York's evidence is more compelling than that of the Sorcerer's Apprentice or Luhrmann since he does not rely on arbitrary and indefensible social classes built on temperament and gives exact figures. However, the measurement of class is notoriously difficult and inviting the subjects to classify themselves is the least satisfactory method.[36]

Reported income levels for Witches in the USA tend to match Scott's characterization. Kirkpatrick also found that the twenty-seven Witches he interviewed were substantially less well-off than the average American, but like so many others undermines the validity of his findings by reporting neither the exact income levels nor the exact numbers reporting these levels.[37]

Witches have generally been characterized as middle class, but the latest research we have would tend to suggest that in both the UK and the USA they are predominately working to lower middle class. Aspirationally, few would see themselves as middle class or subscribe to the attitudes and values usually associated with the middle classes, tending to be more radical and politically left wing. There are some who might even take the term 'middle class' as an insult.[38]

When Shakespeare talked of 'black and midnight hags' he was speaking of the colour of their souls rather than of their skins, and whilst this would not apply to Gardner's Wicca now, today's Witches do at least share one thing with Shakespeare's imagined hags: their skin colour. The ethnic mix of Witches and neo-Pagans is not a varied one. Study after study repeatedly shows a predominance of white Caucasians.

This ethnic picture is broadly similar on both sides of the Atlantic. Kyle reported that American Witches were entirely Caucasian.[39] Berger found neo-Pagans in New England to be predominantly white, a finding she extended to the rest of the USA in her work of 1999. Specifically, she recorded that 90.4 per cent of USA Pagans were white. Most of the non-whites were Native Americans (9 per cent) with a relatively large number of Asians (2 per cent) in contrast to almost negligible Hispanics (0.8 per cent) and African Americans (0.5 per cent).[40] In the UK, Greenwood found that the Witches she surveyed were all of European origin. Crowley reported that neo-Paganism was 'very white', about 99.5 per cent white and only 'slowly changing'. My own findings bear these figures out, but suggest that far from changing, however slowly, things are remaining the same.[41]

We should not be surprised at this nor read too much into it. Wicca was consciously evoked as the ancient indigenous religion of Europe and it draws on the myths and legends of Europe in ways that give it a particularly European appeal (and we would include in this category those of European descent in the New World). It is not, however, a racist religion and does not discriminate against non-whites.

'Women are naturally inclined to witchcraft.'[42] Witches are generally thought of as women. Even though the word itself is not gender specific and evidence from the era of the witch trials shows that men as well as women were accused of being witches, the stereotype, perhaps fed more strongly by the mythic traditions of Greece, Rome and northern Europe, still depicts witches as women. Whilst some of the early research tended to bear this bias out, more recent studies have found that roughly equal numbers of men and women consider themselves to be Witches.

Marcello Truzzi, one of the first sociologists to study modern Witchcraft seriously, simply stated that the typical witch was a 'girl'. Scott found that there were more women than men in the Witchcraft group she investigated by a ratio of three to two. Melton reported that the 'slight majority' of Witches and neo-Pagans were women. *Green Egg* supported this, finding marginally more women amongst their readers than men: 53 per cent to 47 per cent, respectively. Berger, too, found a predominance of women, approximately in the ratio 60:40.[43]

However, in the UK the cult watchdog INFORM[44] stated in 1995 that equal numbers of men and women practised Witchcraft. This general statement has not been borne out by more specific research. Of the neo-Pagans (mostly Witches) that York studied, most were men.[45] In contrast to York, but in agreement with Berger, Crowley stated that there was a 60/40 female to male split in neo-Paganism.[46] I also found a slight predominance of women amongst the Witches I surveyed.[47]

Gender of Witches: US Data

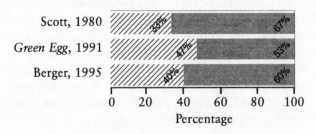

Gender of Witches: UK Data

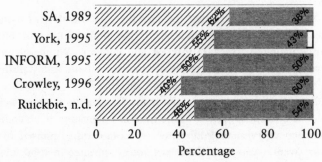

SA (Sorcerer's Apprentice) figures for occultists in general.
INFORM (1995) did not make known the sources for this information
Crowley (1996) is an estimate and not based on statistical analysis

However, popular culture still projects a female identity on to the Witch from *Bewitched* in the 1950s to *The Witches of Eastwick* in the 1980s and *Sabrina the Teenage Witch* and the three witch sisters in *Charmed* in the 1990s. As we have seen the feminist Witchcraft movement consciously draws on the Witch as an image of female power for inspiration, some even going so far as to declare Witchcraft a women's religion. This approach subsumes Witchcraft under a political agenda, however, an agenda that is alien to Gardner's original scheme and contrary to what we know of the history of witchcraft through the trial transcripts of the medieval and early modern periods. Whilst the trial evidence is suspect at the very least, undoubtedly reflecting the Christian bias of the persecutors, it is undeniable that a great many men as well as women were accused and found guilty of witchcraft. Gardner's conception of the priestly partnership of Magus and Witch in the 1950s, reflecting his belief in a divine partnership of God and Goddess, was ahead of its time, bringing women into a central position within religion, which was in the West, dominated as it then was by Christianity, simply unheard of. In contrast, feminist Witchcraft is a reactionary dead end: it demonizes half of humanity and alienates otherwise sympathetic men in a mistaken attempt to empower women by excluding others and isolating themselves.

The Widening Circle

In 1954 Gardner bewailed the fact that Witchcraft was dying out. This was perhaps a calculated part of the plan to launch his new religion: calculated to excite interest and concern. Witchcraft, at least Gardner's Witchcraft, certainly did not die out and today all the indications are that it is growing, if not thriving.[48]

Gardner did not suggest how many Witches he thought were left, which is unsurprising since at the time of publication there could only have been a very small group gathered about Gardner himself. In a little under twenty years after *Witchcraft Today* appeared in 1954, observers of the occult scene were beginning to hazard guesses that there might be as many as one or two thousand active Witches.[49] Since then the guesses have varied widely – and they are all more or less guesses because without a centralized body recording membership of the Craft there can never be any 'official' figures. Both low levels of commitment and drift at the periphery of the 'movement'[50] and high levels of commitment within tightly knit, secret groups make the estimation of the numbers involved difficult. It is also in some instances a point of policy not to disclose numbers. For example, the Oath of Secrecy of the New Wiccan

Church in the USA demands of the Witch 'never to reveal the number of Witches in any given Coven, Order, Tradition, Tribe, Confederation or Nation'. In the UK too, I found that whilst Witches were frequently most willing to discuss intimate personal experiences they were coy, sometimes flatly unwilling, to reveal coven numbers. The situation is further complicated by those practitioners called 'solitaries' who may not take an active part in the movement at all, but who are nevertheless a significant component of it.[51]

In 1980 Russell breezily stated that there were 'several thousand' Witches in Britain.[52] The anthropologist Tanya Luhrmann gives an 'estimated guess' of 3,000 occultists in total; she did not differentiate Witches.[53] In the mid-nineties it was reported in a popular British newspaper that there were an estimated 750 'white witches'.[54]

Witches in the UK: Estimate of Numbers by Decade

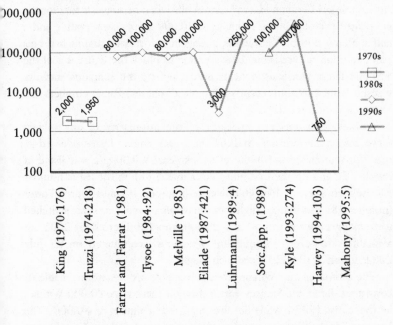

There are no 'official' figures for the number of Witches.
Date of publication is not an exact dating for the figures.
Differing definitions and tools of measurement have been used.

Other sources give much larger estimates. Another British journalist quoted the Witch Nigel Bourne to the effect that there were 100,000 Witches in the UK.[55] The so-called Occult Census of the late 1980s claimed that there were 'over 250,000 Witches/Pagans'. However, this survey – it was not, properly speaking, a census – was of 'slightly over 1,000'. A breakdown of respondents' occult interests revealed that 42 per cent had a 'committed belief' in Witchcraft. A further 26 per cent indicated a serious interest and 16 per cent a curious one, whilst another 16 per cent showed no interest at all. Out of the 1,000 surveyed some 840 showed at least an interest in Witchcraft.[56]

Kyle stated that Witches number from '20,000 to 100,000 worldwide' according to 'more sober estimates' than those of the Witches themselves who 'say their numbers are in the millions'. Unfortunately he does not say who these Witches or sober commentators are. One of the latter may have been the influential Romanian ethnologist Mircea Eliade. World-wide, Eliade thought that there were fewer than 100,000. The British anthropologist Graham Harvey echoes this when he suggests that for the neo-Pagan population an 'estimate of 20,000 seems conservative and a half a million possible'. However, it is again unfortunate that he bases his estimate upon no verifiable data, seeming to pluck the figure out of the air. The latest world estimate is much higher; the religious statistics website Adherents.com recently announced that neo-Pagan numbers had hit the 1 million mark.[57]

A thoroughly modern indicator of the popularity of any subject these days is the internet. In 2001 the search engine Lycos released its top 100 search terms for the previous year. Witchcraft was listed at number 72 and for the first time Wicca made it on to the list at number 91. Related subjects like Hallowe'en (number 19) and Harry Potter (number 38) also figured highly in the results. Lycos has since switched to tracking only the top 50 and thus no top 100 figures for 2001 are available. However, a search on 'Witchcraft' conducted on 27 July 2002, found 1,124,220 listed web pages.

The estimates that Witches themselves give are no more reliable or consistent. Janet and Stewart Farrar thought there were 80,000 Witches in the early 1980s. Melville also reported a figure of 80,000. The London Witch and founder of the House of the Goddess Shan thought that although it was almost impossible to gauge accurately the number of Witches there might be as many as 1 million. 'People often ask me,' said Vivianne Crowley, the Pagan author, psychologist and practising Wiccan, 'how large Wicca is and I have to reply that I have no idea! Wicca has no central organization which can do a headcount, but it is certainly large and growing.' Scott and Adler found a similar problem in gauging numbers in the USA.[58]

I myself abandoned any attempt to assess the number of practising Witches in the UK for exactly this reason. Yet from my own participant observation it is clear that Witchcraft forms a thriving subculture with core and peripheral members and wide diffusion through other youth and subversive subcultural groupings; and having moved in that subculture my own feeling is that interest is growing and the numbers increasing. Its very nature militates against accurate measurement and it is unlikely that we will ever know its full extent.

Witchcraft and, more broadly, neo-Paganism are undoubtedly international phenomena. Witches and Pagans are found all over the world, in Australia, Belgium, Canada, Finland, France, Germany, Holland, Iceland, Italy, Japan, Lithuania, Norway, Poland, Portugal, Romania, Russia, South Africa, Slovenia, Spain, Sweden and the USA – indeed, in almost every country one can think of.[59]

Distribution of Neo-Pagans in the USA

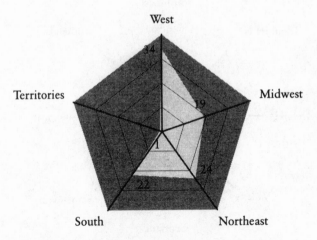

Figures calculated by secondary analysis of Berger (1999:10)
'Neo-Pagan' is Berger's term and includes, but is not restricted to, Witches.

In the USA it is unsurprising, given the state's reputation as a hotbed of new ideas and innovative lifestyles, that the greatest concentration of Witches is to be found in California.[60] If they do not live there the next most likely place is Massachusetts – Salem's reputation is more of a magnet these days – New York, Utah and Ohio. This survey did not find any Witches living in South Dakota, and Tennessee and Washington DC both had negligible communities.

Within the UK the focus of Witchcraft and neo-Pagan activity is in the South-east of England and more particularly within the Greater London area.[61] Roughly a third of the known groups (called 'moots') in England, Scotland, Wales and Ireland are based in the South-east.[62] The Midlands (including East Anglia) is also a hotbed of neo-Paganism with just under a third of the total number of moots active in this area. The North (from the Humber to the Tweed) had just over a quarter of the number of moots operating in the region. The South-west of England had about an eighth. Scotland and Wales each had about a tenth of the total. Ireland (both north and south) had less than a fifth and a single moot was listed for the Channel Islands (based in Jersey).[63]

UK Witchcraft Distribution

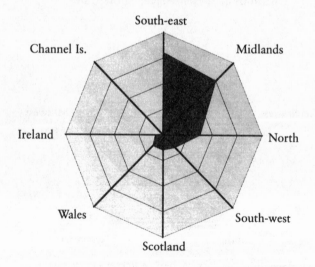

Note: figures based on number of moots advertising per area

The Sorcerer's Apprentice largely supports these findings. The single largest group of those surveyed resided in Greater London, more than a fifth, and over a third of the survey lived in the South-east of England (including Greater London). The South-west saw the least number of those living in England with only about one in fourteen occultists living here. However, in contrast to our earlier findings very few in the Sorcerer's Apprentice's survey lived in the Midlands. The greater number lived in the North. A third of all those the Sorcerer's Apprentice surveyed lived either in the North-east or the North-west of England, with about twice as many living in the East as the West. Of the few remaining, most lived in Scotland or Wales, with only a tiny number residing in Northern Ireland.[64]

Within Europe, the UK is the centre of neo-Pagan activity. The high number of Witches in Germany are, upon inspection, often found to be US military personnel resident in the country. Despite its wide extent, a number of barriers prevent or inhibit Witchcraft's growth in continental Europe. The language barrier is undoubtedly the greatest; few English language books are translated. Given that the principal sources of modern Witchcraft are written in English, this presents a serious impediment. Other barriers include greater religious homogeneity, especially in Eastern Europe where the Catholic and Orthodox churches are resurgent after the fall of the Soviet empire. So both the sources of information for practice and the tolerance of that practice are severely restricted by the prevalent conditions on the Continent.

Coven and Hedgewitch

'The number in a coven never varied, there were always thirteen . . .'[65] In threes or thirteens, Witches always meet in symbolic numbers – or that is what we always thought. Shakespeare's witches in *Macbeth* were three in number, whilst from other sources we are led to believe that a coven is not complete without thirteen members. Thirteen is the number of bad luck. The thirteenth floor is sometimes skipped in skyscrapers. The thirteenth house in a street or hotel room is often either shunned or renumbered. The French call the thirteenth house 12 *bis*, or 12 twice. Friday the 13th still excites superstitious dread as well as inspiring a series of slasher horror films. Thirteen is the baker's or Devil's dozen. But by meeting in groups of thirteen Witches were following an ancient tradition: Christ had his twelve disciples, King Arthur seated twelve of his best knights around the Round Table, Robin Hood's band of merry men comprised twelve and King Edward III enshrined the number in his Order of the Garter.

Triskaidekaphobia

The source of the irrational fear of the number thirteen (triskaidekaphobia) is uncertain. For Christians the number evokes the Last Supper at which Christ and his twelve disciples, including his betrayer Judas, sat down to what would be their last meal together before Christ's arrest and eventual crucifixion. Friday the 13th combines this unlucky number with the day on which he is reputed to have been crucified. However, thirteen's reputation is older than the Christian tradition. According to the myths of northern Europe, Loki, the god of fire and the original Prince of Lies, imposed himself upon a banquet in Valhalla, the home of the gods, bringing the number of guests to thirteen. Balder, the personification of light, was the first to rise from the table and subsequently the first to die (by the machinations of Loki).

On St George's Day, 23 April 1350, King Edward III founded England's highest order of chivalry, the Order of the Garter (also known as the Order of St George). He had first conceived the idea six years earlier when, according to the legend, as he was dancing with the Countess of Salisbury her garter slipped from her leg. Gathering it up and putting it on his own left leg the King cried, '*Honi soit qui mal y pense*' (Shame on him who thinks evil of it). This became the Order's motto and is emblazoned in gold on its blue, gilt-edged ribbon. One can still see it encircling the coat of arms of the British royal family.

The Order comprised twelve knights under the King and twelve under the Prince of Wales, that is, two 'covens' of thirteen. The King as its leader wore a mantle covered in a total of 168 garters which with the one he wore on his leg made 169, or thirteen times thirteen. Margaret Murray, and after her Gerald Gardner, made much of these facts. Gardner especially saw the Countess as a Witch and read Witchcraft into every element in the story. For him it establishes the sacred thirteen at the heart of British aristocracy and demonstrates the use of the garter as a badge of rank amongst Witches. More important, however, this event and the subsequent symbology adopted by the Order appeared to prove that Witchcraft was indeed a religious force within medieval society. None of these conclusions can be regarded as anything other than speculation, although the facts of the matter remain tantalizingly suggestive.

'Twelve women dancing round a man who is stark naked except for garters.'[66] In the dark recesses of an underground chamber, buried beneath the French countryside, a strange scene confronts visitors. In the flickering light of an uncertain power supply, drawings dating from pre-history grace the rough walls, a gartered, but otherwise naked, man stands in the centre of a ring of twelve dancing women. Gerald Gardner took this as evidence of the antiquity of witchcraft and the use of the garter as a badge of authority amongst witches. He did not even consider that the prehistoric painting might show anything other than witches at their worship. We should not be surprised to learn that this piece of archaeological evidence had previously been presented by Margaret Murray in support of her thesis. Closer examination by more careful eyes, however, subsequently revealed the cave drawing to be a number of pictures superimposed upon each other; the women danced on their own and the man appeared to be part of a hunting scene – their meeting was entirely fortuitous.

Others have pointed to the Cave of Bats in Spain as offering evidence of the antiquity of the thirteen-strong coven. Within this Neolithic burial chamber and amongst a clutter of fifty-eight skeletons was discovered a seated female skeleton surrounded by twelve others in a neat semicircle. Needless to say, this arrangement of millennia-old bones might appear to be in line with recent ideas of a witches' coven, but on its own it proves nothing.

It is indisputable that groups of thirteen have indecipherable folkloric meaning, but the evidence that any of these groups were covens of witches rests more upon the desire of the theorists than on reality. Even in the early modern trial records very few accused witches claimed to meet as thirteen. The most prominent of these are the case of Isobel Gowdie at Auldearne, Scotland, in 1662 and that of Ann Armstrong at Newcastle, England, in 1673. Margaret Murray cited the reference to eighteen covens of thirteen,[67] but as with her other arguments, this position has been challenged for relying on evidence obtained under torture and clerical error, and for emphasizing a limited number of cases that support her argument over the greater number of cases that do not. Thirteen remains a number to conjure with, but as we shall see even modern Witches rarely meet in these numbers.

'The witches do say that they form themselves much after the manner of Congregational Churches, and that they have a Baptism, and a Supper, and Officers among them, abominably resembling those of our Lord.'[68] Margaret Murray's tremendous 'Will to Witchcraft' created a universal hierarchy of coven organization drawn from slender and inconclusive historical evidence. At the head of the organisation was the God himself, or a Grand Master acting as vice-regent and sometimes known by the title of 'Devil'. The leader was assisted by a Summoner (or Fetch) responsible for the administration of the group, from calling attendance to the Sabbat to scouting for new recruits. The Grand Master was further assisted by a Maid, or Queen of the Sabbat, who acted as consort. Sir Walter Scott described her in his *Letters on Demonology and Witchcraft* as 'a girl of personal attractions, whom Satan placed beside himself, and treated with particular attention'.

Gerald Gardner's coven structure was patterned on a similar model with a Magus and High Priestess as leaders of the group. He built a special provision into his Wicca, allowing women to take sole leadership of the coven: the High Priestess would symbolically strap on the Magus's magical sword. The Murrayite model was male led and under Gardner's reign was male led, but the coven has subsequently grown further in the direction of female leadership.

> *Ye shall assemble in some desert place,*
> *Or in a forest all together join*

This injunction from Aradia, the Goddess of the Witches, to her followers from *The Gospel of the Witches* would seem to indicate that group involvement is a matter of dogma in Witchcraft.[69] Yet when the journalist Margot Adler surveyed Witchcraft in the USA in the 1970s she found solitary practitioners to be in the majority.[70] The most recent findings from the USA bear this out, but only fractionally: some 50.4 per cent, it was discovered, practise Witchcraft alone.[71] However, the latest research in the UK shows that most Witches are involved in a group, or indeed groups of some sort.[72] Almost three-quarters of those questioned said they were in a group, with around two-thirds of those belonging to two or more groups. These groups might range from three to forty people, but in practice very few had over twelve members. Most had between seven and eleven. On average the British coven consists, not of thirteen, but of ten Witches. Surprisingly, no one mentioned the magic number thirteen at all.

Today's Witch has spent on average some five and a half years in his or her group, which meets once a month for an average of three and a half hours. Witches have described the coven as being like a family[73] and some of their rituals emphasize that through simulated rebirthing psychodramas.[74]

The green-faced, warty hags of our childhood nightmares always met to plot disaster, to cast evil spells and curse their enemies. In the Middle Ages and the early modern period, though they were without the unearthly pallor, they met, it was widely believed, for the same reasons – with the additions of Devil-worship and orgiastic feasting. Now the hags have flown with the cock-crow of reason – as we have seen above, replaced by respectable middle-aged, lower-middle-class folk. But one question still remains unanswered: why do today's Witches meet at all and what do they get up to when they do?

Nowadays Witches only meet with the best of intentions, at least according to the latest research from the UK: 'To celebrate our religion and further our spiritual growth. It's not just about personal growth, but a great religious friendship.'[75] Most of those asked said they met to provide mutual support, facilitate the meeting of like minds, share spiritual experiences or combine magical energies in a common purpose – reasons that can be categorized as 'communitarian'. In contrast, very few met for what could be considered selfish reasons. The percentages are laid out in the pie chart below.

Group Purpose

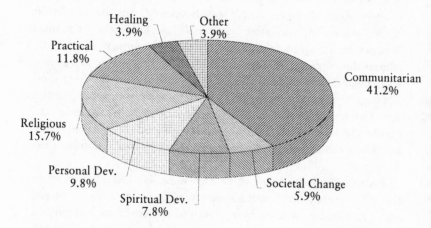

We can see from this that Witches also meet to develop themselves, either spiritually or in some personal way, such as self-discovery, self-knowledge, self-improvement, perfection of the inner self, even 'to make us feel better', or 'to be at peace', with oneself, others or nature. Others gave a specifically religious purpose for the group, ranging across religious expression, religious celebration, seasonal celebration, finding the deities and simply worship.

The remainder identified healing, societal change or some practical purpose as the principal reason for their group meetings. Those who saw their group's purpose as societal change identified several key issues: changing society's perception of the movement in general, which included working for greater official recognition and against hostile others; working for the good of other people generally; working specifically against perceived immoralities such as the arms trade or ecological destruction; and in one case working to bring the force of magic back into the world, a literal re-enchantment. The practical category included some community action such as instruction and training, and more technical issues such as the ability of a group to 'raise more energy'. A very few replied that the group was purely the 'ego-trip' of its leader, or for their own 'selfishness' and personal pleasure (grouped under the 'other' category).

One of the interesting things here is that male and female Witches did not give the same answers. For instance, it was only men who said that the purpose of their group was personal development. On the other hand, women were five times more likely to give a practical purpose for their group. More women gave a religious answer and all of those who said the purpose of their group was healing were women. Yet twice as many men as women gave societal change as their answer and three times as many men said their group's purpose was spiritual development. Notwithstanding this, there was one area of accord: fairly similar numbers gave a community-type purpose.

If we were to draw our portrait of a Witch now, what would we see? A man in his forties, or a woman in her thirties, Caucasian, reasonably well educated, not earning much but probably not too concerned about material things, someone that demographers would call lower middle class. In the USA, our Witch is probably a solitary practitioner, in the UK a member of a coven and more often than not two. They attend once a month and have been doing so for a little over five years, and describe the purpose of their group in communitarian terms.

The explosion of the 'teen witch' phenomenon is media-driven and contrary to the current observable demographics of Witchcraft. The 'naughty schoolgirl', 'St Trinian's' style pranks of the High School Witches in the film *The Craft* and the TV series *Sabrina, The Teenage Witch*, although the product of a male-dominated entertainment industry, are aimed at the female teenage market and in their ruthless pursuit of the teenage dollar accidentally but inevitably draw more and younger people into Witchcraft. Yet where Gardner originally appealed to both sexes with his portrayal of Witchcraft, these modern media images, by exclusively portraying the witch as a female figure, attract only girls. Even as the media moves further from its gleeful misrepresentation of Witchcraft as Satanism and closer to an accurate depiction of its theory and practice, it retains this fantasy of the female witch. It will be interesting to see what the long-term effect of this media distortion will be.

8. CALLING DOWN THE MOON:
BELIEF AND EXPERIENCE IN
MODERN WITCHCRAFT

'If I command the moon, it will come down; and if I wish to with-hold the day, night will linger over my head . . .'[1] Whilst the Witches of the ancient world really were thought to be able to draw the moon down from the heavens, today's Witches see little benefit in pulling the earth's satellite out of its well-established orbit. Instead they seek to connect with the power of the moon and draw into themselves its lunar energy. The Moon, capitalized, also stands for the Goddess herself, a triumvirate of waxing Maiden Diana, full Mother Cybele, and waning Crone Hecate.[2] So when a Witch draws down the moon she is not merely seeking to increase her power, but brings the Goddess into herself in a symbolic counterpart to the Christian Mass.

We have already met many of the gods and goddesses associated with Witchcraft from the Pagan Hecate to the Christian Devil, we have already seen how the 'Father of Modern Witchcraft', Gerald Gardner, presented Celtic Cernunnos and Italian Aradia as the deities of Wicca, but what do today's Witches worship? How do they actually see deity? Is it an impersonal force moving through their lives or do they have a personal relationship with superhuman beings?

God of a Thousand Names

'God is an expression we use to try to explain in everyday language what is not an everyday occurrence.'[3] That was how one Witch explained his idea of the divine to me, but through in-depth research carried out in the UK towards the end of the 1990s I found that Witches' beliefs in deity ranged widely, from impersonal creative forces at one extreme to actual personalities taking a part in the individual's life at the other.[4] The range of belief systems expressed ran the gamut from atheism to pantheism. In all, fifteen categories were identified, not including the ubiquitous 'don't know'.[5] The theistic categories were, in ascending order of theological sophistication:

- goddess monotheism
- unequal duotheism,[6] where one of the deities is accorded greater significance
- equal duotheism
- dualism – what we might think of, to paraphrase Christian doctrine, as the 'Holy Duality', that is the God and Goddess as one god
- trinitarianism, where the God and Goddess are seen as intermediary entities emanating from an ultimate divine source beyond
- metaphorically dualistic monotheism (MDM), where the God/Goddess is a means of understanding the force beyond without existence as separable entities
- metaphorically polytheistic monotheism (MPM), where many gods are seen as the method of understanding the one true God
- metaphorically polytheistic duotheism (MPD), where many gods are essentially expressions of an ultimate God and Goddess
- panentheism, where everything is in God and where deity is both immanent and transcendent
- egoentheism, an admitted neologism to denote the belief that the individual is a part of, or is in deity which consequently and necessarily reciprocates by being part of, or in the individual – distinct from panentheism because only the individual is involved in this relationship with deity
- all-theism, another neologism encompassing all forms of belief in God; whilst 'pan' means 'all' it was clearly not

179

pantheism as it is commonly understood

There was also a number of tacitly atheistic belief systems:

- symbolization, the interpretation of deity in purely symbolic terms as representing balance in the form of a God and Goddess, perhaps including a more psychological interpretation of God and Goddess as archetypal symbols
- constructionism, where deity is seen as a personally constructed conception, possibly with independent action
- naturism, the belief in, worship of or reverence for, nature, but not necessarily as a divine being.

Between the theistic and atheistic positions lay a range of answers that could only best be described as impersonal (the fifteenth category). These people believed in a deity but thought that it did not have a personality, that it was something unknowable, a creative or life force, a power or energy, or an ineffable consciousness.

The largest number of Witches asked (over a quarter of the total) believed that deity was an impersonal entity known through a metaphorical duality of God and Goddess (MDM).[7] Most of these same people also described their relationship with deity as personal.[8] There was no simple differentiation between personal and impersonal deity; instead they expressed a third position in which deity can be both a personal entity or entities, God and Goddess, gods and goddesses, and an impersonal force. Witches refer to the God and Goddess as 'personalizations', 'emanations' and 'intermediaries' of an impersonal force, hence the use of the additional term metaphorical. A Witch in her thirties expressed this position in the following way: 'There are various gods and goddesses within nature that are half gods and half a powerful energy force – a force represented by the deities, they embody and represent the different energies of the force; and the easiest way to contact them is by personifying them.'[9]

Only a tenth of the Witches asked specifically stated in unequivocal terms that they considered deity to be an impersonal force. One man put it thus: 'The whole universe is divine. Being truly in tune one recognizes this. I don't need gods and goddesses.'[10] There were divers other answers that also equated with an impersonal view of deity. One individual saw deity as purely symbolic and three others saw it as a personal construct. However, this did not significantly increase the impersonal viewpoint, rising from a tenth to an eighth of the total.

Other less popular beliefs were equal duotheism, dualism and MPM.[11] There were even fewer naturists, trinitarians, or unequal duotheists. Most of the unequal duotheists were women who accorded more importance to the Goddess; none of them identified themselves primarily as Witches, but more loosely as Pagans.[12] The other persuasions accounted for only a very few of the Witches asked, in most cases only one or two people: two pantheist; one all-theist; an egoentheist; one woman who believed in goddess monotheism; and one person whose answers fell into the MPD category. Only one person did not know what they thought deity was. It is notable that it was mostly women who believed the Goddess was more important a deity than the God.

Witches hold a great variety of beliefs about deity, but how do they describe their relationship with deity? One Witch described it thus: 'In a way we are all part of a jigsaw puzzle; and a personal jigsaw puzzle within a planetary, cosmic jigsaw puzzle.'[13] The largest number of Witches answered in terms best described as 'personal'.[14] This covered relationships that were described as friendships, partnerships, intimate, guiding, even everyday, and of course personal itself. A few described their relationship in strongly emotional terms such as 'very deep', 'loving' or 'powerful'.[15]

Those Witches who did not have a 'personal' relationship most often described it in 'mystical' terms, that is they saw their relationship in terms of achieving union with deity, or believed that there was no separation between man and deity, that deity was everything (and so, in a sense, were already in union). The next most common answer was 'religious', that is they described their relationship in terms of worship, or as being part of a priesthood. Witches also gave other interesting answers; some saw deity as a product of themselves ('constructed'), others saw it in technical or exploitative terms as a resource to be used ('technical').[16]

Finally, there were a very few Witches who gave an 'a-religious' answer, that is, they were non-worshipping, or regarded deity as anthropomorphic representations of nature and as such not subject to a relationship. Two I talked to described their relationship with deity as a form of their own personal development ('developmental').[17]

Witches' Relationships with their Gods

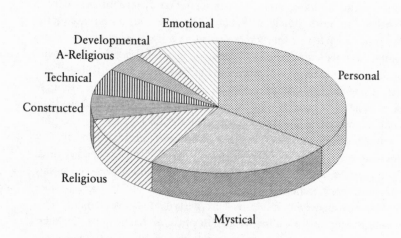

Men and women had different sorts of relationships with their gods. More than double the number of women than men said they had a personal relationship.[18] More women than men also said that they had a religious relationship,[19] whilst more men than women described their relationship in emotional terms, accounting for all of those giving an a-religious answer.[20]

Amongst the other answers given there was far less to differentiate male and female Witches. Most notably about a fifth of both said their relationship was mystical.[21] A 'technical' response was given by equal numbers of men and women, as was a 'constructed' answer.[22] Amongst the few who said their relationship was developmental there were equal numbers of men and women; and there was little difference between the sexes of those who gave no answer at all.[23]

Witches' Relationships with their Gods
Differences Between Male and Female Witches

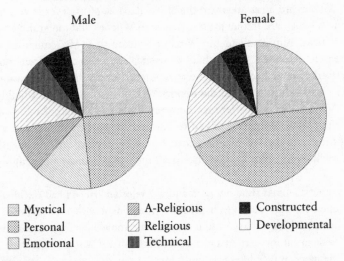

Male   Female

▨ Mystical	▨ A-Religious	■ Constructed
▨ Personal	▨ Religious	☐ Developmental
▨ Emotional	■ Technical	

We see that most Witches, both men or women, conceived of deity as a metaphorical dualistic monotheism (MDM). Most of these same Witches subsequently stated that they had a personal relationship with the deity (of whatever conception), but here men and women gave different answers with only half as many men as women stating that they had a personal relationship.

The Mysteries of Witchcraft

What effect do the rituals of Witchcraft have upon the people who practise them, and what other mystical experiences do they undergo? From my own research and conversations with Witches it is clear that what we might call the mystical has a very profound role to play in their lives. It touches upon their deepest and most intimate experiences, experiences which, by their very nature, can be difficult or embarrassing to talk about. The questions of extent – how many Witches experience something that they would describe as mystical – and valuation – how important this is to them – can be reduced to a simple numerical scale, but the question of what those experiences were requires an open-ended, qualitative approach, and hence probes more revealingly the intimate world of today's Witches.

Witches are no strangers to the unusual. Most of us never have experiences which are frequent occurrences to Witches and integral parts of their lives. Almost all of the Witches I talked to in the course of my research described having had a mystical experience; indeed many claimed to have had several – one reported 'several hundred' (case no. 11) – and almost all rated the importance of these experiences highly.[24]

Again there is a difference between male and female Witches. All of the female Witches I talked to had had what they thought of as a mystical experience, whilst those few who replied in the negative were all men.[25] The women also rated their experiences more highly.[26]

About Lammas time my wife and a few other friends had decided upon a ritual – cutting a hazel stick, threading it with a silver thread and attaching a berry on the end to drag knowledge from a pool. I went to cut the stick in a place we call the Hazel Wood. It was dark, the moon was hidden by clouds, but the tractors were still out with their lights on, going up and down the fields. Perhaps I should tell you a bit about the wood. It was on a slope leading into a gully, a deep gully. It was dark and I couldn't really see where I was going and I thought, 'This is stupid, I could fall down the slope, or anything.' Then I saw this green patch, like lights moving through the trees, and started walking towards it. 'Oh God,' I thought, 'it's a body. What do I tell . . . you know, I'll have to report this.' But as I got closer to it I saw it was too big to be a body. It was like a green energy source in the shape of a being. It turned and smiled, and then rolled into a ball and rolled down the slope. I thought, 'Should I follow it?' Anyway I sat down for a minute, and the moon came out and I could see everything clearly. I cut the stick and put the silver thread and the berry on it. I put it over my shoulder and started back, and then I felt three tugs on it. I turned round and saw nothing there. This was like it saying, 'You don't know everything.' I wasn't going to tell anybody but when I got back they all said, 'What happened?' Because my eyes were shining like crystals.[27]

This dramatic mystical experience was recounted to me by a Wiccan in his fifties. The people I talked to in the course of my research had experienced all manner of feelings, phenomena and events that they described as mystical, ranging from an awareness of the presence of a god to more apparently mundane things. For one woman 'walking through the woods in autumn' aroused a sense of peace and a 'feeling of connection' along with 'gardening and walking the dogs', what she called 'general, everyday things'.[28] Someone else reported both a drop in temperature and the feeling that someone else was there when working with the Egyptian deities.[29] Several of these sorts of experiences were connected with woods, as in the first example. One Witch experienced the spontaneous transformation of a tree into the Horned God (the principal male deity in Wicca) and another felt that there was a strong presence in the trees that regarded her with the intensity of a spotlight.[30]

As I talked to Witches about their mystical experiences it became clear that the largest number of them, just a shade over a quarter, had experienced numinous phenomena, that is, experiences suggesting or revealing the presence of a divine being or preter-human entity. About half as many reported experiencing some form of xenophrenia (altered state of consciousness), which could range from a heightened sense of awareness of their surroundings to a shift in consciousness to another plane of reality involving other-worldly beings (and hence hints of numinosity). Closely related to this, several Witches described experiencing some sort of psychic phenomenon: clairvoyance, telepathy, telekinesis or some auditory or physical manifestation.

But these were not the only mystical experiences they had. The more I talked to Witches the more strange and unusual were the experiences they told me about. Some underwent revelatory experiences that imparted some previously unknown information through mysterious means, others witnessed magical occurrences, which were usually instances in which some magical action was perceived to produce a result. Some achieved theosis, where the individual felt they had become a god or been united with a god, others experienced complete revaluations of the everyday as mystical. Some had mystical encounters with nature, frequently involving a sense of connection, or communion, others experienced synchronicity, the fortuitous coincidence of meaningful events. Some had mystical experiences involving death, either an acceptance of death, often as a specific revelation, or communication with the dead, others underwent transformative experiences that changed their lives in some unspecified way. Still others had ecsomatic experiences, including those described as out-of-body experiences and astral projection. The figures can be seen set out in the pie chart below.

Male and female Witches largely described experiencing the same sorts of things. The largest number of both sexes described experiencing numinous phenomena and the second largest experienced xenophrenia.[31] Fewer male Witches described some sort of psychic phenomenon, whilst fewer women than men reported an experience of nature mysticism. Female Witches were more likely to revalue the everyday as mystical. Most of those who did not know what sort of mystical experience they had had, or who gave no answer, were men.[32]

The Varieties of Mystical Experience in Witchcraft

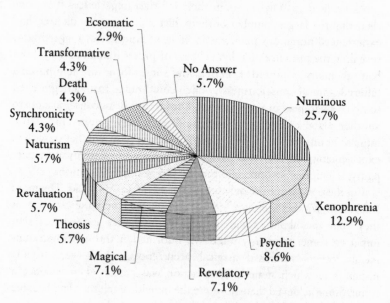

Witches are mystically experienced people. Most of them have had at least one experience that they consider to be mystical and many have had many more. They tend to value these experiences highly; most of them described them as numinous, that is, experiences suggesting or revealing the presence of a divine being. Witches have complex beliefs about the divine, but they mostly see it as something with which they can have a personal relationship; and judging from these findings on mystical experience this relationship is directly experienced in their lives.

Human Rites: The Role of Ritual in Witchcraft

The High Priestess stands skyclad within the circle, arms outstretched, clothed only in the flickering candle-light. The High Priest kneels before her and, drawing an inverted triangle upon her from right breast to left breast to womb, returning to right breast, begins the incantation: 'I invoke thee and call upon thee, Mighty Mother of us all, bringer of all fruitfulness; by seed and by root, by stem and bud, by leaf and flower and fruit do I invoke thee to descend upon the body of this thy servant and priestess.'

He throws out his arms:

> Hail Aradia! From the Amalthean Horn
> Pour forth thy store of love; I lowly bend
> Before thee, I adore thee to the end,
> With loving sacrifice thy shrine adorn.
> Thy foot is to my lip [kisses] my prayer upborne
> Upon the rising incense-smoke; then spend
> Thine ancient love, O Mighty One, descend
> To aid me, who without thee am forlorn.

As he rises and steps back the High Priestess draws a pentagram in the air before her with her wand:

> Of the Mother darksome and divine
> Mine the scourge, and mine the kiss;
> The five-point star of love and bliss—
> Here I charge you in this sign.

They have drawn down the moon.[33]

Our culturally transmitted ideas about witches suggest that they always meet under a full moon to work their magic. But has anyone actually tried to find out if this is true of today's modern Witches? Conducting my research into Witchcraft practices in the UK I discovered that whilst some Witches meet regularly every month, most of them do not. Almost all of the people I talked to attended an organized ritual at least once a year and only 5.7 per cent never took part in such rituals. Only one in eight regularly attended a monthly ritual. Most (27.2 per cent), roughly one in three, attended an organized ritual somewhere between eight and twelve times a year. Slightly less (21.4 per cent), or about one in five, attended only between two and eight rituals a year. A little more than this (22.8 per cent) only ever attended a ritual twice or less per year. A roughly similar number (22.9 per cent), or about one in four, were at the other extreme, attending rituals more often than every month – up to fifty-two times a year, that is every week. Whilst about a third (38.5 per cent) only went to a ritual four or fewer times per year, the majority (61.5 per cent) regularly attended four or more a year. These figures are set out in more detail in the chart below.[34]

Frequency of Ritual Attendance

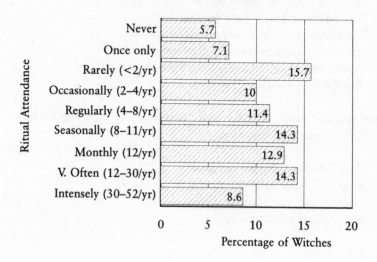

There were noticeable differences between the number of times male and female Witches met. More women than men never or only once attended an organized ritual, but more women than men also attended very often. At the bottom end of the scale there was little difference between the numbers of men and women who never attended rituals or went only once. At the upper end the differences were greater: almost all (80 per cent) of those attending very often were women. One in five women attended very often compared to less than one in sixteen men. Two-thirds of those attending rituals monthly were women, but at the top of the scale we find equal numbers of men and women (but proportionally slightly more men) attending intensely.[35]

Around the middle of the scale more men than women attended seasonally (eight or more times a year but less than monthly). About one in five male Witches attended seasonally as opposed to only one in twelve women. But more women than men attended regularly (between four and eight times a year): about one in six female Witches compared to less than one in sixteen male. Again the tables turn and we find that more men than women attended occasionally (that is, between two and four times a year). Thus, about one in five men compared to only about one in forty women attended occasionally. When we get to those attending rarely the numbers even out. About the same number of male and female Witches, roughly one in six, attended rarely.[36]

Whilst most Witches, in general, attended four or more rituals a year, it was the women who attended most often. Where men were more inclined to attend rituals only occasionally or seasonally, women preferred to attend monthly or very often.

'Eight Sabbats, thirteen full moons and thirteen new moons . . .'[37] When I asked the Witches what rituals they usually attended more than half of them identified the seasonal cycle. The few Witches who did not usually do so mentioned a rite of passage, a convocational meeting or a lunar ritual. A number were not specific, and, of course, there were those who did not attend group rituals at all.[38]

Given the number of different rituals that were mentioned I was curious to know which of them had some special importance for them. Some people made no distinction between any of the rituals they had attended, but most could clearly identify one that held a special place in their memory. Perhaps unsurprisingly, the single largest group again identified a seasonal ritual, that is an event like Beltane or Samhain marking solstitial or ancient agricultural observances. Given the centrality of initiation in most of the literature on Witchcraft it was remarkable to discover how few of the Witches I talked to considered this, the initiation of either themselves or someone else, to be their most important ritual. To those who defined themselves as Gardnerian or Alexandrian Wiccans initiation was more important than it was to those who were non-aligned or more eclectic Witches. Almost three-quarters of all those who said an initiation ceremony had been their most important ritual identified themselves as Wiccan.[39]

Unlike Christianity, which has monopolized the ritualization of many of the major transition points in our lives – principally births, marriages and deaths – Witchcraft appears to play a lesser role during these peak experiences. Few Witches said that a marital ceremony had been the most important to them, and only one mentioned a child's naming ceremony (often referred to as a Wiccaning). This is undoubtedly due to the youth of the religion, but it also reflects its prominence as a mystery religion, having a specialized purpose rather than a life-encompassing role. But, if we group together all those who said some sort of rite of passage – the initiations, marriages and namings – had been their most important ritual we find that fractionally over a quarter gave this sort of answer. This is a little more than those who mentioned only a seasonal rite.[40]

Many Witches also mentioned some non-seasonal ritual, which could range from the Earth Spirit Festival to a Tantric ritual. Also non-seasonal, but more specific, were those few who mentioned a healing ritual. The relative unimportance of healing rituals stands in contrast to the importance of healing as the prime purpose of magic, as we will discover later. Instead we see that the group ritual is primarily a place for seasonal worship and marking significant life experiences with rites of passage.[41]

There was little difference between the sexes on this issue. Most notably more female Witches than male mentioned a marital, naming or healing ritual; almost twice as many women said that a marital ritual had been the most important to them. No men mentioned either a naming or healing ritual. Also, whilst roughly similar proportions of men and women said that a seasonal ritual had been important, fewer men than women said that a non-seasonal ritual had been the most important.[42]

We have discovered what rituals are most important to the Witches, but not why. This was my next question and the largest number, about one in five, gave what we might call a 'social' type of answer. This covered a range of answers including a sense of community, a sense of common purpose, sharing, support, bringing people together, the healing of others, the spiritual development of others and even simply a 'good atmosphere'. As one respondent said: 'The Sabbats are a celebration of life, a connection to the natural cycles through which we understand ourselves better. Also working for others, healing – a sense of unity, togetherness.'[43] The essential element of all these answers was the coming together of people. Excluding those who did not take part in any rituals whatsoever and those who declined to answer, the number giving a social response as a percentage of all those who did attend rituals and did give an answer rises to approximately one in four.[44]

The second largest number – about one in eight of everyone I talked to, or about one in six of all those taking part in rituals and giving an answer – said that the importance of the ritual lay in its being emotionally moving. Beyond these two key areas there was a wide range of additional answers. Some of the remaining Witches cited a mystical experience (mostly a numinous or xenophrenic one), whilst others gave a religious answer (largely to do with the seasonal significance of the ritual). Only one mentioned her own spiritual development as giving the ritual its key importance. Others mentioned the effect of setting them upon their spiritual path, or reinforcing their commitment to their path. Personal satisfaction was also an important factor for some. This category included the ritual being the first the Witch had led or organized, one that they had themselves designed, or one that was in some other way a unique event. Some Witches mentioned personal development (and here this included self-empowerment, which we elsewhere separated from personal development to stand as a category on its own). One Witch noted the sense of meaningfulness that the ritual gave. Another experienced a phenomenal effect, some sort of unexplained and extraordinary occurrence accompanying the ritual. A significant minority were simply indifferent to the effects of organized rituals and in one case there was open hostility to them as a sign of dependence on others and in itself unnecessary to being a Pagan.[45]

Gender is particularly revealing in this instance. The majority of those who gave a 'social' answer were female Witches. Yet this divergence is not carried into the second largest group, where although there is again a gender difference it is not quite so marked. A more marginal majority of those who said the importance of ritual lay in its emotional effect were women. Equal numbers of both sexes who gave no answer, had said previously that no rituals had been of importance, or did not know which ritual had been important or why.[46]

Equal numbers of both sexes also said that the ritual was important for reasons of commitment. However, this is where cross-gender agreement ended. All those giving phenomenal and negative answers were men. Conversely, all those giving as answers meaningfulness or spirituality were women.[47]

More men than women said that their ritual was important because it was personally developmental. More men also gave a mystical answer. Yet slightly more men than women were also indifferent to the rituals they attended. On the other hand, more women than men gave religious answers or said that the ritual had been personally satisfying.[48]

Ritual is undoubtedly important to Witches, but it is by no means necessary to Witchcraft. Whilst most Witches frequently attend some sort of organized ritual many others hardly ever go to one. What was clear was that most Witches when they did attend a ritual went to a seasonal rite of some kind. These sorts of rituals were the most important, but we also saw how the many rites of passage were also significant ritual events for the Witches who took part in them. All the many rituals of Witchcraft, the seasonal festivals, rites of passage and myriad other ceremonies touched them most deeply because of their social effect, the quiet joy that comes of sharing and celebrating with others, or the personal emotional satisfaction that comes of expressing one's religion. Whilst not every Witch attends a ritual, those that do cement the community of Witchcraft with their own joy in doing it.

9. Drawing the Magic Circle: The Definition, Use and Effect of Magic in Witchcraft

'I conjure thee, O Circle of Power, that thou beest a meeting-place of love and joy and truth; a shield against all wickedness and evil; a boundary between the world of men and the realms of the Mighty Ones; a rampart and protection that shall preserve and contain the power that we shall raise within thee. Wherefore I bless thee and consecrate thee, in the names of Cernunnos and Aradia.'[1]

·The chants rose and fell on Samhain night from the lips of the dancers whirling round a blazing bonfire. Under the night sky, bright with winter-sharp starlight and a crescent moon resting on the tree-tops, in a clearing in an orchard at the end of many dark lanes, in a little village within commuting distance of London, Witches worked their magic. They began by opening the magic circle, calling the elemental Guardians or Watchtowers of the four quarters to estab-lish the sacred space of Witchcraft and scene of magical operations.

As she carves the invisible with her Athame, shaping a magic circle where reality becomes unreal and the unreal real, what does our modern Witch mean by magic? What does our modern Witch use this magic for? And what effect does it have upon her? We will examine both written accounts and previously unpublished interview tran-scripts to explore the varieties of definition, to attempt a classification of such variety, to reveal what Witches use magic for and to discover what the effect of practising magic is.

The Pretender's Art

'The pretended art of influencing the course of events, and of producing marvellous physical phenomena, by processes supposed to owe their efficacy to their power of compelling the intervention of spiritual beings, or of bringing into operation some occult controlling principle of nature.' Thus does the *Oxford English Dictionary* define magic. Yet as we shall see the pretence is of the nature of theatre and the influence that it exerts is very real, if only at the personal level. Simply put, magic is real and magic works, but not, perhaps, in the ways that the dictionary suggests.

The history of magic shows a development of the word's definition consonant with the emergence of psychology as a scientific discipline. At the tail end of the Middle Ages Sir Walter Raleigh expressed the view that '(as Plato affirmeth) the Art of Magicke is the Art of Worshipping God'. Hargrave Jennings on the brink of the psychological age called magic 'the unnatural interference with nature'. The most famous modern formulation was given by Aleister Crowley, a man acquainted with the works of Freud and Schopenhauer: 'Magick is the Science and Art of causing Change to occur in conformity with Will.' The language is reminiscent of Raleigh, but the aim is entirely different (or again, perhaps not; those immersed in such things might argue that the will is God, or a part of God). The sense of performing the unnatural is lost, rather things are brought into line with the will as a natural element.[2]

Will was a common ingredient in much of the philosophy of the nineteenth and early twentieth centuries. Schopenhauer's 'big idea' was to redefine Kant's thing-in-itself as will. Will became the reality behind appearance. As time and space are phenomenal, which is to say not real, as Kant taught and Schopenhauer agreed, so must will be beyond them and unaffected by them. Will is therefore an unchanging, unitary and predetermined principle. The separate volitions of man are illusory, the reality is a single, universal will. Schopenhauer's Buddhism and his pessimism made of this will the source of all suffering.[3]

With the development of psychoanalysis the concept of will as one's conscious volition is further problematized by the operation of subconscious and unconscious fields of the personality. When Freud opened up, so to speak, scientific investigation of these areas, he found the dominant processes of psychic life to be instinctual. So far as a man might presume to have a will it was in reality an instinctual motivation whose origins he was unaware of and whose insistency he was at a loss to explain. Again, although whilst the concept of will disappears behind psychic determinism (another form of cosmic determinism?), the unconscious, instinctual motivations are a source of suffering (neurosis).[4]

Philosophy and psychiatric science had made of will something other than the conscious desires and decisions of man. It had become removed from immediate experience and had to be sought out either as a mystical quality to be surrendered or an illusion to be confronted by psychic determinism.

For Crowley, will takes on the connotations of something more like the 'true self'; indeed he refers to a 'True Will' in opposition to a 'conscious will'. His famous maxim, 'Do what thou wilt' is not an injunction to satisfy every passing fancy, but to discover one's true being and purpose and thus to act in accordance with it. The change that his 'magick' is intended to cause takes on psychological and mystical connotations in light of this insight into what is meant by will. Will has to be sought out as the source, not of suffering but of genuine living and authentic being. Though no less deterministic, Crowley at least contributes his optimism.[5]

As a science and art this 'magick' is part psychology, part yoga – Crowley was also much influenced by his study of Eastern mysticism – and part theatre. It is the science 'of understanding oneself and one's conditions' and the art of 'applying that understanding in action'. The theatrical is one technique of that art. In his *Magick* Crowley devotes a short chapter to dramatic ritual, but the greater part of the book is concerned with devices, more or less theatrical, intended to discover one's will and apply it.[6]

Since an understanding of oneself involves a recognition of one's true will, its aim can also be said to be mystical. Crowley concerns himself with attaining to the conversation of his guardian angel, at least in print – some of his actual magical activities were rather more sordid. His guardian angel is also his 'true will' and in seeking to identify with it he seeks to become like 'a force of Nature': his own 'true' nature being at one with Nature (the predetermined order of things).[7]

However, to illustrate his definition, he explodes what might have been a good one and leaves only a cloud of vagueness. Thus:

> It is my Will to inform the World of certain facts within my knowledge. I therefore take 'magical weapons' pen, ink, and paper; I write 'incantations' – these sentences – in the 'magical language' i.e. that which is understood by the people I wish to instruct; I call forth 'spirits', such as printers, publishers, booksellers, and so forth, and constrain them to convey my message to those people. The composition and distribution of this book is thus an act of Magick by which I cause Changes to take place in conformity with my Will.[8]

Doing anything at all, with just one, albeit important qualification, is to do magic: 'Every intentional act is a Magical Act.'[9] The concept of true will is Crowley's only strong point in an otherwise banal explanation and one would have expected more from the 'wickedest man in the world'.

Looking into his commentary upon *The Book of the Law,* perhaps one does indeed get more. 'Magick' is here described as no less than 'the art of life itself'.[10] This is more than aestheticism, although occasionally Crowley was something of a dandy, since its aim is to live in conformity with will and will has been identified with the Freudian unconscious, the Jungian higher self, the mystical Christian holy guardian angel, and with the scientific concept of nature. It is something like Taoism: living in accordance with the way things are.

There is also something like modern self-help psychology in it. Crowley states: 'Magick is the management of all we say and do, so that the effect is to change that part of our environment which dissatisfies us until it does so no longer.'[11] One finds the same sort of philosophy under a different name in the works of Napoleon Hill and the current guru of Neuro-Linguistic Programming, Anthony Robbins.

Gerald Gardner, the 'Father of Modern Witchcraft', was far less satisfying and rigorous than even this in his explanation of magic. He thought it vaguely to be 'the use of some abnormal power', or 'attempting to cause the physically unusual', or even simply 'the art of getting results'.[12] Yet chronic flatulence is an abnormal power, but it is not magic. Cutting off one's nose produces the physically unusual, but it is not magic. Putting up an umbrella in the rain gets results, as does looking at the sports pages of the newspaper, but none of this is magic. Gardner resolutely fails to explain what magic is. His only saving grace is to quote Crowley – in doing so one assumes he was aware of the scope of his definition – and give one or two pointers as to how one might make magic.

Whilst even Crowley's illustration grudgingly lends itself to a mystical interpretation – one must of course have discovered what one's will is before being able to act in accordance with it – Gardner's comments suggest only getting what one wants through mysterious means. Whilst we may not know what we want and Gardner, unlike Crowley, does not suggest anything like contacting one's guardian angel, he does give some indication of the means.

His practical insights into the working of magic depend upon the belief that an energy, unrecognized by science, emanates from the human body, that it can be increased, that it can be stored and that it can be directed. This is the reason behind Witches' nudity, dancing and use of the magic circle. Clothes are believed to obstruct this energy. Dancing, amongst other things such as drug taking, meditation and sexual intercourse, is believed to increase this energy. The magic circle is believed to contain it. Its release and direction depend upon the action and intention of the leader of the coven, most usually the High Priestess.

The idea of a subtle energy inherent in the human body was not a new one, even in the West. Mesmer's animal magnetism and Reich's orgone are but two examples that also highlight the belief that this energy can be utilized for productive ends. More recently the technique of Kirlian photography claims to record it. Yet it remains under the suspicion and censure of the scientific establishment, and indeed of the cultural establishment as the *Oxford English Dictionary*'s reference to 'some occult controlling principle of nature' suggests. However, this energy, as conceived of by Gardner, is not controlling, but controllable, and magic is the name given to the processes by which it is controlled.

Given the unique opportunity to divest himself of all the cumbersome paraphernalia of magic, Gardner chose to retain it. His involvement with the First Rosicrucian Theatre in England had no doubt given him a taste for props.

The whole working of magic involves the utmost theatricality. An elaborate circle is drawn, the participants enter it either naked or dressed in robes. The ceremony proceeds with the whirling of wands and scourges, daggers are dipped into chalices, and so on. Lines learned previously are chanted, or sung or said aloud in a strong clear voice. The nudity, secrecy and worship of proscribed deities gives the whole the atmosphere of carnival: celebratory perversion of norms of conduct, and etymologically 'raising flesh', although probably just goose-bumps, but again with the sense of breaking the norm (in the strict etymological sense this is the forsaking of meat for Lent).[13]

In this art of pretending the object is to forget the element of pretence. One need not believe in the gods, but one should pretend that one does when in the circle and working magic. This is also why the techniques of altering the state of consciousness are so important. In the whirl of the dance and the flicker of candle-light the participants forget that they are middle-aged bankers, unemployed actresses, or whatever it is that they are in the 'outside world', and become Witches.

In a sense it is a form of method acting, of becoming absolutely immersed in the character one is portraying. It is just that here the other character is one's Witch-self. A new name is taken, a transformatory ritualized death is undergone, a rebirth follows, a new identity is constructed, a new character is worked up. A new 'personality' – the word comes from the Latin *persona* meaning a 'mask, particularly one worn by an actor' – is put on.[14]

Whilst this is descriptive of a certain sort of magic, the continuing development of the psychological age has ensured that it is not descriptive of all magic. In her investigation of Witchcraft and neo-Paganism in America the journalist Margot Adler found:

Magic is a convenient word for a whole collection of techniques, all of which involve the mind . . . including the mobilization of confidence, will, and emotion brought about by the recognition of necessity; the use of imaginative faculties, particularly the ability to visualize, in order to begin to understand how other beings function in nature so we can use this knowledge to achieve necessary ends.

This magic [she gave an example of 'Michael's'] did not involve the supernatural. It involved an understanding of psychological and environmental processes; it was a kind of shamanism, a knowledge of how emotion and concentration can be directed naturally to affect changes in consciousness that affect the behaviour of (in this case) humans and fish.[15]

Here we find the art of pretending in the use of the imagination. As with Gardner the notion of supernatural agency is discarded. But the belief in a controllable occult force is also lacking. Magic is motivation plus perception: a technique of true seeing, or intellectual penetration. The theatrical may be involved, but not necessarily. There is no reference to changing self-identity. However, this may yet form the subtext of Adler's account: how did 'Michael' come to be practising magic when he went fishing?

Whilst no one has ever heard of 'Michael', which is in any case a pseudonym, Adler's investigation is both important and widely read. In a field of spiritual endeavour where any number of definitions of magic are forthcoming, it is significant that she should choose to highlight this one account. It is singularly important that the major emphasis of this description is upon the use of mental faculties. 'I think, therefore, I am', therefore I am what I think I am. One detects the supermentalization popularly characteristic of the Californian outlook on life, but tempered with an actual understanding of the 'real' world and thus saved from solipsism.

The Origin of 'Magic'

Where did magic come from? The word is first heard in the English language in the fourteenth century, recorded in Chaucer's *The Man of Law's Tale* (1386), but comes from older tongues. English borrowed the word from the Old French *magique*, which in turn came from the late Latin *magica*. But the trail does not end there. The Latin word derived from the Greek *magike*, a contraction of the phrase *magike techne*, meaning 'sorcerer's art'. *Magike* was the adjectival form of *magos*, a word of Persian origin. Amongst the ancient Medes and Persians the Magi were a priestly class much noted for their occult prowess. Whilst authors such as Ammianus Marcellinus unnecessarily connected the Magi with the Brahmin of India, we, educated by the study of Witchcraft's history, immediately see the link between the Medes, the people founded by the witch-goddess Medea (or by Medea's son, depending on whose account one reads), and this occult art of magic.

This psychologization of magic is also seen in Britain. The 'hedge-witch' Rae Beth calls magic 'the power of thought'. However, she marries this with a more traditional occult view of the universe: 'what we imagine has true astral reality'. Thus 'Visualization is at the heart of all magic.' But magic is not just a mental technique. She also describes it as 'part of the flow of life. It is a kind of dance and a kind of prayer.' She combines the psychological with the occult to produce an account of magic as a natural element that 'controls' the 'three great mysteries' of 'birth and love and death'.[16]

The difference in approach of this hedgewitchcraft stems from the solitary nature of the practice. The practitioner constructs an internal stage upon which to play the Witch and act out the magical fantasy. But this internal action takes on the power and strength of reality. Attempts to define the operation on an astral level seem to be attempts to legitimize the reality of the activity. Beth's interpretation, however, beginning with the psychological, taking in the occult and moving into the natural, ends in the mystical. Always it is a part of life and a way of living.

Magic in Practice

Thus far we have only considered what the vocal, that is published, minority have to say on the subject of magic. Although such definitions carry a great deal of weight amongst practitioners, they do not necessarily hold true in practice. What do ordinary (if there can ever be ordinary) Witches have to say about the magic they themselves practice?

Surprising as it may seem, not every Witch practises magic. Most do – indeed over 90 per cent of those asked said that they did – but it is clearly not essential to being a Witch.[17] When speaking to Witches for this research I asked them to define magic and then asked if they practised it. I did not apply a general definition of magic; the people I talked to defined the term. Thus magic was what the Witches thought it was, and what they practised as magic was this or nothing at all. One said, 'I look at the life I live and the way I live as a magical life.'[18]

Amongst those Witches who did practise magic, most did so frequently. Over half practised 'often', a third practised 'sometimes', less than a twelfth said 'hardly ever' and only one person only practised it in times of crisis.[19]

The Frequency of Magical Practice

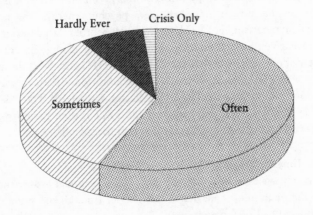

One thing that was immediately noticeable about these findings was a difference in the answers given by men and women. As well as being more likely to practise magic, female Witches also practised it more often, although the difference was slight. The majority of those practising magic both often and sometimes were women.[20] However, more women also practised magic rarely,[21] although all of those who only practised in times of crisis were men.

We may have established that most Witches practise magic and most practise frequently, and that more women than men practise magic and do so frequently, but what is it that they practise?

Witches practise different sorts of magic, but there was a core element to the vast range of definitions that the Witches in my research gave me, that of transformation. Magic is essentially about changing things. As one person said, 'Magic is the unexplained, a miracle, a card-trick, a hundred foot tree having green leaves at the top – how does it do it? The power of it. The quiet power of growing things is magical.'[22] The greatest variation arose in how this transformation was brought about. Thus the typology of magic that I developed focused upon the means used to effect this transformation.

There were two main methods of achieving transformation through magic: transformative mental techniques (TMT), i.e. transformation through the use of some mental ability such as imagination, positive thinking, confidence, concentration or will-power; and transformative energetic techniques (TET), i.e. effecting change through the use and manipulation of energy (natural energy, natural forces, cosmic power, inner power, psychic energy, life power, personal magnetism, etc.). There were two other large groupings: transformative unspecified techniques (TUT), i.e. change in a manner not described; and will-defined TUT (WDTUT), i.e. TUT in accordance, or in compliance with will – the definition closest in spirit to that most famously articulated by Aleister Crowley.[23] The essential difference between this last category and TMT is that transformation is achieved according to will, not through the agency of will.

The Time for Magic

It has always been believed that there was a right and proper time for the operation of magic, as this extract from an old grimoire attributed to Iroë-Grego shows:[24]

An experiment of speaking with spirits or conjuring them should be operated in the day and hour of Mercury. A certain atmospheric condition is also required for the experiment and an obscure, uninhabited place congruous to such an art is even more necessary. But if the experiment be concerned with a theft, it should be performed in the hour of the Moon and on her day. The experience of invisibility should be operated when the Moon is in Pisces. Experiments of love, favour and grace should be accomplished on the day and in the hour of the Sun or Venus. Works of destruction, hatred and desolation should be performed on the day and in the hour of Saturn. Extra-ordinary experiences should be operated in corresponding hours on the day of Jupiter.

Of all these definitions the one used by the largest number of Witches asked was that of TET. The next most used description was TMT. Two people defined magic in terms that cross the boundary between TMT and TET. Next down the list, in terms of the number of people answering, was WDTUT, with TUT coming last in popularity. There was also a number of other definitions. Some of those asked described magic in mystical terms such as being in tune with everything, connected to the divine, or in one well-phrased description as 'spirit in action',[25] and there was a sub-class of theomagic, that is magic, or in this case TMT and TET, with divine intervention or assistance.

The Definitions of Magic

Definition	Abbreviation	Description
Transformative Mental Techniques	TMT	Transformation through the use of mental abilities
Transformative Energetic Techniques	TET	Transformation through the manipulation of energy
Transformative Unspecified Techniques	TUT	Effecting change in a manner not described
Mystical	n/a	Being 'in tune' with everything, connected to the divine, or effecting change with the assistance of the divine
Non-Mystical Transformative Non-Manipulative Techniques	Non-Mystical TNT	Desire ('hopes', 'wishes', etc.) without a divine component or attempt to manipulate current circumstances
Non-Magical	n/a	Magic as a natural or scientific phenomenon, or simply the 'unknown'
Other	n/a	Miscellaneous: magic as a lifestyle; everything as magical
Will-Defined Transformative Unspecified Techniques	WDTUT	Effecting change in accordance with will but in a manner not described

Some people defined magic as a non-mystical transformative technique that did not involve the use or manipulation of mental abilities or energy, such as, in one person's words, 'the conglomeration of hopes, wishes, events'. A few even defined it in what can only be described as non-magical terms, e.g. as science, the unexplained, nature, and so on. Grouped under the catch-all category of 'other' in the chart were the answers given by individuals like the Witch who described magic simply as their 'lifestyle', or another who said that life itself is magical.[26] The broader pattern can be seen in the pie chart.

Witches' Definitions of Magic

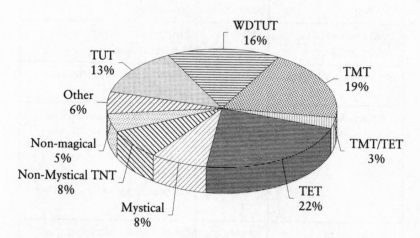

There was a difference between the things male and female Witches said. The largest number of male Witches, a quarter of all the men I talked to, defined magic as WDTUT. This accounted for almost three-quarters of everyone, male and female, who gave this answer. In contrast, the largest group of female Witches, a little over a quarter of all the women, defined magic as TET, again accounting for almost three-quarters. Roughly similar proportions of both sexes defined magic as TUT. The male swing towards WDTUT and the female swing away look all the more significant in this light.[27]

But what do Witches use magic for? Forget love spells, money spells and curses, most use magic to heal. They use it to heal others, to heal the world and occasionally to heal themselves.[28] If they did not use it for healing, then they were next most likely to use it in some developmental way, to change society and to change themselves. Always they sought to change things for the better, whether that be a better world for everyone to live in or a better person for them to be (through self-improvement, problem solving, personal transformation and spiritual development). Fewer used magic for their own advantage: worldly success, material gain, career advancement or even in the general improvement of their circumstances.

The rest of the Witches I talked to gave a variety of different answers (the 'other' category in the chart below). Two people used magic in a technical manner as 'a tool for focusing' and 'a vehicle for exploration', or for fortune telling. Another two used it for spiritual purposes such as 'spiritual development', or 'spiritual solace'. A further two gave miscellaneous answers such as using magic to 'tune into the seasons', to influence the weather and in one case as art. The pattern can be seen in the chart below.

Witches' Uses of Magic

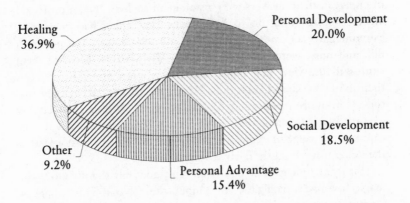

their primary uses of magic. Thus if they had not already said that they primarily used magic for healing, most of them added it as a second use. Again social development featured highly, but strangely, personal development was reduced to two cases of problem solving, and magic for personal advantage rose slightly. There were also a few new types of use such as employing magic for celebration, what we might call the 'religious' uses, mystical uses such as 'being in tune with everything', and finally some miscellaneous spiritual uses.[29] This clearly strengthens the importance of heal-

It would be simplistic to assume that Witches use magic for only one thing. A little under half those questioned also used it for other purposes, but again there were few surprises as they tended to follow the same pattern as revealed in

ing and social development as magical objectives amongst Witches.

This time male and female Witches generally agreed on what they mostly used magic for. Most used it for the healing of others. This is not to say that the sexes were in total agreement. Almost twice as many men used magic for personal development as women, whilst twice as many women used magic for their personal advantage.[30]

Transformations: The Effect of Magic

What effect does practising magic have on the practitioner? When I asked the Witches I talked to this question they most often gave two responses: an emotional one and a factual one. Thus the Witches often began their answers with a statement such as, 'Oh, a profound effect', before going on to detail what that effect had been. Not everyone gave an emotional qualifier, but the majority (60 per cent) did, and most were deeply affected by their magic. Most of them expressed the view that magic had had a momentous effect upon their lives. One described it thus: 'Magic has totally changed my attitude. I'm more open-minded, less sceptical. It has changed my personality.'[31] 'Momentous' is my own term, but it adequately captures the range of expression from 'massive effect', 'vast effect' to the delightfully English 'fairly revolutionary'.[32]

Hardly anyone gave an equivocal reply and only slightly more said magic had had a negligible effect upon their lives.[33] Thus where an emotive reply was given it was predominantly to indicate the depth and profundity of the effect magic had upon the subject's life.

Female Witches were more emphatic than their male counterparts. Most of those who said that magic had had a momentous effect upon their lives were women, whilst most of those who were equivocal in their reply were men. Half of all the female Witches I talked to described a momentous effect, whilst only a little over a third of the men gave a similar answer. Whilst more female Witches said their magic had had a tremendous effect upon them than male Witches, strangely more female Witches also said that its effect had been negligible, although more men than women did not specify any sort of qualitative effect at all.[34]

But what had happened to these Witches that was so profound, so dramatically life-changing? For the largest number it had been a personal transformation. They had discovered themselves, improved themselves, solved their personal problems or expanded their awareness. In a closely related category a further fifth of the Witches I talked to had improved the quality of their lives, by making it more enjoyable, by adding excitement or by making it more fulfilling. A large number specifically stated that practising magic had increased their self-confidence, either giving them more control over life, or enabling them to cope with life better. Some said magic had given them a sense of meaningfulness. Others said that it had had a mystical effect upon them, altering their consciousness, or connecting them to the divine. For some magic had given them a better understanding of others, an increased tolerance of others, or the personal reward of being able to help other people or do some good in the world.[35]

The Emotional Effect of Practising Magic

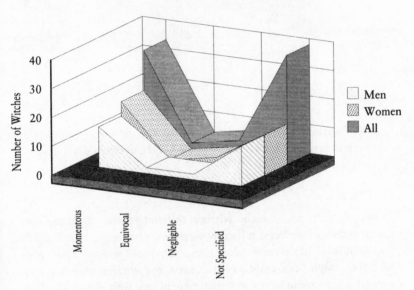

Type of Effect Reported

There were both differences and similarities between male and female Witches on this question. First let us look at their areas of agreement. Both sexes agreed in roughly equal numbers that magic had had an effect on their personal development.[36] Roughly similar numbers of men and women also said that magic had improved their quality of life. For men this was their second most common answer, although it came in third amongst the women.[37] The few who reported a mystical type of effect and those who did not know what type of effect magic had had on them were equally balanced in terms of gender.[38]

The Effects of Magic on its Practitioners

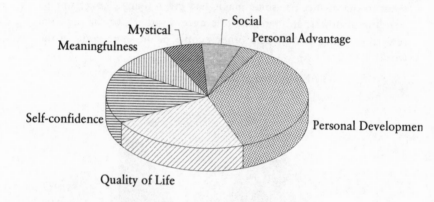

Mystical
Social
Meaningfulness
Personal Advantage
Self-confidence
Personal Developmen
Quality of Life

N.B. Figures recalculated to exclude those who did not know. Spiritual development has been included in the personal development catagory.

Where male and female Witches differed was in the numbers reporting a social effect, self-empowerment, greater meaningfulness and quality of life effects. Most noticeably more women than men said that magic had empowered them.[39] For women this was the second most common answer, for men it was fifth down the list. More women also said that magic had had a social effect; indeed three-quarters of all those who gave this answer were women. Men were more likely to report that magic had provided greater mean-ingfulness. Male Witches also gave a greater range of answers. Thus we find that they accounted for all of those saying that magic had had a spiritual effect or had been personally advantageous.[40]

Magic and Witchcraft go hand in hand, like Hallowe'en and pumpkins, but as we have discovered not every Witch practises magic. Most do, but the magic they practise is not always the magic we thought they did, and it is not always the magic that writers like Gerald Gardner tell us they practice.

Witches define magic in terms of transformation. For most of them this is brought about through the use and manipulation of energies (variously defined), what we called transformative energetic techniques (TET). When we looked at the gender of Witches we discovered that it was the women who were more likely to define magic in these terms, whilst men showed a preference for what we called will-defined transformative unspecified techniques (WDTUT).

However, these differences in definition were not reflected in the two sexes' use of magic. Overall, Witches most often use magic for healing and both men and women were largely agreed on this. They did, however, vary in some of their other answers, especially on the questions of personal development, which men favoured, and personal advantage, which women favoured.

Magic generally had a momentous effect upon those who practised it. This largely expressed itself in the form of personal development and this general trend held for the sexes when viewed separately. The levels of practice, range of definition, varieties of use and types of effect reported all point to magic being a significant factor in the attitude, belief and behaviour of Witches.

Conclusion: Old Ways, New Directions: Evaluating Witchcraft from its Earliest Beginnings to its Future Potentialities

The Old Religion of the past is growing and changing into the New Religion of the future. It will be a happy, constructive religion, and what we now call magic will be a part of it. It will be involved in communication with Mother Earth and with the changing seasons and the elements of life. It will take its stand against greed, cruelty and social injustice. It will help every man to be his own High Priest and every woman to be her own High Priestess. It will be part of the Aquarian Age.[1]

From the Birthplace of All Sorceries to East of Midgard, from Pagan goddesses to anti-Christian Satanists from South of Heaven, we have traced the trajectory of the witch across the European imagination. As Celtic Twilight turned to night and Golden Dawn brightened into day we have charted the emergence of the modern religion of Witchcraft as a craft of invention born out of the imagination of one man, the Wicca man, Gerald Gardner. We have seen how that idea jumped out of the cauldron and landed in the fire, a fire both of enthusiasm and antagonism, and that once out of Gardner's cauldron it grew and mutated into new forms. Now this society of Witches has been studied and understood, we have seen how and why they call down the moon and how and why they draw the magic circle. These old ways, of religious engagement with the natural world, have met with new ways, of gender equality and a religion called Witchcraft, to move in new directions.

Shadows of the Past

We began in ancient Greece, the birthplace of Western civilization and the birthplace of many of our ideas about witchcraft. We saw how the ancient goddess Hecate, 'She Who Works Her Will', was brought into the Greek world by Orpheus and established as an equal of Zeus, the King of the Olympian Gods. We then saw how she declined from such a high office to become a primarily chthonic deity, the snake-haired, three-headed goddess of witchcraft.

Her daughters Circe and Medea appeared to suffer a similar fate as goddesses denigrated to wicked witches by theological developments and literary designs. The original forms of their worship are lost to us now, but still lie faintly and tantalizingly beneath the popular stories: Odysseus's transformative encounter with Circe that bears such a striking resemblance to the medieval witches' Sabbat, and the Greek witchcraft tragedy of Medea that reveals strange mysteries.

These witch-goddesses of the ancient Graeco-Roman world were not the embodiments of evil. They were morally complex deities capable of a wide range of actions and feelings, both good and bad, although as the centuries rolled on their reputations became darker, so that Roman authors would speak of the witch with fear and loathing. Through Hecate, Circe and Medea we met many of the elements more familiar to us as characteristic of later accounts of witchcraft: night as the proper time of magic, the animal transformation of celebrants, feasting, orgy and sexual initiation; and the power of the witch to pervert the normal course of the universe.

The witch figure in ancient northern European culture played a similar role. And yet again we observed a descent from an archaic veneration of the witch as goddess, or the practices of witchcraft as godly activities (in the form of Odin's involvement), to a fear of the evil female magic-user.

The emergent new religion of Christianity took these elements to their extreme. Where Pagans accepted moral diversity amongst, and moral complexity within, their deities, the Christians reinterpreted the Pagan world as entirely evil. The differences between the revered prophetesses and the reviled poisoners were ignored by this perversion of Paganism. Everything Pagan was demonized, or if it was too ingrained (like the midwinter festival that we now call Christmas),

Christianized. The descent of the witch figure was now complete.

The persecution of Paganism was extensive and thorough. Clerical authorities wielded considerable power. There was no separation of Church and State. Christian kings claimed that their authority was from God, but took their orders from Rome. Yet even with the considerable resources of Church and Court at their disposal Paganism proved resistant and difficult to remove. Commoner, noble and cleric alike could be found consorting with sorcerers and practising forbidden arts.

It was when the view of witchcraft changed from an evil magical practice to an evil magical conspiracy, specifically an heretical organization intent on the destruction of Christianity, that its full-scale persecution could begin. Once the village wise-woman had been recast as an agent of the Arch-fiend the diminishing Pagan sympathies of the populace could be finally corrupted by Christian superstition and turned against those last active vestiges of the old ways.

It took several hundred years of the most horrific torture and unprecedented slaughter before the clerical and judicial authorities sickened of the witch hunt they had unleashed and sought to curb, and finally end it. Even after the last judicial sentences for the practice of witchcraft were passed and the Witchcraft Acts were repealed and replaced by more enlightened laws, the common people continued to persecute those suspected of witchcraft. Even now many Witches still hide their religious identity for fear of losing their jobs, their homes and their children.

Only after the ashes of the dreadful pyres had grown cold and been blown away by the winds of human change, only after the memory of the official witch hunts had been dimmed by a hundred or more years could the revaluation of witchcraft begin. The loosening of Christianity's vice-like grip on the human mind heralded by the Age of Enlightenment also allowed a freer expression of the soul in Romanticism. Secular scholars working under the aegis of Rationalism rediscovered witchcraft and reinterpreted it as a Pagan religion, not a devilish perversion.

The boom in Freemasonry and the rationalization of magic created a new class of clear-headed ritualists, serious men who could recast the ancient mysteries in new forms, foremost amongst which was the Hermetic Order of the Golden Dawn. Skilled in the science of this new magic was the single most important figure in the modern history of the occult, Aleister Crowley. It was through his unique drive and ambition, his poetry and prophecy, that the new magic could be connected by Gerald Gardner, the man credited with the birth of Wicca, to the old craft, or more accurately, the new interpretation of the old ways.

Gardner's Wicca was a hodge-podge of cribbed Crowley and copied *Key of Solomon the King* energized by his vision, inspired by Murray and Leland, of a 'craft of the wise', of Witchcraft as the ancient indigenous Pagan religion of the British Isles. Through the industry of his most gifted acolyte, Doreen Valiente, this Wicca was honed and perfected, the obvious plagiarisms removed, re-written or buried deeper, and the inner beauty of the vision polished and made more brilliant.

Despite Gardner's attempts to control his nascent religion, his age, his antagonizing authoritarianism, his ham-fisted dictats, and the spirit of his creation itself made it inevitable that Wicca would escape from his grasp. Once unleashed upon the world it spread slowly at first through the restricting requirements of initiation, but the impatience of people interested in joining combined with both a growing Witchcraft publishing industry and the emergence of new charismatic leaders less concerned about tradition than fame, like Alex Sanders, brought Wicca faster and further to a wider audience.

The gender equality, spiritual radicalism, and libertarian morals as much as the magical adventure and religious mystery of Wicca met with the *Zeitgeist*, that spirit of the times that saw the development of the spiritualized hippy era, to produce a powerful counter-cultural movement. New leaders took Wicca in different directions, back to its roots with spiritualized ecology, or out on a limb with Dianic extremism.

Finally, we went into the heart of Witchcraft to discover those things about it that usually lie hidden in other accounts of the religion. We discovered who the Witches are, what they do, why they do it, and what effect it has upon them. The results were surprising. They overturned the old stereotypes of who Witches are, but they also exposed the new stereotypes of Witchcraft that are emerging through the media.

Contrary to the fairy-tale fantasy Witches are not green-skinned, wart-nosed crones, but contrary also to the new stereotypes of teenage witch-girls, the modern Witches are middle-aged, lower-middle-class men and women. They believe in a personal deity that represents itself as a gender-equal duality of male and female. They are mystically experienced. Most frequently they have numinous or xenophrenic experiences when their gods are directly present or revealed to them, or when they alter their state of consciousness. Most of them are magic users, but again contrary to the stereotypes they do not use magic for cursing or working mischief, but primarily for the healing of other people and the world around them. Witches define magic as a transformative technique most often involving the use of mental faculties or energies. The actual practice of magic itself has a trans-formative effect on the Witches who use it. They change their lives through the practice of magic: they find themselves, improve them-selves, solve their problems and expand their awareness.

It is not the full moon that brings Witches out to worship. The rituals of Witchcraft are primarily seasonal ones and most Witches go to them four or more times a year. Unsurprisingly it is also seasonal rituals that mean the most to Witches, but they also found rites of passage – initiations, hand-fastings (marriage ceremonies) and namings – important. The importance of these rituals lies in their social and emotional satisfaction: they bring people together, create communities, and feed the soul.

Witches and Witchcraft are no longer what they were thought to be. Gone are the pacts with the Devil, the evil imp familiars and toe-curl-ing curses. In their place we find a vital religion practising spiritual equality and seeking the improvement of the world. Witchcraft changes the lives of those it touches and those it touches say it has improved their lives. The shadows of the past still lie over Witchcraft; they always will. As long as mankind retains his historical memory the deaths of untold thousands on the charge of witchcraft can never be forgotten. As long as Witches are still persecuted both in modern and traditional societies these shadows will still have much to teach. Yet not all these shadows are shadows of past iniquities. The shadows cast by Gardner and his initiates are growing longer, the religion of Witchcraft is increasing in size, there are Witches in every walk of life. Born of the 'Book of the Shadows', the people of the shadows are everywhere.

After Christianity

'It is a case of the Church of England or paganism.'[2] The pews are empty, the church doors are locked, the vicar is in retirement, his flock has wandered from the fold. Christianity in the West is in crisis, its message undermined by the machinations of the Vatican, destroyed by the criminal behaviour of its ministers. Its iron hold upon the souls of the people has grown rusty and slack. With increasing access to alternative forms of knowledge Christianity is no longer the only road to salvation. With the spread of free-market capitalism into every aspect of our lives, we are now even free to choose what spiritual path we will follow. And people are choosing Witchcraft.

On the one hand, Christian leaders condemn the rise of new spiritualities and new spiritual ideas, whilst on the other they praise some of their aspects. Whilst the Rt Revd Robert Hardy, Bishop of Lincoln, warned that the United Kingdom would revert to Paganism if the Church of England loosened its hold, Archbishop Carey spoke out in praise of certain aspects of the New Age and the Archbishop of Wales joined the Druids.[3] They are floundering, not knowing whether to reject or embrace the inevitable changes around them. They are now facing their greatest challenge yet.

Since 1990 membership of the Church of England has fallen by 15 per cent according to research carried out by Opinion Research Business in 2000. More than three-quarters of those asked had not attended a church service of any denomination in the last month. Most people (just over half) did not see the decline in traditional religion as a problem. This research confirms the picture drawn by Dr Peter Brierley's statistical analysis of Sunday church attendance in England amongst Catholics, Anglicans, Baptists, Methodists and Pentecostalists. Looking at the period from 1979 to 1998 he found that the percentage of Britons attending church had dropped from 11.7 per cent to 7.5 per cent, which shows a more than one-third decline in attendance of 35.9 per cent.[4]

Scotland in particular has seen a dramatic reversal in Christianity's fortunes. The *Edinburgh Evening News* shocked its readers with revelations that 'Scotland is now a Pagan country' in 2002. Researchers at Aberdeen University had discovered that more than 60 per cent of Scots rarely or never attended church. They warned that Scotland's empty churches were 'just tractor sheds and carpet warehouses in waiting'. For all those who claimed membership of the Church of Scotland (37 per cent) there were as many who identified themselves with no religion at all. They concluded that 'Scotland is not in any sense a Christian country.' However, the researchers themselves found that rather than choosing alternative spiritualities, most Scots were simply indifferent to religion altogether. Only 1 per cent were classified as 'non-Christian' and most people (75 per cent) had never tried things like astrology, the Tarot, or even yoga and alternative therapies like aromatherapy and homeopathy.[5]

Not only are people turning away from the congregation, but also from clerical office itself. In the Lincoln diocese alone there has been a decline in the number of clergy from a total of 620 in 1979 to only 250 in 1998. England's 13,000 parishes are tended by only 9,300 full-time clergy, many of them inevitably overseeing several parishes at once, sometimes as many as five. Overstretched, underattended, the decline of the Church is inevitable.

Nor are these trends restricted to the UK. Census returns collected in Australia in 2001 and published in 2002 reveal a massive surge in the number of Witches and Pagans, despite witchcraft still being outlawed in some states. In 1996 there were only around 2,000 Witches in Australia. By 2001 this number had increased to 9,000 – an increase of almost 500 per cent. Similarly, the number of Pagans more than doubled to 10,632. The Witches come from all walks of life: insurance underwriters, bank clerks, doctors, nurses and lawyers were all mentioned. In marked contrast all of the major Christian denominations lost followers over the same period.[6]

The pattern in the USA has been more difficult to gauge. A telephone poll of 1,008 adults conducted by ABC News in February 2002 found that 83 per cent of them claimed to be Christians. However, only 38 per cent attended church on a regular (weekly) basis. The research gave no historical comparisons, but it suggests that whilst many are happy to call themselves Christian they do not actively engage in it.[7]

Research undertaken for the UK satellite television channel Living TV revealed a widespread belief in ghosts, reincarnation and the power of psychics. Published in 2002, the Paranormal Report investigated the beliefs of a thousand people in the UK and is the largest survey of its kind to date. Two-thirds of those questioned said that they believed in psychic powers. More than half (57 per cent) also said that they believed that the spirits of the dead could return from beyond the grave. Most people (67 per cent) believed in life after death with a further third believing that the soul or spirit could be reborn in successive physical bodies.

Richard Woolfe, speaking for the report, argued that it proves that people are in touch with their mystical sides. He further added that the paranormal has replaced religion (i.e. traditional religion) as the spirituality of choice. 'Instead of going to church,' he said, 'they are visiting psychics, mediums and clairvoyants.'[8]

The consequences are far-reaching and not confined to Christianity alone. The Totally Jewish website, for instance, high-lighted the comparatively low belief in God. Only 36 per cent of those asked said that they believed in God, and bemoaned that 'religion has been eclipsed as the central faith in people's lives'. When two-thirds of those who visit clairvoyants say that their predictions come true, one can see why, when traditional religion now raises more questions than it answers, this should be so.[9]

Witchcraft, and more broadly Paganism, is now the fastest grow-ing religion in the West.[10] Whilst it is not overtly anti-Christian, it implicitly rejects Christianity. Whilst many Witches admire the life and teachings of Jesus they do not regard him as their saviour. The far-reaching and more liberal Wiccan Rede replaces and supersedes the constraints of the Ten Commandments. The dogma of the Holy Bible has been thrown out in favour of the teachings of Nature; the wind and the rain, the land and the ocean are the Witches' 'bible'. The vicar's flock have shorn themselves of the woolly fleece, sprouted goatish horns and found their own path up the mountain.

The Re-enchantment of the World

When a famous and influential pioneer of the study of human society examined the nature and conditions of the modern world he character-ized it as 'disenchanted'. The exact phrase Max Weber used, 'the disen-chantment of the world' (*Entzauberung der Welt*), a consciously poetic use of Schiller's original phrase, expresses a wide variety of interrelated phenomena from the increasing routinization of everyday activity to the bureaucratization of our lives, from the loss of a close relationship with the natural world to the degradation of human being itself.[11]

Weber believed that the original condition of man had been to live in an 'enchanted garden', a Garden of Eden state of intimate connection with the natural world. There is no knowledge of the good and evil of man and the world, no distinction is made between the human and the natural environment. Weber draws upon ancient Judaic, Indian, Chinese and most especially classical Greek examples to develop an idealized picture of this enchanted garden. It is the 'peasant' of 'ancient times' who lives in an ontologically superior state to modern man. Like the Romantic philosopher Rousseau, Weber detested progress, since progress for him was precisely this process of disenchantment. The linearity of progress denies man any satisfaction, any fulfilment. As one thing is achieved, another problem, another challenge, another goal presents itself. The ancient circularity of time and being, of all things in their season, is the natural religion, a deep spirituality of the soil and the cycles of the earth that fulfils man. But more than this the spiritual and the temporal are fused together, work is worship, laughter is prayer, kisses are benedictions, the church is the ploughed field and its steeple the spreading oak. The meaning of life is contained within the conditions of that life. There is no question to ask, no 'Why am I here?' and no answer is necessary.

Disenchantment emerges as the disintegration of the original unity of man and the world. It acts to remove man from his ideal primeval condition to imprison him finally within what Weber calls the 'iron cage' of a particular way of acting, thinking and being in the world. The key features of disenchantment are: rationalization; intellectualization; mastery through calculability; disempowerment; the diminution of human authenticity; the subjectivization of culture; the elimination of magical salvation; the impersonalization of deity; and disenchantment's resistance to re-enchantment.

For Weber, disenchantment and rationalization are almost interchangeable words. Rationalization is disenchanting because it reduces everything to the best, that is most efficient, means of carrying it out. Disenchantment prioritizes the intellect as the only means to knowledge. Disenchantment's intellectualization causes us no longer to believe in the enchanted garden where magic works and all things are possible. Disenchantment seeks to master the world through calculation. It reduces the mysterious forces of a complex reality to numbers and equations. It reduces free choice to mathematical probabilities. It reduces the world to an algebraic expression. Disenchantment disempowers the individual because it has rationalized his existence and mastered him through calculation. We are no longer in control of our lives, we no longer know what our lives are for; the structure of society determines what we do and know. Disenchantment diminishes human authenticity because it reduces human being to rationalized roles within bureaucratic structures and removes us from the 'natural' cycle of existence.

Disenchantment destroys community and the ties that bind it by subjectivizing culture until it is merely the atomized experience of the individual. Disenchantment eliminates magic through monotheism, theodicy and prophecy, the religious rationalizations of ecstatic engagement with the universe. The radical possibilities of magical intervention in the ordered course of things are made redundant by a bureaucratization of the spiritual world. Disenchantment removes the possibility of magic being a route to overcoming physical and psycho-social suffering, that is magic as salvation. Disenchantment reduces deity to an impersonal concept, an intellectualized abstraction that no longer speaks directly to us. Disenchantment actively defends itself against re-enchantment. Both our objective environment, rationalized and bureaucratically administered, and the human condition created by these social structures, resist re-enchantment. Not only are we in an iron cage, but we are wearing an iron mask that blinds us to our condition.

There is, however, hope. The iron mask can be taken off. The iron cage can be opened. Although disenchantment resists re-enchantment it does not rule it out. But re-enchantment, is not simply the return of, or to, magic, as the name alone might suggest. Re-enchantment is the reversal of the whole process of disenchantment, and just as disenchantment was not simply the removal of magic, but a number of interconnected social trends, so is re-enchantment a complex, multi-faceted phenomenon. Re-enchantment involves non-rational modes of knowing, the seeking of magical salvation, mystical experience, mythological explanation and personal empowerment; the belief in personal gods and in a living, spiritual world in which everything is interconnected.

We have already covered some of these areas in our examination of modern Witchcraft and what modern Witches do, but over five years from 1994 to 1999 I conducted a series of interviews across the United Kingdom to explore the question of re-enchantment amongst Witches in more depth. An American sociologist had suggested that Witches might be re-enchanted and I wanted to see if this was indeed true. However, no one had previously developed a theory of re-enchantment – indeed no one had developed a theory that could be 'operationalized', that is turned into a series of easily understandable questions that could nevertheless test complex theoretical propositions. It was a difficult task, but after much trial and error I finally had an operational theory. You can see from the table how I reduced the broad concept of re-enchantment to twelve dimensions, how I specified these and what I proposed would be indicators of these conditions.

The Dimensions of Re-enchantment, their Specifications and Indicators		
Dimensions	Specifications	Indicators
Irrational	Non-instrumentalization Non-intellectualization Emotionalism Experientialism Imaginativeness	Means preferred to ends Rational explanation devalued Emotion preferred to intellect Personal experience valued Imagination preferred to calculation
Mystical	Revaluation of mystery	High value attached to mystical experience
Mythological	Process of mythologization	Use and importance of myth
Magical	Salvational magic	Use and experience of magic as improving life experiences and circumstances
Interconnection	Interconnectedness	Belief that everything is connected with everything else
Worldly	Reunification of spirit and matter Reanimation of the world Respiritualization of the world Resubjectification of the world	Belief that spirit and matter are linked Belief that the world is alive Belief in an alive, spirit/matter linked world Belief that world has meaning independently of man

Power	Re-empowerment of the subject	Feeling of control; influence of spirituality on this feeling
Deity	Personalization of deity	Belief in a personal god or gods
Extent (Totality)	Saturation of the life-world[12]	Influence of religion in everyday life Degree to which beliefs and attitudes are re-enchanted
Cultural	Objectivization of culture	Involvement in groups and ritual communities
Re-	Determinant of structural level of re-enchantment	Perceived change in measured values and attitudes over time
Resistance	Ability to resist disenchantment	The presence and strength of re-enchantment across the other dimensions, excluding 're-'

These twelve dimensions demonstrate varying degrees of intercon-nection, with some being discrete phenomena, and others mutually dependent. The first is irrationalization. This itself is a composite of the sympathetic processes of non-instrumentality, non-intellectualiza-tion, experientialism, emotionalism and anti-calculativeness. In other words, believing that means can be more important than ends, that knowledge can be derived from more than reason alone, that personal experience is as important as rational explanation, and that emotion and imagination are more important than intellect and calculation. The second, mystical, dimension is closely connected, involving as it does the revaluation of mystical experience and hence mysterious forces as against disenchanting calculativeness. The third is the process of mythologization, again a revaluation of non-rational modes of thinking and communication. The fourth is magic, specifically magical salvation, but broadly the reintroduction of magical practice.

Interconnectedness is also a magical concept, but sufficiently distinct to stand on its own. The interconnectedness of all things is the keystone of occult theory and the ground of knowledge in the original undifferentiated man/world of the enchanted garden. The sixth is the worldly dimension, another composite, this time of the interrelated concepts of the reunification of spirit and matter, and the reanimation and resubjectification of the world, that is, the return of agency to a world reduced under disenchantment to the mere scene of human activity. The seventh is re-empowerment, or what could be called the resubjectification of man,[13] that is, the return of control. The eighth is the personalization of deity, where deity becomes a personal entity in a relationship with man instead of an abstraction impersonally ordering the cosmos. The ninth is the extent of re-enchantment in the subject's life, i.e. whether or not it is a total enchantment as experienced in the 'enchanted garden.' The objectivization of culture is the development of a shared set of ideas and actions that bring people together. The eleventh dimension is the time dimension. It is the question of 're-' enchantment, that is whether the enchantment experienced can truly be said to be a re-enchantment of previously disenchanted beliefs and behaviours. The final dimension, the resistance to disenchantment, is a distillation of all the others and an index to the strength of re-enchantment as whole.

Drawing upon the work of Weber and other sociologists it was clear that re-enchantment can manifest itself in three ways: totally, as in the original 'enchanted garden' where its complete pervasion of the life-world of the individual renders it invisible; critically, which is to say in a self-aware manner similar to that ascribed by Weber to the classical Greeks; and falsely, that is, as the mere appearance of re-enchantment whilst in fact it is just another element of disenchantment, such as, for example, the intellectualization of magic, or an enchantment with the techniques and processes of disenchantment itself.[14]

My researches showed that the Witches I talked to were re-enchanted. Their re-enchantment, however, was not absolute. They had not returned to live in Weber's 'enchanted garden', but nor did they experience it only temporarily. Their mystical, mythological, ritual and especially magical practices went beyond the moment of their enactment to produce lasting changes in the experience and conduct of their lives. Nor was it a false re-enchantment. Lasting changes in the Witches' behaviour and outlook had been achieved which led them to believe that they now lived better lives. Instead their re-enchantment was critical, accommodating and partial: critical because they were aware that they were striving to achieve a different way of living; accommodating because as 'real people' in the 'real world' they were faced with decisions that compromised and contradicted that different way of living, and partial of necessity because it was critical, accommodating and, most crucially, on-going.

Occultism, Paganism and Witchcraft have been dynamic, influential forces in the development of Western society and culture, but have remained largely invisible forces.[15] Much attention has been lavished on Christian religion and exotic Eastern imports, and whilst it is also important this emphasis has not given us the full picture on Western religiosity in the post-Christian era. That the Witches I talked to were re-enchanted is an indication that disenchantment has not entirely triumphed, that it is not the final condition of all mankind, that even within disenchanted social structures re-enchantment is possible. It casts doubt on disenchantment: were we ever entirely disenchanted? It gives rise to hope for the future: outside the iron cage there is another enchanted garden.

We have come full circle, from ancient witch-priestess to modern Priestess and Witch. We have plumbed the depths of human wickedness, not through witchcraft, but against it. We have found that despite centuries of the most brutal repression, most ignominious reinvention and most wilful distortion, the Pagan ideals of man in harmony and communication with Nature have re-emerged, as indestructible as the sun, to shine out once more in the new religion of Witchcraft. All the considerable powers of the Inquisition and the basest instincts of mankind were insufficient to root out the irrepressible, magical spirit of us all. The Witches ride again, not on broomsticks to some diabolical orgy of evil, but on wings of the spirit to a better world, a re-enchanted world.

NOTES

Introduction

1. A note on conventions used: following current archaeological preferences the millennia are differentiated as Before the Common Era (BCE) and Common Era (CE) instead of the religiously coloured BC and AD. Where used to refer to a modern religion the words Witch, Witchcraft, Pagan and Paganism are capitalised.

2. Flavius Claudius Julianus (331/332–362 CE), Roman Emperor, called the Apostate by Christians because he attempted to restore Paganism to Rome. He was much regarded for his scholarship and military leadership.

3. Kluckhohn, 1962:72; Clement, 1932:240; although the evidence is suggestive rather than conclusive.

4. Russell, 1980:177; Ayto, 1990:576; *Oxford English Dictionary*.

Chapter 1

1. Lucius Apuleius (125–180 CE) so described Thessaly in his novel *The Golden Ass*. Apuleius was himself the subject of accusations of witchcraft (Kytzler, 1985:14–17).

2. Orpheus, 'Hymn to Hecate', of uncertain date.

3. The lunar association of Hecate is not well attested until the Roman period, that is, after 100 BCE, but it is now an indispensable part of her character.

4. *Brewer's Dictionary*, 1990:534–5; Bulfinch, 1983:160; 'Prayer to Selene for Any Spell', PGM IV:2785–890.

5. Today's Olympic Games keep alive the name: the original Olympic Games were a series of contests held in honour of the Olympian gods.

6. Von Rudloff, 1993; *Encyclopaedia Britannica*; Burkert, 1985; Nilsson,

1967; Kraus, 1960; Pausanias, 1989, XXX. Caria is now in modern Turkey. Orpheus also called Hecate 'Persian' in the 'Hymn to Hecate'.

7. *Brewer's Dictionary*, 1990:806. It is also said that he was torn to pieces because of his excessive grief at losing Eurydice for a second time.

8. Hesiod, *The Theogony*, II, 404–52.

9. Description attributed to Homer (*Brewer's Dictionary*, 1990:1084).

10. Hesiod, op. cit.

11. Ibid.

12. Homer, 1975: II. To Demeter, 19–32.

13. Von Rudloff, 1993.

14. Orpheus, 'Hymn to Hecate' and an unattributed Orphic invocation.

15. Tartarus or Tartaros: in modern usage Tartarus is usually preferred, but there is no general agreement. In this instance the reference is to the title given in the Charm of Hecate Ereschigal.

16. 'Prayer to Selene for Any Spell', PGM IV:2785–890.

17. Hesiod, op. cit.

18. Hecate was often referred to by the same title, but there are enough differences between representations of the two figures to preclude any certain association before the later half of the fifth century BCE (Von Rudloff, 1999:46).

19. Strabo, *Geography*, 14.2.25.

20. Stein, 1997.

21. Graf, 1985:163, 185.

22. To complicate the matter, archaeological finds from the late Bronze Age together with a legend recounted by Pausanias point to an early (c. thirteenth century BCE) settlement of the island by people from Thessaly and hence could indicate a Thessalian origin for the Hecate cult established here (Von Rudloff, 1999:39–40; Stillwell, 1976:20; Pausanias, XXIX).

23. Pausanias, XXX; Dodds, 1963:96. Dionysus was the Greek god of wine and the Corybantes were the Phrygian priests of Cybele, a fertility goddess (*Brewer's Dictionary*, 1990:66, 272).

24. Baroja, 1990:77.

25. Pausanias, XXX. Archaeological evidence also connects Hecate with Eleusis, where she seems to have played a role in the mythic drama celebrated there (Von Rudloff, 1999:37–9).

26. Cf. Circe, who instructed Odysseus to sacrifice a black ewe as part of a necromantic ritual (Homer, 1993:169).

27. 'Prayer to Selene for Any Spell', PGM IV:2785–890. Hecate is identified with the moon goddess Selene in the text.

28. Baroja, 1990:77; Guiley, 1989:135, 156. Guiley also believes *moly*, the herb used by Odysseus to defeat Circe, was garlic, although Homer's description would not seem to support this theory.

29. 'They say that Mormo is a Corinthian woman who knowingly devoured her children one night and then flew away' (scholiast to Aristides' *Panathenaikos*, c. 4 CE, quoted in Johnston, 1997:67) Mormo means 'the frightening one' and she is often described as extremely ugly. Erinna says she has huge ears, a constantly changing face and runs about on all fours, whilst Theocritus

says she is like a terrifying horse (Johnston, 1997:59, n.50). Gorgo, from the Greek *γοργος* meaning 'terrible', is derived from the same word as that which gives us 'Gorgon'.

30. Hippolytus, *Philosophumena*, c. third century CE (Baroja, 2001:30).

31. In Greek ρομβοό, in Latin *turbo*, this device was also known as the bull-roarer for the sound it made (Baroja, 2001:27, 30). Its swirling movement and the direction of this movement were also thought to be magical. Etymologically, Greek *bombos* gives us our words bomb and boom (*Brewer's Dictionary*, 1990:137).

32. *Papyri Graecae Magicae*. Papyrus, though a useful writing material, being organic has not always successfully resisted the ravages of time – hence, perhaps, the rather late date of these spells.

33. 'The Charm of Hekate Ereschigal Against Fear of Punishment,' from the *Papyri Graecae Magicae* a collection of magical papyri from the third or fouth centuries CE. Hekate is an alternative transliteration of Hecate that is currently rather fashionable amongst scholars.

34. Alternative translations of this spell render the first lines as 'If he comes forth, say to him . . .' ending with '. . . and you will avert him.' The 'he' in question is a demon of punishment. The word 'dog' is also given as 'bitch.'

35. The Dactyls were chthonic entities related to the worship of Cybele on the Greek island of Crete and mythically reputed to be the discoverers of iron and copper (*Brewer's Dictionary*, 1990:303).

36. Siculus, 1989: IV, 45.

37. According to Guiley (1989:53) she was also called a daughter of Hecate.

38. Homer, 'Epigrams', XIV. (Homer, 1851) The poet threatens two potters with this curse (amongst others) if they and their goods should prove false.

39. Homer, 1993:159; Hesiod, *Theogony* II:956–62.

40. Graves, 1961:107. The island lay off the west coast of Italy and has been identified as Monte Circeo by Bradford, 1963.

41. Not to be confused with the Samaritans.

42. Graves, 1961:375.

43. Homer, 'Circe', in Trypanis, 1971:85.

44. Milton, *Comus*, (1874) 50–3.

45. Homer, 'Invocation to the Muse', in Trypanis 1971:67.

46. Homer, 1993:163.

47. Hermes was the Greek god of science, commerce, travellers, thieves and vagabonds (*Brewer's Dictionary*, 1990:721).

48. Homer, 1993:163. Despite many attempts (e.g. Guiley, 1989) no one has conclusively identified this plant.

49. Dionysius Scytobrachion (4.45.3) believes her to be Hecate's daughter. Apollonius (1995: 3.251ff) and Euripides (1969), on the other hand, say she was only a priestess of Hecate. Pliny credits her with great magical powers, asserting that she could subject the celestial sphere to her whim.

50. Guiley, 1989: 227; Graves, 1961:769.

51. Euripides, op. cit. like 285.

52. This deed is singularly gruesome, a foretaste of Medea's utter ruthlessness

in the pursuit of her goals. However, other accounts of Jason and Medea suggest that Jason had made a bargain with Apsyrtus (Medea's brother) to hand her over to a local king for judgement (see Apollonius's *Argonautica*). Medea's destruction of him is not so cold-hearted in this light.

53. Ovid, 1989:139–40.
54. Elliott, 1969:104; Johnston, 1997:46.
55. Apollonius, 1995: 3.1069–71.

Chapter 2

1. These territories correspond to modern France and Germany and the many smaller countries of Belgium, Holland, Sweden, Switzerland, Austria, the Czech Republic and Slovakia.
2. Tacitus, 1910.
3. Russell, 1980:42.
4. All references in this section from Tacitus, op. cit.
5. Guiley, 1989: 107–8.
6. Spence, 1920; Rutherford, 1978.
7. Pliny's (1991) description of the Druids' ritual cutting of the mistletoe is our only detailed account of the process.
8. Cunningham, 1983: 163; Guiley, 1989:108, 233; Waring, 1984: 154–5.
9. Mabey, 1988:85.
10. Tacitus, op. cit.
11. du Puget, n.d.:27.
12. Ward, 1997:II.
13. From the *Havamal*, or the Words of the High One, a collection of aphorisms attributed to Odin that encompasses the morals, philosophy and magical beliefs of the ancient Northern peoples. (Palsson, 1998).
14. See Dickins, 1915.
15. J.C. Jones, *Valhalla*, quoted in Guerber, 1986:180. Slightly adapted.
16. Cf. the magical character of the similarly tail-biting Uroborus.
17. Guerber, 1986:90, 180, 229.
18. Quotations from J.C. Jones, *Valhalla*, in Guerber, 1986:181.
19. Grimm, 1883–8; Gloseki, 1989:97.
20. Derivation suggested by Grimm, 1883–8: III, 1047.
21. Ward, 1997:III, V.
22. *Ynglingsaga*, ch. 7, (Detter, 1894).
23. Strömbäck, 1935.
24. Guerber, 1986:155, 155–6; Ward, 1997:V.
25. du Puget, n.d.:188.
26. Tillhagen, 1960:318, talks of men being ridden by the *mara*, or nightmare, and an instance occurs in the *Ynglingsaga*, ch. 13. (Detter, 1894)
27. *Ynglingsaga*, ch. 7. (Detter, 1894)
28. 'Völuspá: The Song of the Sybil', Auden and Taylor, 1981. The title of this piece would be translated more literally as the 'Prophecy of the Volva'. *Volva* or

volve, means 'woman with a magic wand, or wand-bearer' and hence denoted a woman knowledgeable in seiðr (Gordon, 1957).

29. Tegnér, *Frithiof Saga*; Guerber, 1986:312. (Tegnér, 1868)

30. *Vatnsdoela Saga*, ch. 26. (Vigfuson and Möbius, 1960)

31. Quoted in Ward, 1997.

32. The translation of Varðlokur as Warlock Song is misleading since what we now think of as a warlock, a black magician in league with Satan, was a four-teenth-century coinage and the word originally meant an 'oath breaker', hence 'traitor' or 'deceiver', but in Old English, not Norse (Ayto, 1990:567). In this instance, we merely follow convention by using the name by which this passage is most commonly known.

33. *Eiriks Saga Rauða*. (Jones, 1999)

34. *Grettis Saga Ásmundarsonar*, ch. 79. (Foote, 1970)

35. *Voluspa*, alternative translation given by Ward, 1997.

36. *Eyrbyggja Saga*, ch. 20. (Palsson, 1989)

37. Buchholtz, 1971:12.

38. Adalsteinsson, 1978:110–22.

39. Cleasby and Vigfusson, 1957; Ward, 1997; Auden and Taylor (1981) translate the word as 'talisman'.

40. *Kormaks Saga*, ch. 18. (Killings, 1995)

41. Tegnér, trans. Longfellow, quoted in Guerber. 1986:313.

42. *Frithiof Saga*. Longfellow's translation of Tegnér captures something of the wild spirit of the age, but a more prosaic version, from which these quotations are taken, can be found in 'Frithiof's saga', 1928.

43. *Brewer's Dictionary*, 1990:776; Ayto, 1990:365; Tillhagen, 1960:318; Ward, 1997, V.

44. Guerber, 1986:23–6; Russell, 1980:45–6.

45. Quoted in Russell, 1980:46.

46. Guerber, 1986:57–8,140.

47. Ayto, 1990:279; Guerber, 1986:184. Hel's white horse reminds us of the white horses of the sacred groves met with earlier, and indeed in Celtic lands a white horse is a fairy steed, as, for example, in the Scottish ballad 'Thomas the Rhymer'.

48. Haas, 1903:24; a similar prize is recorded by von Tettau and Temme, 1837:244.

49. Quoted in Guerber, 1986:25–6.

Chapter 3

1. For example, the so-called Satanic ritual abuse scandal of the 1980s and 1990s. The Witchcraft Information Centre & Archive website (www.witch-craftinfo.info) carries regular news about cases of discrimination and persecution of witches today.

2. Gibbon, 1776–88.

3. Augustine, 1975:79.4.

4. Russell, 1980:39; Thomas, 1997:165.

5. St Theodore was Archbishop of Canterbury from 668 to 690.

6. Quoted in Russell, 1980:45.

7. St Theodore, 'De Idolatria et Sacrilegio', *Liber Pænitentialis*, quoted in Summers, 1947:6, 134.

8. Quoted in Maxwell-Stuart, 2000:46.

9. Russell, 1980:53; Maxwell-Stuart, 2000:44.

10. Quoted in Russell, 1980:52-3.

11. Quoted in Russell, 1980:45.

12. Baluze, 1677.

13. Baluze, 1677, I, cols 251-2.

14. Baroja, 1990:100-1.

15. Baroja, 1990:55.

16. Agobard's 'Liber contra insulsam vulgi opinionem de grandinem' is reproduced in Migne, 1965:CIV, cols 147ff.

17. Russell, 1980:53.

18. Russell, 1980:53; Baroja, 2001:98-9.

19. Council of Paris, 829 CE quoted in Baroja, 1999:56.

20. Summers, 1947:121, Ginzburg, 1990:89, Maxwell-Stuart, 2000:51. Russell, 1980:53, and Guiley, 1989:52, give only c. 900.

21. For example, by both Russell, 1980:53, and Guiley, 1989:52.

22. Quoted in Guiley.

23. Kramer and Sprenger, 1996.

24. Wakefield and Evans, 1969:254; Russell, 1980:62.

25. Russell, 1980:62; Watson, 1991:138.

26. See *Brewer's Dictionary*, 1990:343, and Summers, 1996:42, for the derivation of the Dominican nickname and the symbol of St Dominic.

27. Summers, 1947:46; Russell, 1980:70, 71.

28. Russell, 1980:76; Summers, 1996:xii.

29. Russell, 1980:90.

30. Russell, 1980:77-8.

31. Whilst Russell (1980:79) sees the importance of the Pope's seal of authority he makes little of it; and Thomas (1997:440) is too parochial in his interpretation of Kramer and Sprenger's role – the Catholic Church was an international organization and even events in Germany had their wider consequences.

32. Summers (1996:xiii, xvii) doubts the 1485 dating of the British Museum's earliest edition, and internal evidence, a reference to the year 1485 (Kramer and Sprenger, 1996:111), would appear to make this an unlikely date for publication, especially since on page 230 1485 is referred to as 'last year'; Russell, 1980:79, gives 1486; Maxwell-Stuart, 1999:55, translates the title more literally, but less poetically, as 'The Hammer of Women who work Harmful Magic', and gives the date of publication as 1487, which would not be supported by internal evidence.

33. Despite the many European editions an English edition of the work was late in coming. Some have suggested that this lessened its effect in England, but

they overlook the fact that Latin was the international language of the period. The lack of an early edition in the vernacular simply indicates that there was no need for one and not that the work itself was without influence. Although some of its arguments were taken up in England, what lessened its effect was the difference between judicial and ecclesiastical prosecution of cases of witchcraft in England and the Continent, a result more of Protestantism than the want of a book in English. An English edition did not come out until 1548.

34. Kramer and Sprenger, 1996:42.

35. Ecclesiasticus xxv; Kramer and Sprenger, 1996:43; St John Chrysostom, St Matthew xix.

36. Kramer and Sprenger (1996:44–5, 47) specifically cite Genesis xxx; I. Kings i, Numbers xii, St Luke x, Ecclesiasticus xxxvii, Proverbs xi, xxx, and Apocalypse vi, 8. I have used Kramer and Sprenger's original referencing.

37. Kramer and Sprenger, 1996:74, 75, 77, 82.

38. 'But let no one think that, because we have enumerated the various methods by which various forms of witchcraft are inflicted, he will arrive at a complete knowledge of these practices; for such knowledge would be of little use, and might even be harmful.' (Kramer and Sprenger, 1996:95). It seems that Kramer and Sprenger are trying to deflect criticism that their 'Hammer' could be wielded by witches themselves and turned upon its head, from a manual of their destruction to an instrument of their increase, or indeed to deter anyone who might think of using it for such a purpose.

39. Kramer and Sprenger, 1996.

40. Pt III, Qn 2; Kramer and Sprenger, 1996:208.

41. Of course estimates vary, but this range of dates encompasses most of them, including, for example, Russell, 1980:83, and Maxwell-Stuart, 2000:69.

42. Gage, 1893; Gardner, 1954:102; Guiley, 1989:369; Llewellyn-Barstow, 1994:179–81; Hutton, 1999:132.

43. Russell, 1980:81; *Brewer's Dictionary*, 1990:357, 909. Guiley, 1989:342, states that it was never used in England, which is surely wrong.

44. Sociologists like Max Marwick have propounded the theory that accusations of witchcraft are an indication of strain within a society. See Marwick, 1990:300ff.

45. Andrews, 1892; Deacon, 1976. The usually enthusiastic anti-witch, Montague Summers, pronounced him an 'unmitigated scoundrel' (Summers, 1947:4).

46. Quoted in Thomas, 1997:460.

47. Quoted in Thomas, 1997:462.

48. Porter, 1999:195; Gijswijt-Hofstra, 1999:146–7; Guiley, 1989:373.

49. Levack, 1999:77–8; Maxwell-Stuart, 2000:110–11; Porter, 1999:195; Gijswijt-Hofstra, 1999:151; Guiley, 1989:373; Russell, 1980:103.

Chapter 4

1. Jarke, 1828:450.

2. Mone, 1839.

3. Russell, 1980:133, gives the year of publication as 1869; Hutton, 1999:137, and Cohn, 1990:145, give the date as 1862.

4. Matriarchal theories of religion were derived from a sociological interpretation of a then current biological proposition that the development of the individual recapitulates the development of the species. Thus, just as all individuals come from a mother, so must all societies originate in a matriarchal culture.

5. Haac, 1982:138.

6. Michelet, 1969:1–2.

7. Leland, 1990:101.

8. Leland, 1990:1, 4, 5.

9. From 'How Diana Gave Birth to Aradia' Leland, 1990:6–7.

10. Leland, 1990:41.

11. Pennell, 1906:310, 341, 404.

12. Leland, 1990:116.

13. The order of the Sabbat varies in Leland's account: in chapter 1 *Benevento* comes before the Supper; in chapter 2 it precedes the Conjuration of Diana, who blows out the lights (Leland, 1990:7, 14).

14. Quoted in King, 1989:45.

15. The MacGregors had been a Jacobite thorn in the English side, and after the rebellion of 1745 the name was outlawed.

16. King, 1989:49.

17. Regardie, 1989.

18. Regardie, 1989:xvii.

19. Mathers, 1997:5.

20. Crowley, 1989:373.

21. Crowley, 1989:385.

22. Crowley, 1988.

23. Crowley, 1989:394. The Boulak Museum no longer exists; its exhibits are now in the National Museum in Cairo.

24. The stele is that of the priest Ankh-f-n-Khonsu and dates from the Twenty-sixth Dynasty. Horus has two, twin aspects: Harpocrates whose magical formula is Silence and Ra-Hoor-Khuit, whose formula is Outpouring (Crowley, 1987:307).

25. Had: Hadit (Behdety), is another name for Horus.

26. Crowley, 1987:164.

27. The term 'autohagiography' was Crowley's little joke: a hagiography being the account of the life of a saint, Crowley, 1989:839.

28. Hutton (1999:177) incorrectly gives this as the 20th of January.

29. Quoted in Symonds, 1989:188.

30. Letter from Crowley to Jones, quoted in Symonds, 1989:203.

31. Ibid.

32. Murray, 1963:104.

33. Murray, 1921:11, 12.

34. Murray, 1921:77–96.

35. Murray, 1921:97–109.
36. Murray, 1921:112–13.
37. Murray, 1921:130–52.
38. Burr, 1922:780–3; Halliday, 1922:224–30; Summers, 1926:32; Ewen, 1938; Butler, 1948; Robins, 1959:116–17; Rose, 1962; Macfarlane, 1967:16–18; Cohn, 1975:102–25; Simpson, 1994:89–96; Oates, 1998.

Chapter 5

1. Gardner, 1949:7.
2. Gardner, 1954: title page, 13.
3. Gardner, 1954:102 and 1959:9.
4. Except perhaps his monograph on the Malay Kris (1939), which has been described as definitive (Bracelin, 1960:8, 81, 84).
5. Gardner, 1949:8.
6. Most especially Crowley, 1912 and 1919. This view is supported by Hutton, 1999, Kelly, 1991, and Melton, 1987.
7. Moody, 1971:437; Russell, 1980:148; Guiley, 1989:134; Crowley, 1993:128; Kyle, 1993:271; and Purkiss, 1995:14.
8. Eliade (1987:421) supports this argument. He explicitly states that 'Gardner . . . invented the religion.'
9. Hobsbawm and Ranger (1983:1) famously defined an invented tradition as 'a set of practices, normally governed by overtly or tacitly accepted rules and of a ritual or symbolic nature, which seeks to inculcate certain values and norms of behaviour by repetition, which automatically implies continuity with the past. In fact, where possible, they normally attempt to establish continuity with a suitable historic past.'
10. J.G. Frazer was immensely popular at the time for his theory of the ritual origins of kingship, his delineation of magic and his cataloguing of exotic rituals (see *The Golden Bough*, 1922). Leland's works proved invaluable to Gardner. The poet and novelist Robert Graves wrote his influential pseudo-historical and largely inspirational account of the magico-religious nature of poetry, *The White Goddess*, in 1948. Gardner was so impressed with Graves's work that he took the trouble to visit him in Majorca. Gardner did little more than borrow a few lines of verse from Kipling's 'A Tree Song' in *Puck of Pook's Hill* (see Kipling, 1994:498) to pad out a calendrical festival.
11. The phrase requires some explanation since it is not rendered with the greatest accuracy in English translation. The Hebrew word *ob*, which we find translated as 'witch', denoted someone skilled in herbalism, poisoning and mediumship, or additionally an astrologer, diviner and juggler (Melton, 1986:211; Guiley, 1989:382). As early as the sixteenth century it was pointed out that *ob* meant something other than the Satanist the Christian Church denounced the witch as (Scot, 1584). Kramer and Sprenger (1996:6), authors of the definitive witch-hunters' handbook, specifically separate witchcraft from fortune-telling and soothsaying. However, the

description of the *ob* would fit the English cunningmen and wise women who were undoubtedly the victims of witchcraft persecution. The Witchcraft Acts of 1542, 1563 and 1604 outlawed fortune-telling, conjuring spirits, making charms and magically finding stolen goods. So that whilst the terms are not synonymous, by virtue of that distinction between folk magic and diabolism, the description 'witch' was more loosely applied to both. In spite of this semantic distinction both the folk magician and the diabolist often met with the same fate.

12. Baroja, 1990:100; Kramer and Sprenger, 1996:6; Rhodes, 1954:45; Bovet quoted in Summers, 1946:18. Witchcraft became a felony under English law in 1563. In 1564 the act of causing death by the use of witchcraft became a capital offence in both England and Scotland (*Brewer's Dictionary*, 1990:1183).

13. Gardner, 1954:105.

14. Ibid: 17.

15. As first pointed out by Rose, 1962.

16. Gardner, 1954:51.

17. Burr, 1922:780–3; Halliday, 1922:224–30; Summers, 1926:32; Ewen, 1938; Butler, 1948. All had made public their criticisms prior to Gardner's publication of *Witchcraft Today* (1954).

18. Robbins, 1959:116–7; Rose, 1962; Macfarlane, 1967:16–18; and still the criticisms mount up, e.g. Simpson, 1994:89–96, and Oates, 1998; although some choose to give Murray the benefit of what little doubt remains, e.g. Lewis (1996:2) generously refers to what he calls her 'speculative scholarship'.

19. Bracelin, 1960; Gardner, 1954: title page.

20. Farrar and Farrar, 1984:3.

21. Kelly, 1991.

22. Gardner, 1954:26.

23. Crowley, 1987:379–82; Regardie, 1989:53–4, 280–4.

24. Nataf, 1991:93; *Concise Handbook*, 1896.

25. Kelly, 1991:52.

26. Farrar and Farrar, 1984:67.

27. Crowley, 1987:427.

28. Mathers, 1909:16.

29. Lugh, 1994:79. 'Lugh' is the pen-name of William Liddell.

30. Knoop and Jones, 1949:90–1.

31. Quoted in Kelly, 1991:53.

32. Kelly, 1991:54; Farrar and Farrar, 1984:16, 297.

33. Crowley, 1987:426–9.

34. Leland, 1899:6–7; Crowley, 1988:50 (I:58), 52 (II:20), and 1987:427.

35. The technical term is theocrasy, the mingling of various deities into one personality, first used by Faber (1813, II:248) to describe a mystical practice of 'the old mythologists'. As such it demonstrates that Rose's (1962:206) observation is not compelling proof of the modern authorship of the passage in question. A much more telling line is Gardner's (1954) belief that the gods need human

help, unheard of in Pagan mythology or Christian theology.

36. Rose, 1962:206, 207.
37. Kelly, 1991:55-8.
38. Cf. *Concise Handbook*, 1896.
39. Crowley, 1998:19.
40. For the record it should be noted that Gardner counts three passwords in the ceremony, but the first two are analytically, if not literally, one, hence the numbering used here.
41. *Concise Handbook*, 1896.
42. Quoted in Kelly, 1991:61.
43. See Crowley, 1987:426-7.
44. *Concise Handbook*, 1896.
45. See Kelly, 1991:56, 58, 60.
46. Kelly, 1991:64-5.
47. Mathers, 1991:64, 88.
48. Regardie, 1989:221, 258, 354.
49. Crowley, 1987:56.
50. King, 1989:114.
51. Symonds, 1989:166, 168-9.
52. Kelly, 1991:65. For an uncritical use of Kelly's argument see Greenwood, 1995.
53. Gardner, 1954:46-7.
54. Gardner, 1954:46-7. Mathers called *The Key of Solomon the King* the 'fountain-head and storehouse of Qabalistic Magic' (1989:vii).
55. Gardner, 1954:47. Crowley's supposed admission to Gardner sounds like a typical Crowleyan joke. Crowley had had an unhappy childhood; his family were members of the strict Plymouth Brethren.
56. Melton, 1987; Jones and Pennick, 1995.
57. Kelly, 1991; Greenwood, 1994; Melton, 1987; Jones and Pennick, 1995.
58. It is interesting to note as an aside that academe also operates a three-degree system of initiation, namely bachelor, master and doctor.
59. Smyth, 1970:30; Bracelin, 1960:213. Jack Bracelin is credited with the authorship of *Gerald Gardner: Witch*, but there is some suggestion that he did not, in fact, write it. Valiente (1989:69) claims to have heard this first hand, but unfortunately does not name her source. Fred Lamond, who was initiated into Witchcraft by Gardner in 1957, believes that the true author was the occultist Idries Shah. Reflecting upon the work, Shah apparently did not want his name to appear on it (Kelly, 1991:169). This seems to have been accepted in some academic quarters: Baker (1996) takes the liberty of directly ascribing the work to Shah.
60. Valiente, 1989:41-2, 43; Smyth, 1970:30; Bracelin, 1960; Field, 1954; Andrews, 1951.
61. Gardner, 1959:11.
62. Nataf, 1991:34; Kelly, 1991; Bracelin, 1960:35.
63. King, 1989:177. One of these sources may have been Patricia Crowther, an attractive, elfin woman, Gardnerian initiate and writer on Witchcraft. She also

said that she had met Crowley, in 1945 or 1946, and had heard from him the same story: that as a young man he had been offered initiation into the Witch Cult, but rejected it because of its female leadership (Crowther, 1970). Unfortunately Crowley's diary for the period does not record a Patricia Crowther (or, as she was then, a Patricia Dawson). During the 1970s almost everybody claimed to have met Aleister Crowley, as if meeting him conferred some mystical benediction. The idea of Crowley having been approached by the Witch Cult was put about by Gardner himself in order to justify his use of Crowley's writings as having originally derived from the Cult.

64. King, 1989:177.
65. Valiente, 1989:36.
66. Torrens, 1973; Regardie, 1989.
67. Valiente, 1989:58, gives the date as 1946.
68. Medway, 1995; King, 1989:176; Valiente, 1989:57–9. Valiente recalls that Gerald Yorke told her that Gardner had paid £300 for this charter, a not inconsiderable sum in 1947.
69. Crowther, 1999.
70. Evidence of Yorke having lent Gardner this book rests upon a note to that effect made on the title page of Yorke's copy of *The Key of Solomon the King* (now in the possession of the Warburg Insitute, London).
71. Letter to John Symonds from Gerald Gardner, 1950, in the Gerald Yorke Collection, Warburg Institute, Scrapbook EE2, fo. 340.
72. Murray, 1954; Kelly, 1991; Valiente, 1989.
73. For example, Medway, 1995.
74. Lewis, 1996:3.
75. Voigt, 1992:174.
76. Farrar and Farrar, 1984:2.
77. Harrow, 1996:15.
78. Adler, 1989:89.
79. Starhawk, 1989:16–17.
80. Campanelli, 1992:53; Farrar and Farrar, 1984:109; Starhawk, 1982:xii.
81. Kelly, 1991:6.
82. Harrow, 1996:13–14.
83. Carpenter, 1996:46, 47.
84. Carpenter, 1996; Griffin, 1988.
85. Orion, 1990; Carpenter, 1996:49.
86. Wright, 1994:24.

Chapter 6

1. Kelly, 1991:165, although Lugh (1994:156) contests this list. North was more widely known as Madelaine Montalban, and somewhat humorously to her friends as the Witch of St Giles because she lived in the St Giles district of London. Reid was Chosen Chief of the Druid Order. Besant-Scott was Annie Besant's daughter and co-founder of the Rosicrucian Theatre. Sullivan was co-

founder and director of the Rosicrucian Theatre.

2. Rhyming version of 'The Charge', Valiente, 1989:61.

3. A year or so prior to the publication of his first non-fiction work on Witchcraft, *Witchcraft Today*, Gardner had established himself in Cecil Williamson's Museum of Witchcraft and Magic near Castletown on the Isle of Man as its resident witch.

4. Known as Mrs Woodley-Grimes to the outside world (Crowther, 1999).

5. Valiente, 1989:37, 39.

6. Ibid: 47.

7. Ibid: 63.

8. Fuller, 1926:231.

9. Farrar and Farrar, 1984:325, 299; Hutton, 1999:232.

10. Quoted in Gardner, 1959:225–6.

11. Valiente, 1989:72.

12. Farrar and Farrar, 1999.

13. Valiente, 1989:135–6.

14. This attribution is said by T.C. Lethbridge (1962) to be characteristic of traditional as opposed to modern Witchcraft, although his evidence comes from correspondence with people claiming to be traditional Witches at that time.

15. Valiente, 1989.

16. Graves, 1961:401.

17. These terms derive from Murray, 1921 and 1933.

18. Graves, 1961:401.

19. The version used by Isobel Gowdie, recorded during her trial, Auldearne, 1662. Quoted in Graves, 1961:401.

20. Cochrane, 1963.

21. Valiente, 1989:121.

22. Jones and Clifton, 1997:164–5; Valiente, 1989:127.

23. Valiente, 1989:130. Hutton, 1999:300, claims that it was founded by Sybil Leek.

24. Valiente, 1989:129.

25. Quoted in Valiente, 1989:133.

26. The number 1734 is said to be of numerological significance and does not refer to an actual date. The key apparently lies in *The White Goddess*.

27. Leek was born in the Midlands area of the UK in 1923 and died in Melbourne, Florida, USA, in 1983.

28. Guiley, (1989:197), gives the spelling as George du Loup; Valiente, (1989:145), as Gorge.

29. Guiley, 1989:197.

30. Leek, 1968:122.

31. Ibid.

32. Ibid: 11.

33. Quoted in Parker, 1993:62.

34. Gardiner, 2000:356.

35. Guiley; 1989:301; Parker, 1993:62.

36. Parker, 1993:63.
37. Crowley, 1989; for one of Crowley's better biographers see Symonds (1989).
38. Russell, 1980:154; Guiley, 1989:301; Parker, 1993:63–4.
39. Parker, 1993:65.
40. Parker, 1993:64, 70–1, 74; Kemp, 1993:42.
41. Guiley, 1989:302; Kemp, 1993:42–3.
42. Parker, 1993:75.
43. This council has an unsupportable and quite ridiculously disproportionate membership for a body of 'elders'; according to Guiley (1989:302) many Witches (whom she does not specify) have considered this council a mere figment of the imagination.
44. Whilst Parker, (1993:63), repeats this without comment, Guiley, (1989:302), asserts that no existing records of these trials mention anyone called Nick Demdike.
45. Guiley, 1989:302; Sanders, 1995.
46. Quoted in Parker, 1993:66.
47. Farrar and Farrar, 1984:245; Kemp, 1993:42; Parker, 1993:65–6.
48. Quoted in Ibid.
49. Farrar and Farrar, 1984:4; Adler, 1986:120; Guiley. 1989:302.
50. Parker, 1993:67.
51. Parker, 1993:66–7.
52. Parker, 1993:67–70.
53. Parker, 1993:71.
54. Farrar quoted in Guiley, 1989:302; Maxine quoted in Parker, 1993:71.
55. Parker, 1993:75; personal communication, 6 September 1995.
56. Guiley, 1989:40.
57. Adler, 1986:92,118; Guiley, 1989:41.
58. Gardner had bought the museum from Cecil Williamson, but the sale ended acrimoniously and caused a permanent split between the two men.
59. Guiley, 1989:41.
60. Adler, 1986:92–3; Guiley, 1989:41.
61. Guiley, 1989:47–9.
62. Anderson was born in New Mexico, c. 1900.
63. Adler, 1986:78–9; Guiley, 1989:10.
64. Quoted in Guiley, 1989:10.
65. Pendderwen was born in Berkeley, California, 1946. He died in 1982. It is unlikely that Gwydion Pendderwen was his given name.
66. Guiley, 1989:264.
67. Adler, 1986:386–7; Guiley, 1989:264–5.
68. Adler, 1986:315; Guiley, 1989:265.
69. Budapest was born Zsusanna Mokcsay in Budapest, Hungary, on 30 January, 1940.
70. Quoted in Guiley, 1989:43.
71. Adler, 1986:76–7; Melton, 1987:215; Guiley, 1989:41–3.
72. Guiley, 1989:327; Leibrock, 2001.

Chapter 7

1. Summers, 1947:2, with some modifications.
2. Gardner, 1954:45.
3. Murray, 1921, 1933; Leland, 1899.
4. Leland, 1990:103.
5. Sorcerer's Apprentice, 1989.
6. Thirty-seven per cent had gone on to higher education and 21 per cent had been to university.
7. Luhrmann, 1989.
8. York, 1995. The figures quoted are based upon a secondary analysis of his raw data.
9. 35.7 per cent (42.9 per cent of those answering).
10. Some 28.6 per cent were graduates: 22.9 per cent had a first degree and 5.7 per cent a master's degree (Ruickbie, n.d.).
11. Scott , 1980:127.
12. Adler, 1986:443–65. Adler's research was carried out in the summer of 1985 by distributing questionnaires amongst the attendees of three Pagan festivals (Rites of Spring, Massachusetts; the Pagan Spirit Gathering, Wisconsin; and the Festival of Women's Spirituality in Oregon).
13. Fritscher, 1985:362.
14. All charts, unless otherwise indicated, are based on data taken from Ruickbie, n.d.
15. York surveyed forty-two people: 45.2 per cent were aged between thirty and forty-nine; 19.1 per cent were aged over fifty and only 35.7 per cent were aged between eighteen and twenty-nine (York, 1995).
16. Greenwood, 1995. The three covens she studied had a total core membership of twenty-three.
17. Crowley, 1996, sample drawn from her Wicca Study Group.
18. Kemp, 1993:133.
19. Ruickbie, n.d.
20. They found that 22 per cent were aged between thirty-one and thirty-five and 18 per cent between thirty-six and forty (*Green Egg*, 1991).
21. Kyle, 1993:275.
22. Berger, 1995. Berger's imprecision impedes her attempt to chart the maturation of the Pagan movement.
23. Thirteen per cent were aged between twenty and twenty-four, 33 per cent between twenty-five and twenty-nine, 16 per cent between thirty and thirty-four, 26 per cent between thirty-five and forty-four, and 10 per cent forty-five and older (Rabinovitch, 1996).
24. See Ruickbie, n.d.
25. Men: 21.9 per cent unemployed/unwaged; 18.8 per cent retired; 3.1 per cent student. Women: 5.3 per cent unemployed/unwaged; 5.3 per cent retired; 7.9 per cent parent/home-maker; 5.3 per cent student (Ruickbie, n.d.).
26. 15.8 per cent of women in management/proprietorship compared with only 9 per cent of men; 18.4 per cent in health care, 87.5 per cent of every-

one in this group (Ruickbie, n.d.).

27. Women represented 66.7 per cent of those in the unskilled category, 66.7 per cent of those in education, 66.7 per cent of those in personal services and 100 per cent of those in sales. As a percentage of women, 5.3 per cent were in unskilled work, 7.9 per cent were in sales, 10.5 per cent each in education and personal services, and 5.3 per cent in clerical or administrative positions (Ruickbie, n.d.).

28. 12.5 per cent of men in skilled/semi-skilled work, 3.1 per cent in health care; 9.4 per cent of the men and 2.6 per cent of the women employed in the technical professions (Ruickbie, n.d.); Crowley, 1996; Adler, 1986.

29. Adler, 1986:446–9; Luhrmann, 1989:99; Sorcerer's Apprentice, 1989:14; Greenwood, 1995; Crowley, 1996. Crowley's group has been independently identified as the Wicca Study Group.

30. Melton quoted in Adler, 1986:446; Scott, 1980:127; Luhrmann, 1989:101.

31. Luhrmann, 1989:100. *The Cauldron*, 1990:9. Although Kyle (1993:275) also noted a particular psychological profile displaying the character traits of independence and creativity he did not try to make a social class out of it. So whilst Luhrmann's conclusions are wrong her observations may not be.

32. Sorcerer's Apprentice, 1989:15.

33. Ruickbie, n.d. £18,000 is approximately US$28,500.

34. Sorcerer's Apprentice, 1989; Luhrmann, 1989; York, 1995. According to York, 19 per cent earned less than £5,000, 35.7 per cent £5,000-£10,000, and, in total, 71.4 per cent earned £15,000 or less.

35. 17.9 per cent poor; 46.4 per cent lower-middle class; 23.8 per cent upper-middle class; 4.8 per cent wealthy; 7.1 per cent refused to answer (York, 1995).

36. See Roberts et al., 1977, and Martin, 1954.

37. Kirkpatrick, 1984.

38. Exchanges in *The Seax* (1995:4), a local Pagan Federation journal, demonstrated that 'middle class' is often interpreted as a term of abuse even if it is warranted.

39. Kyle, 1993:275.

40. Including the 2.2 per cent who replied 'other' to this question and the 5 per cent who refused to answer, Berger's figures unfortunately add up to 109.9 per cent (Berger, 1995:8).

41. Greenwood, 1995; Crowley, 1996; Ruickbie, n.d.

42. Talmud, paraphrased by Baroja, 2001:80.

43. Truzzi, 1974:217; Scott, 1980:127; Melton, 1986:214 and in the 1992 edition, p. 327; *Green Egg*, 1991; Berger, 1995.

44. The Information Network Focus on Religious Movements. Based at the London School of Economics this organization has on occasion received official funding from the Home Office.

45. Twenty-three (54.8 per cent) were men and eighteen (42.8 per cent) women with one (2.4 per cent) who 'did not know' (York, 1995).

46. York, 1995; Berger, 1995; Crowley, 1996.

47. Ruickbie, n.d. The Sorcerer's Apprentice (1989) does not give the male/female distribution for either neo-Paganism or Witchcraft, although reported that for occultists generally (i.e. including both neo-Pagans and Witches) there was a predominance of men (62 per cent of the sample). However,. the authors try and explain this by pointing to the distorting effect of Satanism. Most of the Satanists in their sample were men, more so than occultists on average, at 83 per cent.

48. Russell (1980), Tysoe (1984:94), Crowley (1989), Farrar and Farrar (1990:191), Kelly (1991:ix–x), Kyle (1993:271), Greenwood (1995:47) and Sanders (1995) all report that the numbers of Witches are increasing.

49. King (1970:176) believed that from personal experience, or so he said, there were 'one or two thousand individuals who are . . . active members of covens'. Truzzi (1974:218) thought that 'Great Britain and the United States probably can claim no more than 1,950 coven members'.

50. York (1995:41), although York's low commitment model is corrected by the more sophisticated analyses of Greenwood, et al. (1995) and Ruickbie (n.d.).

51. Oath of the New Wiccan Church quoted in Russell, 1980:165; Ruickbie, n.d.; Adler, 1986.

52. Russell, 1980:140. He does not tell us how he arrived at this figure, so it would seem that he merely plucked it out of the air.

53. Luhrmann's (1989:4, n.3) estimation of the numbers involved is vague. She looks to book sales, but book sales only demonstrate the level of general interest and not of committed or even casual involvement.

54. Mahoney, 1995:5.

55. Tysoe, 1984:92.

56. Sorcerer's Apprentice, 1989:3, 9, 17.

57. Kyle, 1993:274; Eliade, 1987:421–2; Harvey, 1994:103.

58. Farrar and Farrar, 1981; Melville, 1985; Shan, 1988:4; Crowley, 1989:240; Scott, 1980:99; Adler, 1986:107.

59. Based on Farrar, Farrar and Bone (1995:195) and my own research undertaken for this work. Mexico, South America, Africa and India all have what are often termed 'witches', although these individuals are either traditional healers, or those accused of using supernatural powers to harm their neighbours, i.e. not modern Gardnerian Witches (or any neo-Pagan variation thereof).

60. Berger (1999:10) reporting on the Neo-Pagan Census findings, which she points out was not based on a random distribution sample and therefore can only be regarded as suggestive and not conclusive.

61. This can be established fairly crudely by looking at the moots listings in an issue of the Pagan Dawn (No. 125, Samhain 1997, pp. 41–3) where we find a total of 186 such events in the UK and Ireland. 'Moot' is the term given to a meeting, usually in a public house, that is open to all interested parties. It rarely engages in ritual activity at such locations and is usually not considered to be a group in itself and hence tends to have an ecumenical or multi-traditional character, although it will often be the meeting-place of various group members in the district. Its primary purpose is to bring together people of a

like mind. It may have guest speakers and other events are likely to be organized around it. It is often run by a member of the Pagan Federation, or
PaganLink, although such 'official' status is not compulsory. *The Pagan Dawn*
moots list also contains a number of specific ritual groups. The list is not
exhaustive as many groups, for reasons of privacy, prefer not to publish details
of their meetings.

62. Sixty moots, or 32.2 per cent of the total, were based in the South-east of
England. Within this area, Greater London has the lion's share of moots, some
eighteen – being 10 per cent of the total, or 30 per cent of the moots in the area
However, the listing was misleading in this regard. Only fourteen moots and
groups were given for the 'London Area', but three London telephone codes
were incorrectly listed under Surrey, and Middlesex, usually considered a part
of Greater London, was listed separately. The figures have been recalculated to
take account of these discrepancies.

63. Midlands (and East Anglia), fifty-six moots (30.1 per cent); North,
twenty-eight moots (15 per cent); South-west, thirteen moots (7 per cent);
Scotland, eleven moots (6 per cent); Wales, eleven moots (6 per cent); Ireland,
six moots (3.2 per cent); Jersey, one moot (0.5 per cent).

64. Percentage distribution: Greater London, 24 per cent; South-east
England (inc. Greater London), 37 per cent; South-west, 7 per cent;
Midlands, 10 per cent; North-east, 21 per cent; North-west, 12 per cent;
Scotland, 7 per cent; Wales, 5 per cent, Northern Ireland, 1 per cent
(Sorcerer's Apprentice, 1989:10). The Sorcerer's Apprentice cautions that
these figures may be biased in favour of the North-east because their operations are based there and also because occultists in this area had been galva-
nized into responding by the contemporaneous Satanic ritual abuse scandal in
the locality.

65. Murray, 1931.

66. Gardner, 1954:121.

67. Murray, 1921:VII, §2.

68. Cotton Mathers on the Salem witch trials of 1692, quoted in Guiley,
1989:76.

69. Leland, 1899:6.

70. Adler, 1986.

71. Berger, 1999:50. However, so-called 'solitary' practice also seems to
cover couples practising Witchcraft together.

72. Ruickbie (n.d.). The sample used, however, was drawn from those
publicly advertising their willingness to contact other people, and therefore
has a bias towards group involvement.

73. Starhawk, 1989; Berger, 1999.

74. For example, the inauguration ceremony of the Circle of Light coven
(Berger, 1999:48–9).

75. Ruickbie, n.d., case no. 77.

Chapter 8

1. Guiley, 1989:107, attributed to an unnamed antique text.
2. This is a modern interpretation. Hecate herself was a tri-form goddess and could express all three of these characteristics.
3. Ruickbie, n.d.: case no. 64.
4. Ruickbie, n.d., is the only known in-depth exploration of Witchcraft theology.
5. Whilst some of these categories held few cases they could not be combined except under that banner of vagueness, 'other', where countless contradictions may lurk undisturbed. It is entirely because of this unpardonable action of the 'other' category to swallow the dissimilar and make them appear similar that an almost unwieldy number of small categories was preferred to an inordinately large 'other' category. The danger, and one cannot tire from stressing it, is to give the appearance of association between the cases collected under 'other' which is entirely lacking.
6. The correct construction of words using the Greek would give us ditheism and so on, but I think my meaning is better and more easily conveyed by the incorrect duotheism and in the midst of such terminological convolutions ease of understanding must take precedence over correctitude.
7. Some 27.1 per cent of those asked expressed this view (Ruickbie, n.d.).
8. Of those subscribing to the MDM view, 63.2 per cent also described their relationship with divinity as personal.
9. Ruickbie, n.d.: case no. 6.
10. Ruickbie, n.d.: case no. 28.
11. 10, 10 and 8.6 per cent, respectively.
12. 7.1, 5.7 and 5.7 per cent, respectively.
13. Ruickbie, n.d.: case no. 36.
14. 31.4 per cent of those asked.
15. 7.1 per cent.
16. 'Mystical' answers accounted for 21.4 per cent, whilst 11.4 per cent answered in 'religious' terms and 5.7 per cent in each case gave 'constructed' and 'technical' answers.
17. 4.3 per cent a-religious, 3 per cent developmental. The remaining 10 per cent gave no response.
18. Proportionally the difference was less pronounced, with 21.9 per cent of the men and 39.5 per cent of the women giving this answer.
19. 13.2 per cent of women and 9.4 per cent of men.
20. 12.5 per cent of men and 2.6 per cent of women 'emotional', 9.4 per cent men and no women 'a-religious'.
21. In raw numerical terms there were slightly more women, but, proportionally more men than women gave this answer: 21.9 per cent of the men to 21.1 per cent of the women.
22. Proportionally this worked out at 6.3 per cent of the men and 5.3 per cent of the women.
23. Again this meant a greater proportion of men to women giving a 'devel-

opmental' response: 3.1 per cent of men and 2.6 per cent of women – while 9.4 per cent of men and 10.5 per cent of women gave no answer.

24. Some 97.1 per cent of Witches reported a mystical experience or experiences, and 77.9 per cent rated the importance of their mystical experience(s) as a 5 on a scale of 1–5. None rated it lower than 3. The rest rated it as a 4 (nine people, or 13.2 per cent), or 3 (six people, or 8.8 per cent), giving an average of 4.7. Including those who did not report having a mystical experience the average falls to 4.56.

25. The 2.9 per cent who had not had a mystical experience were male.

26. Some 81.6 per cent of women put it at 5, or 58.5 per cent of this rating. Whilst the majority of the men also rated their experience as 5 (68.8 per cent), proportionally more of them also rated it lower. Where 15.6 per cent of the men rated their experience as 4, only 10.5 per cent of the women did so. The men accounted for 55.6 per cent of this category. Again, whereas 9.4 per cent of the men rated it 3, only 7.9 per cent of the women did so, although in this case men and women each accounted for exactly half of this category. On average women rated their mystical experience at 4.7, whilst the men only rated it at 4.3.

27. Ruickbie, n.d.: case no. 67.

28. Ruickbie, n.d.: case no. 6.

29. Ruickbie, n.d.: case no. 7.

30. Ruickbie, n.d.: cases no. 11 and 47 respectively.

31. Of the men 21.9 per cent reported numinous experiences; and 28.9 per cent of the women; 15.6 per cent of the men and 10.5 per cent of the women had a xenophrenic experience.

32. A total of 10.5 per cent of women and 6.3 per cent of men reported psychic phenomena, while 9.4 per cent of men reported some sort of nature mysticism compared to only 2.6 per cent of women, accounting for 75 per cent of this category. Three-quarters of those who revalued the everyday as mystical were women; although this represented only 7.9 per cent of women it was still more than double the 3.1 per cent of men who gave this answer. Seventy-five per cent of those who did not know or gave no answer were men: 9.4 per cent of men and 2.6 per cent of women.

33. Based upon the ritual given in Farrar and Farrar, 1984:296–7.

34. The overlap in attendence between 1–2, 2–4, 4–8 and 8–11 times was caused by the sorts of answers given, thus some would say that they attended only once or twice a year, whilst others would say they attended twice or three times, and so on.

35. 13.2 per cent of women and 12.5 per cent of men never or only once; 15.8 per cent of women and 9.4 per cent of men monthly; 21.1 per cent of women and 6.3 per cent of men very often; 7.9 per cent of women and 9.4 per cent of men intensely.

36. 15.6 per cent of men and 15.8 per cent of women rarely; 18.8 per cent of men and 2.6 per cent of women occasionally; 6.3 per cent of men and 15.8 per cent of women regularly; 21.9 per cent of men and 7.9 per cent of women seasonally.

37. Ruickbie, n.d.: case no. 123.

38. 64.3 per cent seasonal; 8.6 per cent other; 7.1 per cent rite of passage; 7.1 per cent convocation; 2.9 per cent lunar; 4.3 per cent unspecified; 5.7 per cent 'don't know'.

39. 14.3 per cent no distinction; 22.9 per cent seasonal ritual; 11 per cent initiation, of whom 62.5 per cent were Wiccans.

40. 12.9 per cent marital ceremony; 1.4 per cent naming ceremony; in total 25.7 per cent a rite of passage.

41. 18.6 per cent non-seasonal rituals; healing ritual 2.9 per cent.

42. 9.4 per cent of men and 15.8 per cent of women marital ritual; 2.6 per cent and 5.3 per cent of women either naming or healing ritual; 25 per cent of men and 21.1 per cent of women seasonal ritual; 15.7 per cent of men and 21.1 per cent of women non-seasonal ritual.

43. Ruickbie, n.d.: case no. 81.

44. 21.4 per cent social; 7.1 per cent did not take part in rituals; 15.7 per cent did not answer; excluding non-relevant categories the percentage giving a social answer rises to 27.8 per cent.

45. 13 per cent (16.7 per cent excluding non-relevant categories) emotionally moving; 7.1 per cent (9.2 per cent) mystical; 4.3 per cent (5.6 per cent) religious; 1.4 per cent (1.8 per cent) spiritual development; 5.7 per cent (7.4 per cent) path related; 5.7 per cent (7.4 per cent) personal satisfaction; 4.3 per cent (5.6 per cent) personal development; 1.4 per cent (1.8 per cent) meaningfulness; 1.4 per cent (1.8 per cent) phenomenal; 3 per cent (4 per cent) did not know; 7.1 per cent (9.2 per cent) indifferent; 1.4 per cent (1.8 per cent) hostile to ritual.

46. Some 73.3 per cent of those giving a social response were women; 55.6 per cent of emotional answers given by women; 18.8 per cent of men and 15.8 per cent of women gave no answer; 6.3 per cent of men and 5.3 per cent of women said no rituals had been of importance; and 3.1 per cent of men and 2.6 per cent of women did not know why a particular ritual had been important.

47. 6.3 per cent of men and 5.3 per cent of women 'commitment'.

48. 6.3 per cent of men and 2.6 per cent of women personal development; 12.5 per cent of men and 2.6 per cent of women mystical; 9.4 per cent of men and 5.3 per cent of women indifferent; 3.1 per cent of men and 5.3 per cent of women religious; and 3.1 per cent of men and 7.9 per cent of women personally satisfying.

Chapter 9

1. Wiccan circle-casting ritual (Farrar and Farrar, 1984:295).
2. Raleigh, 1614:201; Jennings, 1884:8; Crowley, 1987:131.
3. Russell, 1983:722–7.
4. Rycroft, 1972:172.
5. Crowley, 1987:133.

6. Ibid. 137, 283–4.

7. On Crowley's less salubrious magic see Symonds, 1989; Crowley, 1987:138.

8. Crowley, 1987:131.

9. Ibid. 132.

10. Crowley, 1988:94.

11. Ibid. 94.

12. Gardner, 1954:19, 99.

13. Ayto, 1990:89.

14. Ibid. 390.

15. Adler, 1986:8.

16. Beth, 1990:22, 44, 45, 60, 114.

17. Ruickbie, n.d.; 94.3 per cent said they practised magic. Of the 5.7 per cent who did not the majority (75 per cent) were men.

18. Ruickbie, n.d.: case no. 36.

19. These periods were subjective and not objectively measured, thus one person's 'sometimes' is not the same as another's, but it measures more accurately how often they think they practise. Figures calculated excluding those who do not practise magic: 56.1 per cent practised often, 33.3 per cent sometimes, 7.6 per cent hardly ever, 1.5 per cent only in times of crisis and the remaining 1.5 per cent did not know.

20. Of those practising often 56.8 per cent were women, as were 59.1 per cent of those practising sometimes.

21. 7.9 per cent of women compared to 6.3 per cent of men.

22. Ruickbie, n.d.: case no. 70.

23. 'Magick is the Science and Art of causing Change in conformity with Will.' (Crowley, 1987:131). However, Crowley's Magick is not just any magic and his use of the final 'K' is more than stylistic affectation. It is the quintessence of his theory of applied metaphysics (Symonds and Grant in the Introduction to Crowley, 1987:xvi). So when Crowley defined Magick he did more, and less, than define magic.

24. Iroë-Grego, also Iohé Grevis and Iroe Grevis, is mentioned in a manuscript thought to date from the sixteenth century held in the British Museum (Add. MSS. 10862). He is described as a Babylonian philosopher of post-Solomonic times (Mathers, 1989:viii–ix, 3).

25. Ruickbie, n.d.: case no. 105.

26. Ibid. Cases 15, 112 and 40.

27. Twenty-five per cent of men and 7.9 per cent of women defined magic as WDTUT; 28.9 per cent of women and 12.5 per cent of men defined it as TET; 12.5 per cent of men and 13.2 per cent of women defined it as TUT; 72.7 per cent of those defining magic as WDTUT were men and 73.3 per cent of those defining magic as TET were women.

28. Only 2.9 per cent of those questioned used magic exclusively to heal themselves.

29. Of those asked, 42.4 per cent gave a multiple answer to the question of what they use magic for. Of these 44.8 per cent used it for healing, 17.2 per

cent for social development, 17.2 per cent for personal advantage, 6.9 per cent for 'religious' purposes, 6.9 per cent for problem solving, 3.5 per cent for mystical reasons, and 3.5 per cent for spiritual purposes.

30. The largest groups of both men (28.1 per cent, or excluding non-practitioners, 31 per cent) and women (31.6 per cent, or 32.4 per cent) used magic for the healing of others. Some 21.9 per cent (or 24.1 per cent) of men used it for personal development, whilst only 13.2 per cent (or 13.5 per cent) of women did so; 18.4 per cent (or 18.9 per cent) of women used it for personal advantage whilst 9.4 per cent (or 10.3 per cent) of men did so.

31. Ruickbie, n.d.: case no. 10.

32. Some 47 per cent of the sample or 78.6 per cent of those giving an emotive qualifier gave this sort of answer.

33. Only 7.1 per cent (4.5 per cent), gave an equivocal emotive reply, and only 14.3 per cent (7.6 per cent) said magic had had a negligible effect upon their lives.

34. As many as 63.3 per cent of 'momentous' answers were given by women; 66.7 per cent of equivocal emotive responses were given by men. 34.4 per cent of men said magic's effect had been momentous. 60 per cent of those who said that magic's degree of effect had been negligible were women. More men (43.8 per cent) than women (36.8 per cent) did not specify any sort of qualitative effect.

35. Personal development 33.3 per cent, quality of life 21.2 per cent, self-confidence 16.7 per cent, sense of meaningfulness 9.1 per cent, mystical effect 6.1 per cent, social effect 6.1 per cent, personal advantage 3 per cent, spiritual development 1.5 per cent, and 3 per cent did not know what effect magic had had on their lives; figures recalculated to include only those who practised magic.

36. 31.3 per cent of men and 31.6 per cent of women.

37. 21.1 per cent of the women and 18.8 per cent of men gave this answer.

38. Although the numbers were equal because there were more women than men amongst those asked, the percentage proportion of men giving these answers was fractionally higher.

39. 23.7 per cent of women as opposed to only 6.3 per cent of men, accounting for 81.8 per cent of all those who gave this answer.

40. A social effect was reported by 7.9 per cent of women and 3.1 per cent of men. Two-thirds of all who reported greater meaningfulness were men, accounting for 12.5 per cent of men compared to only 5.3 per cent of women who answered similarly. Spiritual effect and personal advantage only represented 3.1 per cent and 6.3 per cent of men respectively. The remainder (9.4 per cent of men and 2.6 per cent of women) did not practise magic.

Conclusion

1. Valiente, 1989:218.
2. Robert Hardy quoted in Combe, 1998.

3. Combe, 1998; BBC News, 2002. The then Archbishop of Wales (now Archbishop of Canterbury), the Most Revd Rowan Williams, tried to get a foot in both camps by becoming an honorary Druid of the Welsh National Gorsedd of Bards in August of 2002.

4. Petre and Cobain, 2000; Petre and Southam, 2001.

5. Swanson, 2002. The research was conducted by Steve Bruce and Tony Glendinning of Aberdeen University and published in the Church of Scotland's magazine, *Life and Work*, c. 2002.

6. At the time of writing witchcraft was still banned under the 1966 Vagrancy Act in Victoria and under Section 432 of the 1899 Criminal Code in Queesland. Both laws have been subjected to recent judicial review. Petrys, 2002; Walker, 2002.

7. Sussman, 2002.

8. Quoted in Ferrer, 2002.

9. All references and quotations are taken from Ferrer, 2002.

10. The 'West' should be interpreted in terms of the 'First World', i.e. the most developed countries, which would also include Australia.

11. Weber uses this phrase or variations of it throughout his work, but see in particular Weber, 1987, and Weber, 1989.

12. The 'life-world' is a concept developed by Husserl (1970). Warnke (1987:35) explains this most succinctly: the life-world is 'the horizon of subjective modes of givenness'.

13. This is the phrase used by Bauman, 1992.

14. See Barthes (Myerson, 1997), Germain (1994), Postman (1993) and Ellul (1964) for a discussion of the enchantment of disenchantment.

15. See Webb (1971) for one of the few insightful investigations of the socio-history of the occult.

BIBLIOGRAPHY

Adalsteinsson, Jón *Under the Cloak: The Acceptance of Christianity in Iceland with Particular Reference to Religious Attitudes Prevailing at the Time.* Acta Universitatis Upsaliensis, 1978

Adler, Margot, *Drawing Down the Moon: Witches, Druids, Goddess-Worshippers, and Other Pagans in America Today,* revised and expanded edn. Beacon Press, 1986

Agobard, Saint, Archbishop of Lyons, 'Liber contra insulfam vulgi opinionem de grandinem', in *Opera omnia. Agobardi lugdunensis,* ed. L. van Acker. Typographi Brepols, 1981

Andrews, Allen, 'Witchcraft in Britain', *Illustrated,* 1951

Andrews, William, *Bygone Essex.* J. Forster, 1892

Apollonius, Rhodius, *Jason and the Golden Fleece (The Argonautica),* trans. Richard Hunter. Oxford University Press, 1995

Apuleius, Lucius, *The Golden Ass,* trans. William Addington, revised S. Gaselee. Wordsworth Editions, 1996

Auden, W.H., and P.B. Taylor (trans), *Norse Poems.* The Athlone Press, 1981

Augustine, Saint, Bishop of Hippo, *Opera: Pars 13, ii. De diversis quaestionibus octoginta tribus. De octo dulcitii quaestionibus,* Brepols, 1975

Ayto, John, *Dictionary of Word Origins.* Bloomsbury, 1990

Baker, James W., 'White Witches: Historic Fact and Romantic Fantasy', in James R. Lewis (ed.), *Magical Religion and Modern Witchcraft.* State University of New York Press, 1996

Baluze, Etienne, *Capitularia regum francorum.* F. Muguet, 1677

Baroja, Julio Caro, 'Witchcraft Amongst the German and Slavonic Peoples', in Max Marwick (ed.), *Witchcraft and Sorcery.* Penguin, 1990

Baroja, Julio Caro, *The World of the Witches.* Phoenix Press, 2001

Bauman, Zygmunt, *Intimations of Postmodernity.* Polity Press, 1992

Berger, Helen A., 'The Routinization of Spontaneity', *Sociology of Religion,* vol. 56, no. 1, 1995

Berger, Helen A., *A Community of Witches: Contemporary Neo- Paganism and Witchcraft in the United States.* University of South Carolina Press, 1999

Beth, Rae, *Hedge Witch.* Robert Hale, 1990

Bracelin, J.L., *Gerald Gardner: Witch*. Octagon Press, 1960

Bradford, Ernle, *Ulysses Found*. Hodder & Stoughton, 1963

Brewer's Dictionary of Phrase and Fable, 14th edn, revised by Ivor H. Evans. Cassell, 1990

Buchholtz, Peter, 'Shamanism: The Testimony of Old Icelandic Literary Tradition,' *Medieval Scandinavia* 4, 1971

Bulfinch, Thomas, *The Myths of Greece and Rome*. Penguin Books, 1983

Burkert, Walter, *Greek Religion*. Basil Blackwell, 1985

Burr, George Lincoln, 'A Review of M.A. Murray's Witch-Cult in Western Europe', *American Historical Review*, vol. 27, no. 4, 1922

Butler, E.M., *The Myth of the Magus*. Cambridge University Press, 1948

Caesar, Julius, *The Conquest of Gaul*, trans. S.A Handford and J. Gardner. Penguin Classics, 1951

Campanelli, Pauline, 'Seasonal Rites/Magical Rites', in Chas Clifton (ed.), *Witchcraft Today, Book One: The Modern Craft Movement*. Llewellyn, 1992

Carpenter, Dennis D., 'Emergent Nature Spirituality: an Examination of the Major Spiritual Contours of the Contemporary Pagan Worldview', in James R. Lewis (ed.), *Magical Religion and Modern Witchcraft*. State University of New York Press, 1996

The Cauldron, no. 55, Winter, 1990

Cleasby, Richard, and Gudbrandr Vigfusson, *An Icelandic-English Dictionary*, 2nd edn. Clarendon Press, 1957

Clement, F.E., 'Primitive Concepts of Disease', *University of California Publications in American Archaeology and Ethnology*, vol. 32, 1932

Clifton, Chas S., 'A Quick History of Witchcraft's Revival', in Chas S. Clifton (ed.), *Witchcraft Today, Book One: The Modern Craft Movement*. Llewellyn, 1992

Cochrane, Robert, 'Genuine Witchcraft Defended', *Psychic News*, 9 November 1963

Cohn, Norman, *Europe's Inner Demons*. Sussex University Press, 1975

Combe, Victoria, 'Bishop Warns of Pagan Threat to Rural Parishes', *Daily Telegraph*, 20 November 1998

A Concise Handbook for the Instruction of Students and Officers in Craft Freemasonry. Containing the Ritual Used in the Three Degrees. J. Boazman & Co., 1896

Crowley, Aleister, 'The Book of the Law', *The Equinox*, no. 8, 1912

Crowley, Aleister, 'Liber XV', *The Equinox*, 1919

Crowley, Aleister, *Magick*. Guild Publishing, 1987

Crowley, Aleister, *The Law is for All*, ed. Israel Regardie. Falcon Press, 1988

Crowley, Aleister, *The Confessions of Aleister Crowley*. Arkana Books, 1989

Crowley, Vivianne, *Wicca: The Old Religion in the New Age*, Aquarian Press, 1989

Crowley, Vivianne, 'Women and Power in Modern Paganism', in P.B. Clarke and E. Puttick (eds), *Women as Teachers and Disciples in Traditional and New Religions*. Edwin Meller Press, 1993

Crowley, Vivianne, 'Contemporary Paganism in the UK and Europe', unpubished paper presented to the Social Sciences and Religion Seminar, King's College, London, 10 October 1996

Crowther, Patricia, 'The Day I Met Aleister Crowley', *Prediction*, November, 1970

Crowther, Patricia, Foreword, to Gerald Gardner, *The Meaning of Witchcraft*. Mercury Publishing, 1999

Cunningham, Scott, *Magical Herbalism*. Llewellyn, 1983

Deacon, Richard, *Matthew Hopkins: Witch Finder General*. Muller, 1976

Detter, Ferdinand, 'Zur Ynglingsaga. 2: Der Baldermythus; König Hygelac', *Beiträge zur Gescgichte der deutschen Sprache und Literatur*, 19, 1894

Dickins, Bruce, *Runic and Heroic Poems of the old Teutonic Peoples*. Cambridge University Press, 1915

Dodds, E.R., *The Greeks and the Irrational*. University of California Press, 1963

du Puget, R., *Les Eddas traduites de l'ancien idiome scandinave*. Paris, n.d.

Eliade, Nircea, *The Encyclopedia of Religion*, vol. 15. Macmillan, 1987

Eliade, Mircea, *Occultism, Witchcraft and Cultural Fashions*. University of Chicago Press, 1976

Elliott, Alan, 'Periegesis', in Euripides, *Medea*. Oxford University Press, 1969

Ellul, Jacques, *The Technological Society*, trans. John Wilkinson. Vintage, 1964

Euripides, *Medea*, ed. Alan Elliott. Oxford University Press, 1969

Ewen, C.L., *Some Witchcraft Criticisms: A Plea for the Blue Pencil*. Privately printed, 1938

Faber, George Stanley, *A Practical Treatise on the Ordinary Operations of the Holy Spirit*. Kessinger, 1813

Farrar, Stewart and Janet Farrar, *Eight Sabbats for Witches*. Robert Hale, 1981

Farrar, Stewart and Janet Farrar, *The Witches' Way: Principles, Rituals and Beliefs of Modern Witchcraft*. Robert Hale, 1984

Farrar, Stewart and Janet Farrar, *Spells and How They Work*. Robert Hale, 1990

Farrar, Stewart, Janet Farrar and Gavin Bone, *The Pagan Path*. Phoenix, 1995

Farrar, Stewart and Janet Farrar, 'Doreen Valiente Passed into the Summerlands on the 1st of September', *www.iol.ie/~jsfarrar.index/html*, accessed 11 September, 1999

Ferrer, Richard, 'Godforsaken Survey', www.totallyjewish.com, 12 June 2002

Field, Arnold, [Interview with Gerald Gardner], *Daily Despatch*, 5 August 1954

Foote, Peter (ed.), *The Saga of Grettir the Strong*, trans. G.A. Hight Dent, 1970

Frazer, J.G., *The Golden Bough: A Study in Magic and Religion*. Macmillan, 1922

'Frithiofs saga hins Fraekna', trans. Margaret Schlauch, in *Medieval Narratives*. Prentice Hall, 1928

Fritscher, John, 'Straight from the Witch's Mouth', in A.C. Lehman and J.E. Myers (eds), *Magic, Witchcraft, and Religion*. Mayfield Publishing Co., 1985

Fuller, J.F.C., 'The Black Arts', *The Occult Review*, no. 43, 1926

Gage, Matilda Joslyn, *Woman, Church and State: A Historical Account of the Status of Woman Through the Christian Ages*. Kerr & Co., 1893

Gardiner, Juliet (ed.), *The History Today Who's Who in British History*. Collins & Brown and Cima Books, 2000

Gardner, Gerald, *The Keris and Other Malay Weapons*. Progressive Publishing, 1936

Gardner, Gerald B., *High Magic's Aid*. Michael Houghton, 1949

Gardner, Gerald B., *Witchcraft Today*. Rider, 1954

Gardner, Gerald B., *The Meaning of Witchcraft*. Aquarian Press, 1959

Germain, Gilbert G., 'The Revenge of the Sacred: Technology and Re-enchantment', in A. Horowitz and T. Maley (eds), *The Barbarism of Reason: Max Weber and the Twilight of Enlightenment*. University of Toronto Press, 1994

Gibbon, Edward, *The History of the Decline and Fall of the Roman Empire*, 6 vols. T. Cadell, 1776–88

Gijswijt-Hofstra, Marijke, 'Witchcraft After the Witch-Trials', in Bengt Ankarloo and Stuart Clark (eds), *Witchcraft and Magic in Europe: The Eighteenth and Nineteenth Centuries*. The Athlone Press, 1999

Ginzburg, Carlo, *Ecstasies: Deciphering the Witches' Sabbath*. Hutchinson, 1990

Gloseki, Stephen O., *Shamanism and Old English Poetry*. Garland, 1989

Gordon, E.V., *An Introduction to Old Norse*, 2nd edn. A.R. Taylor, 1957

Graf, F., *Nordionische Kulte*. Schweizerisches Institute in Rome, 1985

Graves, Robert, *The White Goddess*. Faber and Faber, 1961

Green Egg, vol. 24, no. 93, 1991

Greenwood, S., G. Harvey, A. Simes and M. Nye, 'Current Research on Paganism and Witchcraft in Britain', *Journal of Contemporary Religion*, vol. 10, no. 2, 1995

Greenwood, Susan, 'Wake the Flame Inside Us: Magic, Healing and the Enterprise Culture in Contemporary Britain', *Etnofoor*, vol. VIII, no. 1, 1995

Greenwood, Susan, 'The British Occult Subculture: Beyond Good and Evil', in James Lewis (ed.), *Magical Religion and Modern Witchcraft*. State University of New York Press, 1996

Griffin, David Ray (ed.), *The Reenchantment of Science, Postmodern Proposals*. State University of New York Press, 1988

Grimm, Jacob, Teutonic Mythology, 4 vols. Swan Sonnenschein & Allen, 1883–8

Guerber, H.A., *The Norsemen*. Guild Publishing, 1986

Guiley, Rosemary E., *The Encyclopedia of Witches and Witchcraft*. Facts on File, 1989

Haac, Oscar A., *Jules Michelet*. Twayne, 1982

Haas, Hippolyt J., *Rügensche Sagen Märchen*. Burmeister, 1903

Halliday, W.R., Review of Murray, The Witch Cult, *Folk-Lore*, no. 33, 1922

Harrow, Judy, 'The Contemporary Neo-Pagan Revival', in James R. Lewis (ed.), *Magical Religion and Modern Witchcraft*. State University of New York Press, 1996

Harvey, G., 'The Roots of Pagan Ecology', *Religion Today*, vol. 9, no. 3, 1994

Hesiod, *'The Theogony' and 'Works and Days,'* trans. M.L. West. Oxford Paperbacks, 1999

Hobsbawm, Eric, and Terence Ranger (eds), *The Invention of Tradition*. Canto, 1992

Homer, *The Odyssey*, trans. E.V. Rieu. Guild Publishing, 1993

Homer, *The Odyssey of Homer, with the Hymns, Epigrams, and Battle of the Frogs and Mice*, trans T.A. Buckley. 1851

Homer, *The Homeric Hymns. A Verse Translation*. W.W. Norton & Company, 1975

Husserl, Edmund, *The Crisis of European Sciences and Transcendental Phenomenology*. Northwestern University Press, 1970

Hutton, Ronald, *The Triumph of the Moon: A History of Modern Pagan Witchcraft*. Oxford University Press, 1999

Jarke, Karl Ernst, 'Ein Hexenprozess', *Annalen der Deutschen und Auslandischen Criminal-Rechts-Pflege*, 1, 1828

Jennings, Hargrave, *Phallicism: Celestial and Terrestrial, Heathen and Christian*. George Redway, 1884

Johnston, Sarah Iles, 'Medea and the Cult of Hera Akraia', in James J. Clauss and Sarah Iles Johnston (eds), *Medea: Essays on Medea in Myth, Literature, Philosophy, and Art*. Princeton University Press, 1997

Jones, Evan John, and Chas Clifton, *Sacred Mask, Sacred Dance*. Llewellyn, 1997

Jones, Gwyn, (ed.), *Eirik the Red and Other Icelandic Sagas* (Oxford World's Classics). Oxford Paperbacks, 1999

Jones, Prudence, and Nigel Pennick, *A History of Pagan Europe*. Routledge, 1995

Kelly, Aidan A., *Crafting the Art of Magic, Book I: A History of Modern Witchcraft, 1939–64*. Llewellyn, 1991

Kemp, Anthony, *Witchcraft and Paganism Today*. Michael O'Mara, 1993

Killings, Douglas B., (ed.), 'The Life and Death of Cormac the Skald' (*Kormak's Saga*), trans. Willaim G. Collingwood and Jon Stefansson. Holmes, Online Medieval and Classical Library Release 7, 1995

King, Francis, *Ritual Magic in England*. Neville Spearman, 1970. Revised edition published as *Modern Ritual Magic: The Rise of Western Occultism* by Prism Press, 1989

Kipling, Rudyard, *The Works of Rudyard Kipling*. Wordsworth Poetry Library, 1994

Kirkpatrick, R.G., 'Feminist Witchcraft and Pagan Peace Protest: Sociology of Counter-Cultures and Social Movement Intersections', unpublished paper given to the American Sociological Association, 24 August 1984

Kluckhohn, C., *Navaho Witchcraft*. Beacon Press, 1962

Knoop, Douglas, and Gwilym P. Jones, *Passing the Bridge*. Published privately, 1949

Kramer, Heinrich, and James Sprenger, *Malleus Maleficarum*, trans. Montague Summers. Bracken Books, 1996

Kraus, T., *Hekate*. Winter, 1960

Kyle, Richard, *The Religious Fringe: A History of Alternative Religions in America*. InterVarsity Press, 1993

Kytzler, Bernhard, *Die Klassiker der römischen Literatur*. ECON Taschenbuch Verlag, 1985

Leek, Sybil, *Diary of a Witch*. NAL Signet Library, 1968

Leibrock, Rachel, 'A Passage Into Paganism: Author Shares Wiccan Ways', *The Sacramento Bee*, 24 January 2001

Leland, C.G., *Aradia: Gospel of the Witches*. Phoenix Publishing, 1990

Lethbridge T.C., *Witches: Investigating an Ancient Religion*. Routledge & Kegan Paul, 1962

Levack, Brian P., 'The Decline and End of Witchcraft Prosecutions', in Bengt Ankarloo and Stuart Clark (eds), *Witchcraft and Magic in Europe: The Eighteenth and Nineteenth Centuries*. The Athlone Press, 1999

Lewis, James R. (ed.), *Magical Religion and Modern Witchcraft*. State University of New York Press, 1996

Llewellyn-Barstow, Anne, *Witch-Craze: A New History of the European Witch Hunts*. HarperCollins, 1994

'Lugh,' Liddell, W.E., and M. Howard, *The Pickingill Papers: The Origin of the Gardnerian Craft*. Capall Bann, 1994

Luhrmann, T.M., *Persuasions of the Witch's Craft*. Basil Blackwell, 1989

Mabey, Richard, *The Complete New Herbal*. Hamish Hamilton, 1988

Macchioro, Vittorio D., *La Villa dei Misteri in Pompeii*. Published in Naples, 1925

Macfarlane, A.D.J., 'Witchcraft Prosecutions in Essex, 1560–1680: A Sociological Analysis', unpublished PhD thesis, University of Oxford, 1967

Mahoney, John, 'Hallowthere', *Daily Star*, 31 October 1995

Martin, F.M., 'Some Subjective Aspects of Social Stratification', in D.V. Glass (ed.), *Social Mobility in Britain: A Study in Intergenerational Changes in Status*. Routledge and Kegan Paul, 1954

Marwick, Max, 'Witchcraft as a Social Strain-Gauge', in Max Marwick (ed.), *Witchcraft and Sorcery*. Penguin, 1990

Mathers, S.L. 'MacGregor', *The Key of Solomon the King*. G. Redway, 1889

Mathers, S.L. 'MacGregor', *The Key of Solomon the King (Clavicula Salomonis)*. Weiser, 1989

Mathers, S.L. 'MacGregor', *The Kabbalah Unveiled. Translated into English from the Latin Version of Knorr von Rosenroth and Collated with Original*

Chaldee and Hebrew Text. Arkana, 1991

Mathers, S.L. 'MacGregor', *The Goetia: The Lesser Key of Solomon the King (Clavicula Salomonis Regis)*, ed. Aleister Crowley. Weiser, 1997

Maxwell-Stuart, P.G., *Witchcraft: A History.* Tempus, 2000

Medway, Gareth J., 'Gardner, Crowley and Lugh', *Aisling*, no. 8, 1995

Melton, J.G., *Encyclopedic Handbook of Cults in America.* Garland, 1986

Melton, J.G., *The Encyclopedia of American Religions.* Gale Research Co., 1987

Melville, Joy, 'That Old Black Magic', *The Guardian Weekly*, 17 March 1985

Michelet, Jules, *La Sorcière*, trans., R.A. Allinson. Tandem Books, 1969

Migne, Jacques Paul, *Patrologia Latina.* N.J. Ridegewood, 1965

Milton, John, *Milton's Paradise Lost, Books I and II, Comus, Lycidias, etc.* William Collins, Sons, & Co., 1874

Mone, Franz Josef, 'Uber der Hexenwesen', *Anzeiger fur Kunde der Teutschen Vorzeit.* 1839

Moody, E.J., 'Urban Witches', in J.P. Spradley and D. McCurdy (eds), *Conformity and Conflict: Readings in Cultural Anthropology.* Little, Brown, 1971

Murray, Margaret, *The Witch-Cult in Western Europe.* Oxford University Press, 1921

Murray, Margaret, *The God of the Witches.* Sampson Low, Marston and Co., 1933

Murray, Margaret, Preface, to Gerald Gardner, *Witchcraft Today.* Rider, 1954

Murray, Margaret, *My First Hundred Years.* William Kimber, 1963

Myerson, Jeremy, 'Cutting a Dash', *Weekend Financial Times* How to Spend It Magazine, 1 and 2 March 1997

Nataf, André, *The Wordsworth Dictionary of the Occult*, trans. J. Davidson. Wordsworth Editions, 1991

Nilsson, Nils Martin Persson, *Geschichte der griechischen Religion*, 2nd edn, 2 vols. Beck, 1967

Oates, Caroline, *A Coven of Scholars: Margaret Murray and Her Working Methods.* Folk-Lore Society, 1998

Orion, Loretta Lee, 'Revival of Western Paganism and Witchcraft in the Contemporary United States'. Unpublished PhD thesis, University of New York, 1990

Orpheus, *The Mystical Hymns of Orpheus*, trans. T Taylor. B. Dobell, 1896

Ovid, *Ovid's Metamorphoses*, trans. Charles Boer. Spring Publications, 1989

' "Pagan" Archbishop Claims Dismissed', *BBC News*, 19 July 2002

Pagan Dawn, No. 125, Samhain, 1997

Palsson, Hermann, (ed.), *Eyrbyggja Saga* (Penguin Classics), trans. Paul Edwards. Penguin, 1989

Palsson, Hermann, (ed.), *Words of Odin: Havamal*, trans. Paul Edwards. Lockharton, 1998

Papyri Graecae Magicae. Die griechischen Zauberpapyri Herausgegeben und übersetzt von Karl Preisendanz. Zweite verbesserte Auflage. Mit Erganzungen von Karl Preisendanz. Durchgesehen und herausgegeben von Albert Henrichs, (PGM)B.G. Teubneri, 1973

Parker, J., *At the Heart of Darkness*. Pan, 1993

Pausanias, *Description of Greece*, ed. Maria Helena Rocha-Pereira, 3 vols. Teubner, 1989

Pennel, Elizabeth Robins, *Charles Godfrey: Leland: A Biography*. Houghton Mifflin, 1906

Petre, Jonathan, and Ian Cobain, 'Survey Charts the Soul of Britain', *Sunday Telegraph*, 28 May 2000

Petre, Jonathan, and Hazel Southam, 'Revealed: The Prayer Map of a Nation in Religious Decline', *Sunday Telegraph*, 20 May 2001

Petrys, Leisha, 'Witchcraft Soaring in Popularity', www.news. com.au, 21 July 2002

Pliny the Elder, *Natural History: A Selection*. Penguin, 1991

Porter, Roy, 'Witchcraft and Magic in Enlightenment, Romantic and Liberal Thought', in Bengt Ankarloo and Stuart Clark (eds), *Witchcraft and Magic in Europe: The Eighteenth and Nineteenth Centuries*. The Athlone Press, 1999

Postman, Neil, *Technopoly: The Surrender of Culture to Technology*. Vintage Books, 1993

Purkiss, Diane, 'Coming Out of the Broom Closet', *Times Higher Educational Supplement*, 22 December 1995

Rabinovitch, Shelley T'Sivia, 'Spells of Transformation: Categorizing Modern Neo-Pagan Witches', in James R. Lewis (ed.), *Magical Religion and Modern Witchcraft State*. University of New York Press, 1996

Raleigh, Sir Walter, The History of the World. Walter Burre,1614

Regardie, Israel, *The Golden Dawn*, 6th edn, Llewellyn, 1989

Regino of Prum, *Reginonis abbatis Prumiensis libris duo de synodalibus causis et disciplinis ecclesiasticis . . .*, ed. F.W.H. Wasserschleben. Lipsiae, 1840

Rhodes, H.T.F., *The Satanic Mass: A Sociological and Criminological Study*. Rider and Co., 1954

Roberts, K., Cook, F.G., Clark, S.C., and Semeonoff, E., *The Fragmentary Class Structure*. Heinemann, 1977

Robbins, R.H., *Encyclopedia of Witchcraft and Demonology*. Crown, 1959

Rose, Eliot E., *A Razor for a Goat: Witchcraft and Diabolism*. University of Toronto Press, 1962

Ruickbie, L.P., 'The Re-Enchanters: An Inquiry into the Social Significance of Modern Witchcraft', unpublished Ph.D. thesis, King's College, London, n.d.

Russell, Bertrand, *A History of Western Philosophy*. Allen & Unwin, 1983

Russell, J.B., *A History of Witchcraft*. Thames and Hudson, 1980

Rusten, Jeffrey S. (ed.), 'Dionysius Scytobrachion *(Papyrologica Coloniensia)*, Westdeutscher Verlag, 1982

Rutherford, Ward, *The Druids: Magicians of the West*. Gordon and Cremonesi, 1978

Rycroft, Charles, *A Critical Dictionary of Psychoanalysis*. Harmondsworth, 1972

Sanders, Alex, *The Alex Sanders Lectures*. Magickal Childe, 1995
Scot, Reginald, *The Discovery of Witchcraft*. Centaur Press, 1964
Scott, G.G., *Cult and Countercult: a Study of a Spiritual Growth Group and a Witchcraft Order*. Greenwood Press, 1980
The Seax, no. 7, June 1995
Shakespeare, William, 'Macbeth', in Stanley Wells and Gary Taylor (eds), *The Complete Oxford Shakespeare*, vol. III: Tragedies. Oxford University Press, 1987
Shan, *Which Craft?* Houseof the Goddess, 1988
Shan, *Pagan Index*. House of the Goddess, 1994
Siculus, Diodorus, *The Antiquities of Asia*, trans. Edwin Murphy. Transaction Publishers, 1989
Simpson, Jacqueline, 'Margaret Murray: Who Believed Her, and Why?' *Folklore*, no. 105, 1994
Smyth, Frank, *Modern Witchcraft*. Macdonald, 1970
Sorcerer's Apprentice, *The Occult Census*. Sorcerer's Apprentice, 1989
Spence, Lewis, *An Encyclopedia of Occultism*. G. Routledge & Sons, 1920
Starhawk, *Dreaming the Dark: Magic, Sex & Politics*. Beacon Press, 1982
Starhawk, *The Spiral Dance: A Rebirth of the Ancient Religion of the Great Goddess*. Harper & Row, 1989
Stein, Diane, *The Goddess Book of Days*. Llewellyn, 1997
Stillwell, R., (ed.), *The Princeton Encyclopedia of Classical Sites*. Princeton, 1976
Strabo, *Geography* (Loeb Classical Library). Loeb. 1969
Strömbäck, Dag, *Sejd: Textstudier I Nordisk Religionshistoria*. Hugo Gebers Forlag, 1935
Summers, Montague, *The History of Witchcraft and Demonology*. Kegan Paul, Trench, Trubner and Co., Ltd, 1926
Summers, Montague, *The History of Witchcraft*. The Mystic Press, 1947
Summers, Montague, Introduction to H. Kramer and J. Sprenger, *Malleus Maleficarum*. Bracken Books, 1996
Sussman, Dalia, 'Who Goes to Church?', *ABC News* (abcnews.com), 1 March 2002
Swanson, Ian, 'Scots Turn Backs on the Kirk', *Edinburgh Evening News*, 18 May 2002
Symonds, John, *King of the Shadow Realm*. Duckworth, 1989

Tacitus, 'Germania', in *Voyages and Travels*, vol. XXXIII. P.F Collier & Son, 1910
Tegnér, Esaias, *Frithiofs Saga*. Norstedt, 1868
Thomas, Keith, *Religion and the Decline of Magic*. Oxford University Press, 1997
Tillhagen, Carl-Herman, 'The Conception of the Nightmare in Sweden', in Wayland D. Hand and Gustave O. Arlt (eds), *Humaniora: Essays in*

Literature, Folklore and Bibliography Honouring Archer Taylor on his 70th Birthday. J.J. Augistin, 1960

Torrens, Robert George, *The Secret Rituals of the Golden Dawn*. Aquarian Press, 1973

Truzzi, M., 'Towards a Sociology of the Occult: Notes on Modern Witchcraft', in I. Zaretsky and M.P. Leone (eds), *Religious Movements in Contemporary America*. Princeton University Press, 1974

Trypanis, Constantine (ed.), *The Penguin Book of Greek Verse*. Penguin, 1971

Tysoe, Maryon, 'The Great British Witch Boom', *New Society*, 18 October 1984

Valiente, Doreen, *The Rebirth of Witchcraft*. Phoenix, 1989 Vigfusson, Gudbrandt and Theodor Möbius (eds), *Vatnsdoelasaga, Hallredarsaga Flóamannasaga*. Hinrichs, 1860

Voigt, Valerie, 'Being a Pagan in a 9 to 5 World', in Chas S. Clifton (ed.), *Witchcraft Today, Book One: The Modern Craft Movement*. Llewellyn, 1992

Von Rudloff, I. Robert, 'Hekate in Early Greek Religion', *Hecate's Loom*, 21, Beltaine/Litha 1993

Von Rudloff, I. Robert, *Hekate in Ancient Greek Religion*. Horned Owl, 1999

von Tettau, Wilhelm, and Jodocus Temme, *Die Volkssagen Ostpreussens Litthauens und Westpreussens*. Nicolai, 1837

Wakefield, Walter, and Austin P. Evans, *Heresies of the High Middle Ages*. Nicolai, 1969

Walker, Frank, 'Snatch Your Cape and Broom and Join the Trend', www.smh.com.au, 14 July 2002

Ward, Christie L., 'Women and Magic in the Sagas', unpublished paper presented to the Alexandrian Company Symposium on Medieval Women, Southwest Texas State University, San Marcos, Texas, 30 August 1997

Waring, Philippa, *Dictionary of Omens and Superstitions*. Treasure Press, 1984

Warnke, Georgia, *Gadamer*. Polity Press, 1987

Watson, Donald, *Dictionary of Mind Spirit*. Andre Deutsch, 1991

Webb, James, *The Flight from Reason*. Macdonald, 1971

Weber, Max, *The Protestant Ethic and the Spirit of Capitalism*. Unwin, 1987

Weber, Max, *Max Weber's 'Science as a Vocation'*, ed. P. Lassman and I. Velody. Unwin Hyman, 1989

Wright, Geoff, 'Modern Magic and Human Potential', *Talking Stick*, XVII, Winter 1994

York, Michael, 'A Sociological Profile on the New Age and Neo-Pagan Movements', unpublished PhD thesis, King's College London, 1992 Published as *The Emerging Network: A Sociology of the New Age and Neo-Pagan Movements*. Lowman and Littlefield Publishers, 1995

INDEX